M000310389

# The **DORIS DAY** Companion
## A Beautiful DAY

# The **DORIS DAY** Companion
## A Beautiful DAY

*One on One with Doris and Friends*

**By Pierre Patrick and Garry McGee**

BearManor Media
2009

TheDoris Day Companion: A Beautiful Day
© 2009 Pierre Patrick and Garry McGee
All rights reserved.

For information, address:

**BearManor Media**
P. O. Box 71426
Albany, GA 31708

bearmanormedia.com

Cover design by John Teehan

Typesetting and layout by John Teehan

Published in the USA by BearManor Media

ISBN—1-59393-349-5

# Table of Contents

# Acknowledgments

Thank you to Ben Ohmart and BearManor Media for the patience and publishing this work; MAD Magazine/DC Comics Group; and Jim Pierson for many of the photos, help with our research and for bringing Doris Day's television work back into the public's consciousness.

*Television Chronicles'* Bill Groves; Bill Glynn; Dominic, Marie-Pierre, Kevin, Julie and Michel Villmaire; Lise and Sylvain Diotte; Maurice and Richard Lavigne; Jacques Despins; Thérese and Réjean Patry; Regine Patry; Anik, Charlotte, Felix-Olivier et Jean Coté; Bernice McDonald; Winnie Batch; Norma Stockwell; June Penner; Theresa Majestic; Anne-Marie Tessier; Catherine Barton; Gerald and Marian McGee; Perry McGee; Linda Tasse; Larry McGee; William Suretté; Charles and Amélie Despins; Stephen Munn and his www.dorisdaytribute.com; The Films of Doris Day at www.dorisday.net; Reno Venturi; Jeremy Hetzler; Tyson Kasfeldt and Loraine Salik for their help and support with this book.

To Kaye Ballard, Philip Brown, Don Genson, James Hampton, Jackie Joseph, Sid Melton, Bernie Kopell and Rose Marie for giving their time and sharing their memories of working on *The Doris Day Show*, and a bouquet of endless daisies to Doris Day for her participation in this book.

If Portrait of a Bookstore was our champion on the West Coast, then Atticus Bookstore Café in New Haven, Connecticut by Yale University, was our champion on the East Coast. Atticus sold more copies of this book's original edition than any other book store. So special thanks to Colleen Carroll, Jean Marcel Recapet, Elroy Lira, the cafe staff and Charles Negaro.

Photographs and illustrations are courtesy of Arwin Productions, CBS Television, Doris Day, Jim Pierson, Jackie Joseph, Cameron Murley, Jennifer Andrews and the authors. 'Academy Awards', 'Oscar' and 'Grammy' are registered trademarks.

Doris Day and son Terry Melcher.

# Dedication

To Terry Melcher, Don Genson and Martin Melcher, whose guidance and support of Doris Day's journey from the film and music fields to television brought another layer of success to her unparalleled career in the entertainment field.

# Foreword
## by Jackie Joseph

I'm pleased to introduce you to Doris Day, the Doris I worked with on the last two years of her television series, *The Doris Day Show*.

Although I was lucky enough to work briefly with Doris on *With Six You Get Eggroll,* that was not the time to start up a casual chat. It was a busy set with a large cast preparing for a party scene. I do remember when I first saw her. She came onto the stage for a rehearsal with giant rollers in her hair, in a chenille sort of bathrobe, snacking on something and chuckling. I remember thinking: this is one comfortable, accessible, darling movie star...

This is the same Doris Day I really got to know while working on *The Doris Day Show*, on her big soundstage at CBS Studio Center. Maybe no rollers or chenille, but the essence never changed. Easygoing, relaxed, professional and always friendly. Each week's working schedule started with an informal reading of the script. My shooting schedule for the rest of the week was thoughtfully assigned, a kindness I'll always remember. Being a mommy with young children, they never called me in before I was needed; it was that kind of company. Doris really set a tone. Consideration...

Even when we worked a full day, we didn't have to report to duty until noon. (Unheard of on most sets, where a 5:30 or 6:00 A.M., call was the norm.) Doris thought it was dumb to make people get up at four in the morning to come to work. I've never heard of another show that worked a sane schedule like hers. And, it always worked.

Instead of a lunch break, which would have been silly starting at noon, Doris had sandwiches (we're talking monster sandwiches from

Art's Deli in Studio City) brought in for the cast and crew. It was easy for anyone to grab a bite, a big bite, when they weren't doing their stuff. It felt like a constant picnic. We'd finish the day by around seven and go home to a fairly normal life. And every week, after the last shot on Friday, she threw a little party on the set for everyone. It was a special way to become friends with everyone we worked with. More consideration…

Doris would always come to work with a selected group from her many dogs. She'd bring, maybe six or seven. At the end of the day, for the last shot or so, three of the dogs (who knew their set manners) would be invited to come and watch us work, sitting in tall director's chairs, no barking, maybe a wagging tail. It was such a comfy way to end the day. Again, what other company could experience such a thing? Only *The Doris Day Show*.

A cottage-style dressing room, white picket fence and all, was attached to her soundstage. A welcoming place. In my memory, it was a little house where Doris lived while working. The room was decorated with comfy furniture and was a great place to hang out. She liked to eat cantaloupe filled with a scoop of Rocky Road ice cream. It may have been a long time ago, but these memories stand out.

Doris was a magnet for terrific guest stars. As a fan, it was such a tickle to work with Van Johnson, Andy Griffith, Peter Lawford and so many others. (Her character had a lot of nifty boyfriends.) She gave Peter Lawford his first directing opportunity. I'll never forget the first show he directed, mainly because I developed a nightmare of a cold sore on my lip. It looked like a burnt marshmallow. Doris decided to make it "okay" by referring to it as "that thing" in the script, and we shot this café scene with lots of closeups. A few weeks later, I got a call sheet to reshoot that scene. It said, "Reshoot due to ugliness." How mortifying—but necessary—was that!

Like all people doing any sort of job, life happens while work happens. Doris Day encountered some major life challenges while shooting her series, family illness, a disheartening trial. Her son Terry's motorcycle accident was truly serious. But, here's the thing: she never brought any of her grief to work. When life was down, Doris was not. If we heard anything about her goings-on, it would be a light reference to something that tickled her. For instance, she got a big kick out the hairstyles she saw in Hemet where she was spending a lot of time visiting Terry in the hospital. She had Barb, her good friend and hairstylist for the show, start piling high and abundant hair all over my head. Just for fun. It's funny to watch the last year of the show with all my varied Hemet hair.

Something very big and important happened during the last season. Doris and I became allied with Richard and Diana Basehart and a group of people who were forming a humane organization that they called Actor's and Others For Animals. We met on evenings or weekends and discussed a course of action to improve the staffing of the animal shelters and to really change the way people treated their animals, encourage the spay and neutering of pets, and halt illegal puppy mills. Her activities with the group went from dramatic rescues, speaking to city councils and creating celebrity fund-raisers. All this during shooting *The Doris Day Show*, where she sold peanut brittle in nice tins to the crew in order to raise a few dollars for the cause. She was on the phone between shots getting personal goods to auction from James Garner and other pals.

We did a Celebrity Fair at my kids' grade school with Kris and Ricky Nelson making sandwiches, Lucille Ball posing for Polaroid pictures for a donation. Lucy Arnaz was the photographer. Doris was the auctioneer and sold Desi's old tuxedos. Sixteen thousand people showed up! We were swamped. Nothing like this had ever happened to bring the public

Billy De Wolfe, Doris Day, Jackie Joseph and friends while working on the series.

Jackie Joseph

together with the stars. And, to put the spotlight on the animals. Her hope was that if macho men saw leading men, who were really masculine role models, saying that it was cool to neuter their pet, then old ideas might change and the soaring pet population could be reduced. It worked. Because of Doris, TV star by day and activist by night (and day), the shelters were staffed with people who met humane criteria. (Before, some workers played baseball with kitties.)

The only anger and tears I ever saw from Doris was due to cruelty to animals. I believe that her star power gave light to a new way to treat animals, something she continues to this day with her Doris Day Animal League.

She called me Jocko. She gave me a birthday cake with a frosting picture of me peeking out a door, making a typical entrance on the show. I found a little buck-toothed dog on the street and she adopted him, calling him Bucky. Just a tip of the iceberg of caring instances that filled my life during the show and after.

As a teen, I got her autograph at a "Coke Sesh" at the Broadway Hollywood department store. She was just a young girl on the threshold of her career, but the glow was there. Who would have dreamed she would call me on my 70th birthday. I was at El Buco, an Italian Restaurant crowded with my friends to surprise me and watch David Lawrence propose to me. I had to say yes. After all, he managed to have Doris call me during the party so everyone I loved could be there. She was the frosting on an unbelievable cake. More recently I was in England and called her on her birthday. She said, "Is it cold there? I get fan letters that they complain about the weather." She had recovered from a back injury; having tripped over a dog in the dark. "I forgot they don't always stay on their little rugs."

When I think of Doris at home in the Carmel Valley, I picture her stepping over her boxes of fan mail, taking inventory of the sweet gifts and messages sent, so she can give her heartfelt thanks. Very important to her.

I'll leave you with a favorite memory of Doris at home, sitting on a high stool, wearing a special long apron, front and back, with over a dozen dog bowls in front of her. Each dog with its own special diet. Most of the dogs waited patiently for their meal on their own little throw rugs. Those not physically able were in their special crib on one side of the pet kitchen. Her days are full of dog walking and dog dishing.

There is no "Secret Love" in this book. The writing comes from devotion and respect. And a desire to share treasured memories and interesting details of Doris Day's work and life. We'll all love this book because it loves her, loves her work, and brightens our memories by bringing us inside and closer to her world. I'm proudly one of her legion of fans worldwide.

# The Doris Day Show:
## "What Will Be..."

*The Doris Day Show* (which was known as *Que Sera, Sera* in French Canada and France) is probably the only show in the history of television to have been brought on the air without the star's knowledge or approval who turned it into a major hit.

Doris Day succeeded in television where virtually no other movie star ever had (Fred MacMurray in *My Three Sons* being the other notable exception). Lana Turner, Debbie Reynolds, Bing Crosby, James Stewart, Judy Garland, Henry Fonda and Jean Arthur were unsuccessful in creating a hit series. But Doris was magic. Viewers not only welcomed her, but felt comfortable having her in their homes.

*The Doris Day Show* television series was an innovative, fast-moving, and creative television series. It is sometimes noted for having the most changes in the history of television, which is not true at all. According to *Vanity Fair* (Dec. '95), "one of the best working women in television," the character of Doris Martin evolved and developed. She moved from location to location and worked her way through her chosen profession not unlike true-life individuals, but unlike most television characters who primarily "stay put."

For years, CBS-TV had to deal with the unshakable Lucille Ball, then on her third series with the network. She was CBS's biggest superstar, and was making more incredible demands with each passing year. Doris Day, being a major movie star and recording artist, would create a certain balance within the CBS empire, giving the network some negotiating power with Ball. The feeling was that Day would be an unbeatable value for the network. The only problem was Doris Day was not interested in working on television. Her only previous television appearances had been at the televised Academy Awards and on the game show *What's My Line* in the mid-1950s. She had made major efforts to stay away from the medium primarily because she had two successful careers in films and music. However, she had no idea she would soon be working hard in it and that it would, arguably, bring about the end of Doris's other careers due to the time constraints required of her in television.

CBS-TV signed Doris Day exclusively in the spring of 1967, without her knowledge, through her husband and manager, Martin [Marty] Melcher. *Variety* called it "One of the industry's all time plush talent deals." Doris and Marty, through their company Arwin, would own the negatives of the show, plus all rerun rights, and the rights to produce movies for CBS. (The movies were later switched for two extraordinary specials featuring the vocal talents of Doris Day.) CBS was ecstatic.

In April 1968 Doris' husband/manager of 17 years suddenly died, having not told her he had officially signed her to a major television deal. Although she knew Marty had wanted her to do a television series, Doris did not feel he would go against her wishes, regardless of what had been announced in the trade papers. In the weeks after Marty's death, while still suffering from her loss, she found by accident a few completed scripts for a Doris Day television show. She was shocked, surprised and baffled! Barely recovered, Doris discovered from her son Terry (who became executive producer of the show) that she was locked into a television series for five years. "I was not prepared to go into television, and I didn't know a thing about it," she later told Barbara Walters.

Far worse was that her husband had invested all her money from 20 years of hard work with a crooked attorney, who took it all after her husband's death. Doris needed to work and needed to fight back to reclaim her fortune. And yes, she was successful at both. Throughout her life she has many times been able to turn tragedy into gold. She did that with her series, her life, and fought her attorney—and literally triumphed on all levels.

Without input from the star, it was decided by the creator of the show, James Fritzell, that Doris would play Doris Martin, a recent widow with two children, having left the city to return to her father's ranch. CBS knew how to make those small farm community shows—*Petticoat Junction, The Andy Griffith Show*, et cetera—successful, so perhaps the thinking was why not put Doris Day in one?

Casting decisions were made before Doris even knew she was going to star in her series. James Hampton and Fran Ryan were both selected by Marty Melcher before his death, and it is probable that Denver Pyle was as well. Auditions for the roles of Doris Martin's sons were held as far back as January 1968. Philip Brown recalled he was among 500 youngsters who auditioned five months before production started. In the few short weeks before filming the first episode, the field was narrowed to a third and then to 30 who all read with Doris Day. The final selection for the roles were Philip Brown and Tod Starke.

From the beginning, Doris made the show very real and very human, as opposed to the other farm shows which were a little off the wall—but funny—like *Green Acres*. Still, Doris was apprehensive with the format, but dealing with the loss of her husband, she accepted the situation... at least for a while.

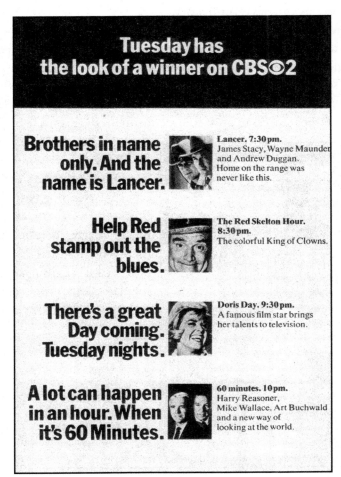

Before Norman Lear and MTM Productions changed the face of CBS and television in the 1970s, the landscape of the medium itself was changing in 1968. Not only was the most successful film actress joining the ranks, but groundbreaking series including *The Mod Squad, Julia* and *Rowan & Martin's Laugh-In* were presented. *The Doris Day Show* simply evolved with the changing times.

CBS was so sure that Doris Day would be an instant hit, scheduling would be important for the program which would follow Day's. As it happened, *The Doris Day Show* was to serve as the lead-in to another new series: a serious one with journalists doing major investigations. The show was called *60 Minutes. The Doris Day Show* was scheduled for 9:30 (EST) Tuesdays, and *60 Minutes* followed, hoping to keep a large portion of her audience. The news magazine show eventually became one of the longest running series in television history.

September 24, 1968 was the day we all met Doris Martin—beautiful widow, talented journalist, fashion trendsetter, wonderful singer, animal lover, and a determined, caring person. It is no coincidence that those are also some of Doris Day's best qualities. As stated in the 1996 *Encyclopedia of Fictional People*: "Doris Martin is perfect. Blonde hair, blue eyes. She favors coat dresses and color coordinated ensembles. She smiles through her problems and always looks nice."

Doris wanted a situation comedy that was not based on jokes. Problems were not always solved in the matter of one episode either, which added to its uniqueness. A lot of time was spent on selecting locations, sets

**Tuesday**

Everybody's all-American girl has finally come to TV with her own series. She is, of course, Doris Day, who plays a young widow (with sons, Billy and Toby, played by Philip Brown and Todd Starke respectively; and a large sheep dog). She is Doris Martin, singer, and, fed up with the big city (they don't say which), she returns to the ranch of her father (Denver Pyle), outside of a small town of about 20,000 population (they don't say which). Also living there are a housekeeper (Fran Ryan) and a hired hand (James Hampton). During their stay in the wilderness Miss Day and group become involved in the town's activities (political and otherwise), meddle in each other's romances, get embroiled in humorous tragedies (like the children take Mom out for a steak and discover that they have no money), and mercifully help out the poor locals in their bucolic trials. Debut: Sept. 24.

and backgrounds. The look of each show was like a mini-movie in a period when television was turning to the less expensive videotape format. A show like this today would easily cost $2 million to produce without the inclusion of a major name attached.

*The Doris Day Show* was brilliantly filmed by Richard Rawlings, and never in front of a live audience. The lack of an audience was primarily due to the fact that the series was shot on film using one camera, not unlike how a movie is filmed. A three- or four-camera setup allows the actors to deliver their lines similar to a stage play [more or less in real time with each scene], with each camera focusing on different preplanned shots. The one camera technique is more time consuming—and arguably more intimate—in that a scene with multiple characters is filmed, then the scene is repeated, usually with close-up shots of each actor delivering their lines. These are then edited to comprise the final scene. The choice of film over videotape proved a wise decision in that the look of the series was fuller, with depth and color, and also the original masters were better preserved over the years since videotape has a much shorter lifespan than negative film.

The first season opening credits, showing Doris and the cast, was shot at the Disney Ranch in a vast, beautiful field with the sun shining brightly behind them, as Doris sings "Whatever Will Be, Will Be (Que Sera, Sera)" on the soundtrack with a choir of children. While different arrangements of the piece would follow in the ensuing seasons, this would remain the theme song throughout the run of the show.

In the first year of *The Doris Day Show,* which was shot at Golden West Studios in Hollywood, we discover Doris Martin recovering from her husband Steve's death at her father's ranch with her two young sons, Billy and Toby. Living far from their city home, this new loving environment on the ranch would be provided by grandfather extraordinaire Buck Webb, farm help Leroy B. Simpson, plus two housekeepers, Aggie followed by Juanita.

The ranch was located at 32 Mill Valley Road, near the town of Cotina in Mill Valley, a community about a 40-minute drive outside of San Francisco. The house was huge. It had four bedrooms and two stairways (one from the kitchen and one from the living room) leading to the second floor. A barn with ducks, pigs, horses and cows completed the farm setting.

Doris Martin was where she needed to be, at least for a while. She was involved with the community. She directed a school musical and helped with local clubs. She even went back to New York for a short time to work for *Women's World* magazine. Doris worked on the farm, brought important values to the kids, and dated a bit.

Doris Day helped with the sets for the TV series and frequently rewrote lines of dialogue, or at least put them the way she'd say them. But after the first year, she and Don Genson made some changes in the series' format. Doris Martin got a job with the San Francisco magazine, *today's world*, where she would remain until the end of the series. Doris still lived on the ranch and had the life of a commuter. The episodes in season two were split between the magazine offices and the farm.

For the second season, a new opening was created where Doris Martin says goodbye to her family and drives in her new red convertible to her new job. Interestingly, Mary Tyler Moore would have a similar opening with her show the following year, walking among the sites of Minneapolis. While in her title credits, Moore tossed her hat in the air with a devil-may-care attitude, Doris literally held onto hers as if to prepare for the bumps in the road ahead. And there were several.

To some extent, the addition of the San Francisco setting mirrored the move made by the production company to the CBS Studio City facility where Doris was very happy to be working. The theme song was sung solo this time by Doris, with a new arrangement by Jimmie Haskell, the series' new music director who would stay with the show in its remaining years.

Doris' first job at the magazine was as executive secretary to *today's world* managing editor Michael Nicholson, played by McLean Stevenson in his first regular series. Veteran actor Paul Smith as Assistant Editor Ron Harvey and Rose Marie as Ron Harvey's secretary, Myrna Gibbons, were added to the cast.

The changes Doris Day created helped the series tremendously, as did CBS moving the show to Monday nights at 9:30 P.M. (EST), where it jumped into the year-end top ten. Suffice to say, CBS was thrilled with the success.

The third season found Doris Martin secure in her job and ready to stop commuting. A move to San Francisco was needed and Doris found the perfect place at 965 North Parkway, Apartment 207. Rent was $140 a month and conveniently located above Pallucci's Italian Restaurant (San Francisco's best kept secret). The owners of the building were Angie and Louie Pallucci, played by veteran actors Kaye Ballard and Bernie

Kopell. Angie was always eating, and always on a diet. Her husband, Louie, did not like children until he met Doris' boys and learned they loved his pizza better than any other food—even hot dogs.

Again, a new opening was created with Doris Martin greeting her audience by coming down the now-famous spiral staircase of her apartment, sequenced with the cast credits and shots from the fashion show episode.

Another new and important cast member would be Doris' old friend from her Warner Bros. days, Billy De Wolfe, who was introduced in the second season. He played Doris Martin's nemesis and next door neighbor, Mr. Jarvis.

Season three also saw a departure for Day with her first television musical special, *The Doris Mary Anne Kapplehoff Special,* with guests Perry Como and Rock Hudson. Doris sang some of her greatest songs: "It's Magic," "Sentimental Journey" and "Everybody Loves a Lover." The show was a huge hit.

With the fourth season, Doris Martin became a full-time reporter and an associate editor for *today's world* as an associate editor. Interestingly, this was not the first time Doris Day played a writer. She had already done so in her film *Teacher's Pet* with Clark Gable; however, that character was light years from Doris Martin, who was writing for a major national magazine. At *today's world,* Doris no longer worked for managing editor Mr. Nicholson, but for City Editor Cyril "Cy" Bennett, played by John Dehner. Another addition to the cast was Jackie Joseph, who played Jackie Parker, Cy's secretary.

Changes were important to Doris Day—give the audience something new every year; keep the show fresh and entertaining. Doris, who was used to making two or three movies a year where everything would change, was always looking to find new horizons.

Season four brought the most changes in personnel yet as a major new and permanent love interest was brought into Doris' life, Dr. Peter Lawrence (beginning with "Doris and the Doctor"). Peter Lawford played Doris' new love interest, and the chemistry between the two worked well. They achieved a perfect balance of humor, love and entanglement.

The major change of the fifth and final season was that Doris Day became executive producer of her show. Despite her wanting little to do with television four years earlier, now she was ready to do it all. Although she had a hand in many aspects of her series, including set design and costumes, Doris was now in charge of the budget, music, casting, et cetera...and loved it all.

In this final season, Mr. Jarvis became Doris's hard-to-deal-with land-lord, while the Palluccis perhaps left for Italy on a well-deserved vacation, although their restaurant business remained. The only regular cast member added to the last season was Patrick O'Neal (Doris's leading man in *Where Were You When the Lights Went Out?*), who played foreign correspondent Jonathan Rusk, another serious boyfriend for Doris Martin. During the last year, Doris dated both Jonathan and Dr. Lawrence, leaving the audience wondering which one she would pick.

After this fifth season and sixth year, CBS wanted desperately to keep Doris Day on the air after she fulfilled her series commitment to the network. Doris kindly said, "I have done everything I can with the series. My contract is up. Thank you very much," and made a graceful exit from prime time.

When *The Doris Day Show* was first offered in syndication in 1976, it was sold to a fair amount of local stations across the US. However, the show's visibility in domestic syndication was affected by the fact that it was not offered to stations sooner, while it was fresh off its network run in the fall of 1973.

Another factor was the series' frequent change in cast and format. This disruption in continuity works against a show's repeatability in syndication. Firstly, it gives an impression—though falsely in the case of *The Doris Day Show*—that a program was not particularly successful and was in search of a formula that worked. Perhaps more important, it confuses audiences who want familiarity with characters. More than any other show that was a hit and had a long run, *The Doris Day Show* was a chameleon and a rather unique situation now considered "normal."

Doris Day returned to CBS once more to satisfy her contract with the network. In February 1975, the musical special *Doris day toDay*, was applauded by critics and was a ratings hit. It featured guest stars John Denver, Rich Little, and Tim Conway. Like her earlier special, *Doris day toDay* included a combination of classic and current songs, as well as short comedy sketches.

In 1985 Doris returned to television when she hosted an informal talk show with music and occasional skits called *Doris Day's Best Friends*, which featured Denver Pyle, Kaye Ballard, and costumer Connie Edney from *The Doris Day Show* among the guests. The series also featured new, previously recorded songs by Doris, but the main focus was animals: what they are, their contributions to humans and nature, and our responsibilities toward them.

With Billy DeWolfe, John Dehner and friends.

In the following years, Doris made infrequent appearances on television, but primarily kept them to a minimum, selectively choosing nonperforming shows. In 1976, Doris did a talk show tour promoting her book *Doris Day: Her Own Story*, which included *Today* and *The Tonight Show*. In 1983, she agreed to a week-long stint on *Good Morning, America*, and in 1993, a *Doris Day Best Friends* event was staged in Carmel with media coverage presented on Vicki Lawrence's talk show *Vicki!*. Doris also appeared in a few documentaries including *Doris Day: A Sentimental Journey* in 1991, co-produced by her company Arwin.

The main focus of this book is *The Doris Day Show* series and includes information on each episode. This consists of the first US televising of the episode; directors, writers, guest stars and their characters as listed in the credits; a synopsis of the show; Groovy Day Facts lists items about or connected to the episode; stories or ideas that *today's world* magazine was working on; Doris Day Album and Music Finds are mentions of Doris's songs rearranged as incidental music or newly performed songs in the episode; Movie Finds are connections the episode has to Doris or her series co-stars; and in later shows, a nod to some of the far-out looks of Jackie Parker are included.

# Speaking With Don Genson, the Producer

*You started with the show in the very beginning and you were with it for all of its seasons.*

I had known Marty Melcher when he was with The Andrews Sisters, and then I was with the firm in 1962. So it was for some years before Doris did the TV show. She was only doing pictures at that time. Then, in 1967, Marty made a deal with CBS for the television show. But he did it with Doris being completely unaware of the whole thing. And then he passed away and we were left with a show to do, and she was a widow. And it was quite a mess, quite a mess the first year. But we thought we did a pretty good show.

*Was it difficult the first year since it was a new medium for Doris to work in?*

Yes, it was. She had to get used to that sort of a show. It was tough because she didn't know she was going to do it. And she was suddenly thrown into this, [with] new ideas and concepts. She had to do it because she had a contract—Marty had done that. So she had no alternative except to do the best she could—and she did.

*You were involved with the casting for the series?*
Yes, I did all the casting.

*How did you decide which actors would be selected for the show?*
I guess it was an innate feeling that I had. As it turned out, I had a great feeling for it. And the gal who ran the [casting department] at CBS

called me and said, 'I can't believe you've never done that before. You're really a genius at it.' But no, I really had a feeling for it and it turned out very well.

*In addition, you wrote several scripts for the show.*
Well, I'd read the scripts and I knew we could do better. I had a talent for that too, so it turned out quite well.

*Did you make script changes to those that were chosen to be filmed?*
Oh, sure, lots of changes. I changed almost every script that passed our desk.

*In regard to scripts, were there ever times that you decided, 'no, we're not going to do this one?'?*
No, because we always had time to rewrite it, or the writers had time to rewrite it. It depended, too, on who the producer was at the time. We had four of them all together.

*It took five or six days to produce an episode the first year and by the last you could do a show in four days, correct?*
Yeah, we could, and later we also started around noon so Doris wouldn't have to get to work at six in the morning like she always did. We had a great show. It ran very smoothly and we had good people. Doris had people there she had known for years, so it was a happy show.

*How much input in the scripts were the actors allowed? For example, Billy De Wolfe was such a great character...*
And a great friend for Doris...

*...How much of his personality, like using his finger to check for dust or his quotes like "ne-vah touch!," was his or were they already written in the scripts?*
"Ne-vah touch!" He, of course, embellished, it was so natural for him. He was so great with Doris, and he really played that part to the hilt. It was just great. And Van Johnson was a good friend of Doris's. We loved having him on the show. Peter Lawford was okay. There were a few problems.

Doris Day, with Tod Starke, Van Johnson and Philip Brown, preparing to film the season three episode, "Cousin Charlie."

*And there was Patrick O'Neal as well.*
Patrick O'Neal was very good.

*The fashion shows were almost a yearly event. Were they difficult to pull off?*
Yes, they were because they involved the selection of clothes and the fittings, but she enjoyed doing those. She had a great figure and could model anything with style.

*You also produced Doris Day's first television special. Was that part of her contract with CBS or was it something she wanted to do?*
It was a combination. That was part of the deal and Doris wanted to do it. It was a great show.

*The show was distinctive because Doris Day sang for the first time in a special.*
Yes, but she did get to sing in the series with Tony Bennett.

*Where did the idea for the Palluccis and their restaurant come from?*
We got Kaye Ballard and Bernie Kopell for the roles. Bernie had a great accent for everything. I don't know how that actually came about, but we thought of putting them in a restaurant downstairs from where

Doris lived. And it turned out to be great and they were so good to-gether. Bernie's such a talent, and so is Kaye, of course.

*Doris liked to be surrounded by people whose company she enjoyed—as well dogs. Were they always around?*
Always. They were fine. We had a few on the special as a matter of fact. But on the series she'd bring a couple with her. They were no problem at all.

*We noticed some of the extras were used and reused in the series many, many times. Was there a reason for this?*
No. I just thought they were very good so we'd call the same ones back.

*There was a Genson in an episode* ["Doris, the Model"]. *Was she related to you?*
The one with the models? That was my wife. She was a model and I got her friend, who was also a model, and put them in the show. She passed away a long time ago.

*Jimmie Haskell provided a lot of terrific incidental music to the series, as opposed to a few bars from three or so unfinished songs that sitcoms use over and over through their shows. How'd you decide on him to do the music?*
He was terrific, and I thought he was very talented and I could depend on him. It worked very well.

*Many songs Doris sang on her albums and in her films were heard in the series as instrumental music.*
I put those in so that she'd receive performance rights; the background music belonged to Arwin so that's why you heard all of that. Of course, we lost "Que Sera." That went back to the original writers.

*How many years did you work with Doris?*
I was, altogether, with Doris and Terry for about 15 years. First I ran the music division of her company and then I was in charge of Doris's record deal with Columbia. Then Marty had made the deal with CBS for the television show, and he had hired the producers. Doris was not too happy with them—nothing personal, but because of the direction the

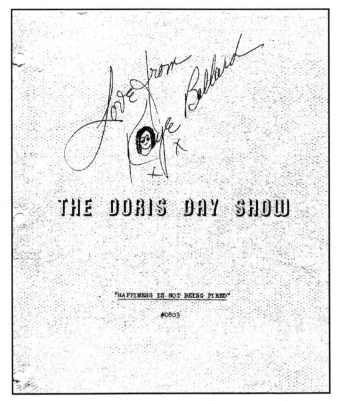

An original script for the series signed by Kaye Ballard.

series was going. We changed producers, and finally Terry and I took over. The last year we had a few little differences and I didn't want to do it anymore. And that wasn't personal either because we've stayed close. Of course, I spend every summer with her up in Carmel, but I haven't been feeling all that great the last couple of years, so I haven't made the drive up there. But we're in constant touch. She's a great gal, and my wife and I love her. And she's one of the great talents of all time.

# The Doris Day Show

| | |
|---|---|
| Executive Producers | Martin Melcher, Terry Melcher, Don Genson, Doris Day |
| Producers | Jack Elinson, Norman Paul, Edward H. Feldman, George Turpin Bob Sweeney, Richard Dorso |
| Associate Producers | Jerry London, George Turpin |
| Music | Jimmie Haskell, William Loose, Robert Mersey |
| Theme Song | "Qué Sera, Sera" by Jay Livingston & Ray Evans |
| Creator | James Fritzell |
| Art Direction | Perry Ferguson II |
| Supervising Film Editor | Howard French, A.C.E. |
| Film Editor | Michael Kahn |
| Director of Photography | Richard L. Rawlings |
| Production Manager | Abby Singer |
| Set Decorator | James Hassinger |
| Sound Mixers | William M. Ford, Woodruff Clark |
| Assistant Directors | Robert Daley, Louis B. Appleton |
| Story Editor | Sid Morse |
| Script Supervisor | Maggie Lawrence |
| Dialogue Coach | Kay Stewart |
| Makeup | Harry Maret |
| Hairstyles | Barbara Lampson |

| | |
|---|---|
| Ms. Day's Costumer | Connie Edney |
| Women's Costumer | Joy Turney |
| Men's Costumer | Leonard F. Mann |
| Property Masters | Sam Loreno, V.E. "Ted" Ross, Wm. "Speedy" Skamres |
| Music Editor | Earle Dearth |
| Sound Effects Editors | Sid Lubrow, Jerry Rosenthal, Jack Finlay |

Titles by John Urie & Associates

Wardrobe Furnished by Joseph Magnin

Automobiles Furnished by the Chrysler Corporation

Office Equipment Furnished by Steelcase

## CAST CREDITS & MAIN CHARACTERS:

*The Doris Day Show* included many veterans of stage and screen, both big and small, in its six-year/five-season run. The following includes brief professional credits and overviews of those actors who received opening title credits, as well as their characters' backgrounds. In addition to those who were deemed regulars, there are some (Edward Andrews, Kaye Ballard, Billy De Wolfe, Bernie Kopell, Peter Lawford and Patrick O'Neal) who appeared several times throughout the series in memorable roles. They are listed here as well:

### Doris Day as Doris Martin, seasons 1-5

On the evening of Friday, October 13, 1937, Ohio's number one dancer is one week away from moving to Hollywood. Doris Mary Anne Kappelhoff was a passenger in a car that was hit by a train. Her leg was crushed and it was the end of the young lady's career as a dancer. But it was the beginning of one of America's best and most important vocalists, Doris Day.

Almost ten years later, she was a hit singer with Les Brown and his Band of Renown and was a solo artist on Columbia Records. While performing her first concert in New York, she received news from her second husband, who felt her star was on the rise. He was afraid of becoming Mr. Doris Day and wanted out of the marriage. Devastated and ready to go back to her hometown of Cincinnati, legendary Hollywood film director Michael Curtiz signed the young star to his company and a contract with Warner Bros. She became a star with her first film, and by the mid-1960s was the world's #1 favorite. Doris was voted a Top Ten box office draw for ten years, and for four of those years was the #1 star.

In May 1956, Doris renewed her contact with Columbia for the extraordinary amount of $1,050,000. It broke all records at the time. Columbia was happy keeping the popular artist, so many (including Frank Sinatra eariler in the decade) had already left the label. She achieved 56 Top 40 hits, including seven #1 singles. Her soundtrack album, *Love Me or Leave Me,* spent more than four months at #1 on the album charts, becoming one the most successful albums of all time.

In 1967, a few days after her third husband's death, Doris discovered two scripts for a new television series she had never heard of called *The Doris Day Show.* This was the dawn of a new Day—in television.

Doris received many awards in her career, including seven million selling singles in the U.S., five Golden Globe Awards, two Oscar-winning songs and the Presidential Medal of Freedom.

Doris Martin is a widow with two sons, who moves from New York to her father's home near Cotina, California and then to San Francisco. A former magazine writer, she rejoins the publishing world with *today's world* as a secretary, where she works her way up the ladder to become associate editor. As a single working mother, she attempts to balance work, family, home and her own personal desires, not unlike many women of today.

Doris finds herself in various predicaments that are not usually of her own doing. She frequently (if not always successfully) helps resolve issues in which she is involved. She is a good friend to those who are the same, and is a dog lover as well.

Upbeat and kind, Doris's sunny disposition, smile and willingness to help, charms many of the people she meets, from millionaires and princes, to pilots and mechanics. She tries to be fair and helpful. But, if ever crossed, Doris retaliates: be it a person with an ulterior motive, a difficult boss, or even a newspaper delivery boy who constantly aims and hits her with each toss of a rolled newspaper.

## Edward Andrews as Col. Fairburn, seasons 2-4

Edward Andrews first appeared on the stage at age twelve and made his Broadway debut in 1935's *How Beautiful with Shoes.* In 1938 he appeared in the Pulitzer Prize-winning play *The Time of Your Life.* Andrews was regularly cast as government employees in his roles, from politicians to military officers, including his film debut in the 1955 drama *The Pheonix City Story*. He preferred comedy roles, and his finger-shaking gesture became a trademark, which included several movies with Doris Day. Andrews' portrayal of an overly ambitious, yet paranoid NASA officer in *The Glass Bottom Boat* led to his recurring role as the neurotic Col. Fairburn on *The Doris Day Show*.

Andrews continued making several television guest appearances in hit shows like *Bonanza, The Streets of San Francisco, Sanford and Son* and *The Bob Newhart Show*, and film roles including Walt Disney's *Now You See Him, Now You Don't* and *The Million Dollar Duck*.

Col. Norton Fairburn's first appearance was in "*today's world* Catches the Measles" and his last was in "The New Boss."

Col. Fairburn, an ex-army officer, is the publisher of *today's world* magazine. He resides in New York and likes to play golf, work on cross-word puzzles, and throw darts. Col. Fairburn likes fish, has an aquarium in his *today's world* California office, and tries to run his operations as if it were a branch of the military. His most common saying is "Eeexaaactly!"

In 1970, he is a widower with two children, Sharon and Clifford. Clifford attended a military academy, followed by four years at Caruther's College of Business Administration, where he graduated at the top of his class—so Col. Fairburn said. Nepotism runs in the Fairburn family since the Colonel starts a new magazine for Clifford to run. Fairburn also has a sister who is involved with charity work and a sister-in-law, Thelma King, who's been engaged to Henry Thurston for 15 years.

By 1972, Col. Fairburn owns 67% of *today's world*. He has remarried, but the marriage appears to be rocky since the Colonel was caught in a raid of a topless-bottomless joint in 1972.

Col. Fairburn is fond of Doris Martin as a person and as an employee. He has bought her flowers, candy and once a diamond jeweled pin. But in later years, their relationship appeared somewhat strained, especially after Doris's self-penned articles sometimes affected Fairburn's business activities. He fired her a few times from *today's world*, but she always returns back to the magazine.

## Kaye Ballard as Angie Pallucci, seasons 3-4

In her hometown of Cleveland, Kaye Ballard made her professional debut singing in a USO show at the age of 15, and has worked as an entertainer every year since then. She was a solo performer on the RKO vaudeville circuit before appearing on the New York stage in 1946 with

*Three to Make Ready.* Ballard was popular in the cabaret circuit and continued stage appearances in such productions as *Carnival* and *The Decline and Fall of the Whole World as Seen Through the Eyes of Cole Porter Revisited.*

A handful of films followed, including *The Girl Most Likely*, *Freaky Friday* and *The Ritz*, but Ballard became a household name through several television shows, including the live televising of *Cinderella* with Julie Andrews and future *The Doris Day Show* alum John Cypher. Her starring in the popular series *The Mothers-In-Law*, with Eve Arden, furthered her standing with television audiences.

As Angie Pallucci, with dramatic Italian nuances, Ballard played the character as comic relief, with a lot of yelling, flapping gestures and dramatized problems, but always put Doris Martin's needs first by helping her as a friend.

Angie Pallucci first appeared in the episode "Doris Finds an Apartment" and was last seen in "The Blessed Event." (Kaye Ballard's first appearance on *The Doris Day Show* was in "Kidnapped.")

Angelina (Angie) Pallucci is married to Louie, with whom she runs Pallucci's Restaurant, an Italian establishment located on the ground floor of their building at 965 North Parkway. She and Louie do not have children, but their Italian food-loving dog Sophie delivered six puppies. The only relative mentioned is her cousin, Vito Garlotti, who headed the Cellini exhibit in San Francisco.

Much of Angie's time is consumed with the restaurant. She goes to Fisherman's Wharf at 4:30 A.M. to get the best lobsters, but confessed she once ran out of marinara sauce at the restaurant. She bought two cans of Chef Bambino's sauce for 59 cents and substituted it for her own.

She works side by side with Louie every day. Perhaps because of the time required at the restaurant, Angie tends to live her life through others and becomes excited when there is change in her day-to-day routine. She cannot keep a secret. For example, Angie tells neighbors and friends Tony Bennett is eating at Pallucci's, which causes Bennett to be overwhelmed by autograph seekers. She also likes to play matchmaker to any single person around; however, her comeuppance is when she's caught in a standoff, the feather in her cap is shot ("Have I Got a Fellow for You").

Angie is outspoken, and her most common phrases are "Are you a crazy person?" and "Rats!" She calls Cy "Mr. Cheap" when he doesn't buy Doris's dinner. And there are several instances when she utters Italian words accentuated with various hand gestures to convey her opinion.

But it was her nose—namely her sense of smell—that helped solve an unsolved crime while at the health spa Meadowbrook. There she caught the scent of a pizza hidden in a wall along with $2 million that had been stolen.

### Philip Brown as Billy Martin, seasons 1-3 (opening title credit)

Philip Brown was born in California and his uncle Peter Brown starred in films and the television series *The Lawman* and *Laredo*. Philip started his performing career when he was eight; he appeared in television commercials, and, within two years, he appeared in more than 20. Films followed, including *Bitter Ash*, *The Playground*, and *Fitzwilly*.

As Doris Martin's oldest son Billy, Brown played the character with conviction and determination. With Tod Starke, Brown not only proved capable but appealing in the series. Brown continued to work long after his childhood on several television shows, including *The Dukes of Hazzard* (with Denver Pyle), *The Love Boat* (with Bernie Kopell), *Matlock*, *Murder, She Wrote*, and recurring roles on *Knots Landing*, *The Colbys*, *Loving* and *The City*. He now regularly appears in many television commercials and in guest spots on various series.

Billy Martin appeared in the first episode of *The Doris Day Show* with his last being "Doris Goes to Hollywood."

Doris Martin's firstborn, Billy is ten years old when we are introduced to him in 1968. Billy is called "William" by his mother when she demands his attention. He has a tendency for being impetuous at times. Among other things, he used Aggie's lipstick to make a sign without her permission. He volunteered Doris to umpire his Little League game ("Doris Strikes Out") and said she would chaperone him and his date to a school dance ("Billy's First Date"). Billy also donated the family's broken toaster for a library fundraiser without first asking his mother. He did not know Doris hid several thousand dollars in it, which was Leroy B. Simpson's rodeo winnings.

Billy likes to earn money. He sold rides on Lord Nelson in San Francisco and lemonade with Toby on the farm and in San Francisco. His lemonade must not have been very good since customer Gertrude Fields yelled to Doris, "Your kids make lousy lemonade!"

Billy is generous, especially to his mother. He bought her a belt ("The Five-Dollar Bill") and he and Toby gave her a gold heart necklace. Like his brother, Billy has a good heart and tells the truth. For example, when Mrs. Loomis accused Billy of stealing five dollars from her purse, he truthfully denied it.

Billy is involved in activities. He is in Cub Scouts in 1969 and later in the year sells candy bars for a fund-raiser. He has a pig named Herman, which was entered in the state fair; takes piano lessons; is a pitcher in the Cotina Little League; plays football with friends; ate four chili dogs at Cubby Weaver's barbecue; likes the TV show *Frogman*; and his idea of a good breakfast is pickles, spaghetti, jam and root beer ("Let Them Out of the Nest").

Billy hauls in wood for the farmhouse's fireplaces, and, like most siblings, argues with his little brother. But he is also close to Toby and they play games together, including Scrabble, Dominos and racing cars. Billy also got the measles from Toby.

When living in the country, the boys sometimes rode their bikes to school and other times took the school bus. Although we see him do his studies on occasion, he had a problem learning fractions and is not very good in geography.

## John Dehner as Cyril (Cy) Bennett, seasons 4-5 (opening title credit)

John Dehner began his career in the entertainment industry not as a performer, but as an assistant animator for Walt Disney. Following work as a disc jockey and a pianist, an Army publicist and radio journalist, Dehner made his film debut in 1945.

He remained busy for the next four decades, alternating work in radio, film and television. Among the TV series Dehner appeared in include *Mission: Impossible*, *Columbo* and *Maverick*. His film work included *The Boys From Brazil*, *Airplane II: The Sequel* and the Academy Award-winning *The Right Stuff*, in which he played publisher Henry Luce.

Dehner usually played the heavy in his work, although *The Doris Day Show* provided him a chance to shine in a comedy role. Regardless, Dehner was seldom a leading man, and his roles precluded any romantic involvements. While acting on *The Doris Day Show*, Dehner noted with pride to *TV Guide* that he never won nor kissed the heroine in any of his roles. As Cy Bennett, Dehner played a driven, ego-tripping, pompous, cheap, hypochondriac. "Get the story done at any cost" was his motto, but Doris Martin was determined not to let him walk all over her. She argued, fought and defended her point of view on any story, and Doris and Cy would go head-to-head on many issues.

Cyril (Cy) Bennett was first seen in the televised episode "And Here's… Doris" and his last appearance was in "Byline… Alias Doris." Known for his exaggerated phrasing with "Mmmm-yellow," when answering the telephone, and "That's a brrrilliant idea," among his most common, he was managing editor of *today's world* in 1972 and then editor-in-chief in 1973.

Cy was in China and North Africa as a foreign correspondent. He also interviewed Winston Churchill. He loves his old trenchcoat, which he calls Old Blood and Guts, and says he was known as "The Tiger." He has a desire to be a television newsman.

Cy was formerly married to Donna to whom he makes monthly alimony payments. There's no mention of him having any children. Although he says he does 100 pushups a day, Cy tends to be a hypochondriac, but does have true illnesses at times and is treated by Dr. Peter Lawrence. He had vision problems and got contact lenses, had Hay Fever, and at times his back went out of alignment.

He plays golf and occasionally gambles on the horse races. Cy drinks bourbon and Coke. Like all the others at *today's world*, has a bad habit of taking and making personal telephone calls during company time. He was once offered a job with a New York magazine but turned it down.

With Cy Bennett at the helm, *today's world* was a less relaxed workplace than under Mr. Nicholson. Under his tenure, Doris was an associate editor, and her relationship with Cy was strictly business. Although he tended to lecture and reprimand Doris much of the time, he did like her and admired her even if his praises were infrequent. Cy Bennett could be ruthless at times in order to get his own way. He once said he was Doris's uncle in order to get into her London hotel room. When an author became smitten with Doris, Cy said he was Doris's boyfriend so that the magazine could obtain the serialization rights to his book; and he also played Doris's favorite uncle in "A Fine Romance" to uncover a computer dating scam.

The workers at *today's world*, however, seem to have less respect for him than those who worked under Mr. Nicholson. Doris called Cy "Mom" after he complained of being a Mother Hen. She also called him a conniver, stinker, faker, fink and dirty rotten...

He is also cheap: He would put Doris into budget hotels while she worked on out-of-town stories, and told her to cut long distance telephone calls when it cost $12 a minute for a call from San Francisco to Rome. He gave Doris a box of peanut clusters only because he loved them. He also fired Doris in almost every episode.

However, at other times, he was generous. When Doris volunteered to organize a fashion show for a hospital benefit, it was turned down by the benefit committee. Cy telephoned the hospital administrator and convinced him to do the fashion show. He bailed Doris and Mr. Jarvis out of jail in the middle of the night when they were sent in for allegedly robbing a jewelry store. He also said he would trade all of the employees of *today's world* to keep Doris with the magazine.

### Billy De Wolfe as Mr. Jarvis, seasons 2-5

Comic character actor De Wolfe first appeared in vaudeville as a teen-ager then moved to many nightclub and Broadway roles in the late 1930s and early 1940s. His best-known routine was of "Mrs. Murgatroyd," in which the mustachioed De Wolfe played a middle-aged woman having lunch after a shopping spree. De Wolfe made a handful film appearance, most notably the *Dear Ruth* trilogy, as well as *Tea for Two* and *Lullaby of Broadway*.

De Wolfe also appeared on the TV shows *That Girl, Good Morning, World* and *The Queen and I*. His recurring role of Mr. Jarvis on *The Doris Day Show* was a highlight. His most famous quote was when Doris would come into physical contact with him: "Ne-vah touch! Ne-vah touch!" The pair was close friends in real life, but on onscreen, the irritation the characters caused each other provided much amusement to the viewer. De Wolfe would remain until the end of the series.

He also was a welcomed guest on *The Tonight Show*, making dozens of appearances on Johnny Carson's talk show, never failing to convulse the host and audience with his catch phrase "Busy, busy, bizzeee!" His last performance was in *Free to Be... You and Me* in 1974.

Every holiday season finds De Wolfe in one of his most-heard roles, that of the villain in the animated cartoon *Frosty the Snowman*, which was first shown in 1969 and every year since.

Mr. Willard Jarvis first appeared in *Doris vs. the Computer* and his last appearance was in *It's a Dog's Life*

In his first appearance, Jarvis works at the electric company and has Doris's power turned off because the computer has no record of her paying her bill. She did pay it and confronts Jarvis—the first of many in the following years. In his first appearance, Jarvis is married; however, in future episodes, he is a bachelor.

After the utility company, he works as an efficiency expert and is hired by Col. Fairburn to remedy *today's world's* problems ("The Office Troubleshooter"). Jarvis is meticulous—so much that he confronts Col. Fairburn over his own inefficiency and is thus removed from the job.

When Jarvis, however, returns in season three, he is now single. It was never explained if he was divorced or widowed, but he rents an apartment with a year's lease. It just so happens to be next door to Doris Martin. He is just as displeased as she is. "Nearly one million people in San Francisco and I get *you* as a next door neighbor!" Doris says. "My sentiments exactly," he retorts.

Perhaps Doris Martin reminds Mr. Jarvis of Doris Day. He hates Doris Day. "Can't stand that woman," he remarks to Doris Martin when Doris Day appears onscreen. Another time when he is talking to Doris Martin he hears a neighbor's television set that has just tuned into *The Doris Day Show*. "Can't stand that woman…" Jarvis says.

Jarvis reads *The Wall Street Journal* (which Doris accidentally drenches while watering her plants); likes to watch nightly cello concerts on public television and play conductor; has problems with nasal passages on rainy nights; and hates tipping the telegram boy. But Mr. Jarvis was elected to the San Francisco City Council.

Jarvis' mother's name is Myra, and he gives the same name to his dog. Jarvis has an unnamed sister who, he says, is "a stunning brunette" and that the two are sometimes mistaken for each other. He has an Uncle Randolph (Randy) Jarvis who visits and so happens to be the complete opposite of his nephew. In the end, Mr. Jarvis purchases the apartment building, thus becoming not only Doris's continued neighbor, but her landlord.

## James Hampton as Leroy B. Simpson, seasons 1-3 (opening title credit season 1)

James Hampton first gained audience recognition with the 1960s TV series *F-Troop* before appearing in *The Doris Day Show*. He followed the series with many television appearances and films, including the highly-rated *Stand By Your Man*, *The Burning Bed* and *The Amazing Howard Hughes*. Hampton was also in the theatrical films *The China Syndrome*, *Teen Wolf* (he reprised his role for a cartoon series based on the movie), and two Burt Reynolds movies, *The Longest Yard* and *Hustle,* in the 1970s.

He also made guest appearances on TV shows, including a reunion with Denver Pyle on *The Dukes of Hazzard*. After acting on *Days of Our Lives* in 1989, Hampton directed several hits shows in the 1990s, from *Grace Under Fire* to *Evening Shade*. He continued acting, including the acclaimed film *Sling Blade*.

As Leroy B. Simpson on *The Doris Day Show*, Hampton appeared as a regular the first season and made guest appearances in seasons two and three. Farmhand Leroy was very clumsy, causing more problems in the ranch than poor Buck could ever imagine. Buck called him a "nincompoop."

Leroy B. Simpson appeared for the first time in the premiere episode of *The Doris Day Show* and was last seen in the episode "Lassoin' Leroy."

Buck believes the "B" in Leroy B. Simpson's name stands for "Bumbler." In fact, Buck once fired Leroy four times in one week.

Leroy is kindhearted, but nonetheless a klutz. He once pushed the kitchen door open which, on the other side, forced Buck into Doris, causing her to drop a pie on the floor. He got Buck caught in the back window of the station wagon while messing with the car's control switches. He accidentally let the pigs out of their pen. And he once burned out the telephone while replacing light bulbs in the porch light fixture.

Once he helped Joe White Cloud for a day and in one hour he stepped into a hornet's nest, fell into the water trough, and backed the tractor over Joe's new suit—which was hanging in the closet as Leroy drove into Joe's bedroom. Leroy also lost Buck's tractor by stacking bales around it.

He plays guitar and has an above average interest in Hollywood and movie and music stars. He also has a large appetite, once eating a record 14 pancakes in one sitting at the Webb kitchen table.

Although Leroy is incompetent with machinery and electrical equipment on the farm—from fixing plumbing to doing laundry—he learned enough to run his own Tidy Service station for a while in Cotina.

Leroy has an Uncle Buster, cousins Edgar, Albert and Herman Simpson from Choctow County and a grandma. He also has a female cousin, Jessie Higgins, whose facial shaving must be the result of a male hormone problem.

Leroy dated Winifred (Winnie) Proxmeyer, the Cotina librarian, but he married Ellie and the couple had three triplets. He and his family then moved to Montana, where he worked on a farm. Leroy started riding in rodeos on the side to earn more money. He returned to San Francisco and entered a rodeo in which he won $20,000. He planned to buy a ranch with the winnings.

**Jackie Joseph as Jackie Parker, seasons 4-5 (opening title credit)**

Jackie Joseph was a chorus dancer who gained recognition in *The Billy Barnes Revue,* which featured her future husband Ken Berry. Perhaps her most famous film work was in the original *The Little Shop of Horrors,* Joseph also appeared in *A Guide for the Married Man, The Cheyenne Social Club* and *With Six You Get Eggroll.* Among her television appearances were *Hogan's Heroes, The Andy Griffith Show* and the first *Bob Newhart Show* (1961-62). Joseph joined the cast of *The Doris Day Show* in 1971 and stayed until the series ended in 1973. Her character, Jackie Parker, was single, assertive, attentive to her boss Cy and friend to Doris. She was also quite imaginative with her hair and wardrobe.

After the series ended, Joseph worked as a Los Angeles TV host and as an animal activist. When her marriage to Berry ended in a costly, traumatic divorce, Joseph founded L.A.D.I.E.S., a support group for ex-wives of celebrities.

The 1980s found Joseph in the successful *Gremlins* and *Gremlins 2: The New Batch,* and the comedies *Police Academy 2: Their First Assignment* and *Police Academy 4: Citizens on Patrol..*

Jackie Parker was first seen in the episode "And Here's…Doris" and her last televised appearance was "Byline…Alias Doris." She is Cy Bennett's secretary, a position Doris Martin had with Mr. Nicholson.

She had a thing for Albert Gramas while the two attended John Marshall High School. She ran into him while in Rome and later at a hotel. Jackie dated a man named Harry for two years, but he cheated on her twice. She was then seeing Sid, who sold watches and also snores. Jackie's mother, who won a trip to Rome but couldn't go because her dog was sick, is Jewish and her father isn't.

Jackie is a competent secretary; however, she tends to visit a lot with Doris, which bothers Cy. She once called in sick on a Friday in order to have a three-day weekend; collected $83 from the staff for Cy's birthday gift (a new trenchcoat); announced the designs at the 1972 fashion show in which Doris modeled works by her tailor; and injured her arm when the elevator at *today's world* stopped abruptly.

She is a good friend to Doris and stayed overnight with Doris after she thinks there's a peeping tom in the neighborhood. She also offered to quit when Doris was fired in "There's a Horse Thief in Every Family Tree."

Her sense of fashion and hairstyles are another thing, however. They frequently changed and weren't always as stylish as her friend's.

### Bernie Kopell as Louie Pallucci, seasons 3-4

The New York native is a veteran of several television shows, but one of Bernie Kopell's earliest screen appearances happened to be an unbilled part as a frustrated television director in *The Thrill of It All*. He guested on many popular TV series: *That Girl, The Odd Couple, McMillan and Wife, Alice, The Six Million Dollar Man, Chico and the Man, The Mary Tyler Moore Show* and *The Fresh Prince of Bel-Air*.

Kopell also appeared on many episodes of *Bewitched* and *Love, American Style*, and his first recurring television role was on the 1960s spy spoof *Get Smart*. After *The Doris Day Show*, where he played the Italian master chef Louie Pallucci, Kopell's fame increased in households by playing the doctor for several seasons in *The Love Boat* and its subsequent reunion shows. Kopell continues working today, recently on the sitcom *Scrubs*.

Louie Pallucci's first appearance was in "Doris Finds an Apartment" and his last was in "The Blessed Event." Bernie Kopell was first seen in the series, however, in "A Woman's Intuition" and his last appearance on the series was as Uncle August Van Kappelhoff in "The Magnificent Fraud."

Louie Pallucci is married to Angie and the couple are the proprietors of Pallucci's Italian Restaurant. The establishment is in the building Louie purchased with his father-in-law's money, so Angie said.

Louie married Angie in 1960, and met her while clamdigging; however, in the 1971 episode, "A Weighty Problem," they've been together for 22 years. Had they dated almost a dozen years before marrying?

Louie is an excellent chef and used to make Angie banana splits and serve them to her in bed when first married. But when Angie gained a few pounds, he called her "Fatso." Although he seldom gives affection or much attention to his wife, he once believed Angie was having an affair with Ron Harvey ("Love Makes the Pizza Go 'Round").

The couple works long hours at the restaurant and seldom retreat from their daily routine; however, they once slipped away for a weekend in Las Vegas. Louie doesn't like children or pets living in the building, even though he and Angie later have a dog named Sophie. He made a concession with Doris's sons after they said they liked his pizza better than anyone else's, and he quickly grew to like the boys.

**Peter Lawford as Dr. Peter Lawrence, seasons 4-5**

In a career that spanned six decades, Peter Lawford was part of Hollywood royalty. A leading man in 1940s and 1950s Hollywood films, Lawford appeared in many classics including *Mrs. Miniver*, *Random Harvest*, *The White Cliffs of Dover*, *The Picture of Dorian Gray* and *Easter Parade*. His poise and looks provided sophistication, but his charm and clipped British accent, which was downplayed at times, made him appealing in films like *Good News*. Lawford outgrew the charming young man image, despite the fact MGM, the studio he was signed to, believed he would become "the new Ronald Colman" as a romantic leading man. By the 1950s, he was appearing in the television series *Dear Phoebe* and *The Thin Man*.

Lawford's marriage to Patricia Kennedy elevated him to a higher level of power and wealth. As President John F. Kennedy's brother-in-law, Lawford continued working in films (*Exodus* and *Advice and Consent*), but his public persona was that of a jet-setter who was part of the infamous partying group, the Rat Pack, with Frank Sinatra, Joey Bishop, Dean Martin and Sammy Davis, Jr. In the years following his divorce from Patricia Kennedy, Lawford made few films but several TV appearances, including the recurring role of the hip and uncomplicated Dr. Peter Lawrence on *The Doris Day Show*.

Dr. Peter Lawrence first appeared in "Doris and the Doctor" and was last seen in "Hospital Benefit." He was introduced to the series when he made a house call to Cy Bennett's home when he is sick in bed. Peter sees Doris and asks her if she's Mrs. Bennett. "Never," she replies. This leads to many dates and a comfortable relationship.

Peter is a general practitioner who performs surgery and delivers babies, as in the case of Mr. and Mrs. Winston. He charges patients $15 for an office visit, but made a few "office calls" to Cy Bennett at *today's world,* which gave him the opportunity to see Doris.

Peter gave Doris an antique, hand-cranked car she called Clara for their one-year anniversary. He says they met at Sandy Crawford's cocktail party and Doris wore a navy suit with a white hat. Doris says it was Cy's apartment and she was wearing a gray dress. She was correct.

Peter was married to Lois Fraser, a surgical nurse, who Peter works with at times at the hospital. Doris never knew about her until well into their romance, which caused some problems in their relationship.

## Patrick O'Neal as Jonathon Rusk, season 5

Florida native Patrick O'Neal started acting in 1944 while a young-ster, and then in his teenage years, he was (surprisingly) directing Signal Corps training films. His training at the Actor's Studio and Neighbor-hood Playhouse followed, as did acting in live television broadcasts in-cluding *Gruen Playhouse*. O'Neal juggled theater (*The Night of the Iguana*), television (*The Twilight Zone*, *The Outer Limits*, *Columbo*) and film roles (*A Fine Madness*, *The Way We Were*) in his long career. As Jonathon Rusk on *The Doris Day Show*, O'Neal was a suave and charming, intelligent and down-to-earth suitor for Doris Martin.

Regardless of the role, O'Neal brought a sense of calm and compe-tence to his parts; however, his personal life was not so. It was in the 1970s when O'Neal publicly admitted his alcoholism and appeared in several public service announcements for Alcoholics Anonymous. O'Neal continued to work after his disclosure, from television commercials to movies, including *Die Hard 2*, *For the Boys* and *Under Seige*.

Jonathon Rusk's first appearance on the series was in "The Press Sec-retary" and the last was in "Welcome to Big Sur, Sir." He was Doris's hometown friend and the two had dated. When Jonathon and Doris meet again, he is running for Congress and he hires Doris as his press secretary. In the episode, Jonathon is married to Louise and she believes Jonathon and Doris are having an affair. She learns they aren't, but the couple later divorce.

Although Jonathon lost the election, he continued his work as a tele-vision news correspondent. One of his more important stories was a series on North African nations.

He and Doris begin dating and have a serious relationship, possibly leading to marriage, but it is put on hold as the series ended.

## Denver Pyle as Buck Webb, seasons 1-3 (opening title credit seasons 1&2)

Denver Pyle did not plan on becoming an actor, but instead the Colorado native studied law and worked his way through school playing drums in a dance band. However, he grew disenchanted with law and quit to work various jobs including shrimp boats in Texas and oil rigs in Oklahoma. His desire to perform came about while working with a mute co-worker in the oil fields who conveyed his thoughts through body lan-guage and expressions.

After studying under Michael Shekhov and Maria Ouspenskaya, Pyle was cast in small roles, usually as a rural character. His breakthrough role came in 1967's *Bonnie and Clyde* as a humiliated sheriff. The following year, Pyle began a three-season stint as Buck Webb on *The Doris Day Show* and also directed several episodes of the series. As Doris Martin's father Buck, Pyle played the character as a good man with old-fashioned common sense and a good heart. Buck worked the farm, which had been in the family for three generations, and felt a closeness to the wide-open spaces.

Pyle's later television work included *The Life and Times of Grizzly Adams*, and he is best remembered as the level headed Uncle Jesse Duke on *The Dukes of Hazzard* from 1979-85.

Buck Webb's appeared on the first episode of *The Doris Day Show* and last appeared in "It's Christmas Time in the City." While his real name is Buckley Webb and his age is unknown, since he said his birth certificate was lost, Buck Webb is a farmer who has lived all of his live on the Webb farm near Cotina. In his youth, Buck was a boy soprano: "When I sang 'Over the Waves,'" Buck said, "there wasn't a dry eye in the house." "That, I believe," Aggie the maid replied.

Other than his unnamed wife, the only other specific mention of women in Buck's life includes Major Emma Flood, whom he dated when he was a sergeant in the Marines. They once had a breakfast of chipped beef, waffles and sweet-and-sour sauce in Hong Kong. Buck also dated manicurist Vera McIntosh in his later years, but that relationship ended and she presumably married Buck's best friend Doc Carpenter.

Buck's favorite actor is John Wayne. He likes playing gin rummy, and smokes a pipe on occasion. He once coerced Doris into putting on an Elementary school musical to raise funds for the traveling library ("The Musical"), and then another show for his lodge. He is involved in many community groups, including being a school board member, is a lodge member and part of the Rotary Club.

Buck's favorite pie is blueberry, and he prefers salted crackers to plain ones. He likes Chinese food and takes the boys out to eat with Doris and Mr. Nicholson. He hates being called "Gramps" by Mr. Nicholson ("Married for a Day"). Is called a "sweet old bear" and "Buckaroo" by Doris, and "Old Timer" by a police officer in "Buck Visits the Big City." Most people address him as Buck or Mr. Webb, while his grandsons call him Grandpa.

He dotes on his daughter and especially his grandsons, who he takes bowling, fishing and camping. He bought the boys new bicycles. Buck helps the boys with their homework, specifically teaching fractions to Billy. But he believes the boys need to learn things on their own, as well. He reminds Doris of this many times, including when Billy and Toby get a temporary job delivering eggs.

While he is slow to admit it, he likes hired hand Leroy B. Simpson. It is not quite a father-son relationship, but more of a friendly distant cousin. Buck, however, dislikes it when Leroy does not listen to his orders and many times calls him a "nincompoop" because of Leroy's incompetence.

Buck once lived on a mountain for two months living off roots and berries. He lost every event in the father-son competition with Toby and Billy, including the three-legged race and the sack race. However, Buck came in first place in the horseshoe tossing tournament with Leroy as his partner.

Buck admitted "drab and dull" are his favorite colors when Doris wants to paint the interior of the house. He likes things to be kept simple. Rarely is he seen wearing anything else but a plaid shirt, denim jeans and boots. In 1969, Doris gave him a wool plaid shirt for his birthday and the boys gave him a football.

After Doris and the boys moved to San Francisco in 1970, Buck made several Sunday visits to the city, bringing produce from the farm.

### Rose Marie as Myrna Gibbons, seasons 2-3 (opening title credit)

Rose Marie Mazetta began her career in entertainment at the age of three when her neighbors entered her in a talent contest. She appeared onstage at New York's Mecca Theater and sang "(What Can I Say) After I Say I'm Sorry?" then danced the Charleston and won the first-prize trip to Atlantic City and a spot on a major radio program. By 1932, Baby Rose Marie was one of the biggest stars on the NBC radio network. Audiences were skeptical that a youngster could possess such a mature voice, that many protested in writing and accused the network of passing off an adult midget as a child. Rose Marie continued performing, however, venturing into vaudeville and appearing in a few movies, including 1933's *International House*.

When she was 12, her parents moved from New York to New Jersey and entered Rose Marie in a convent school where she remained through the age of 17. The transition from child star to an adult performer was difficult, but Rose Marie found a niche after restyling herself as a comedienne and traveled the nightclub circuit for several years. In the 1950s, she began guest appearances on television shows including *Love That Bob* which led to her being cast as a regular on *The Dick Van Dyke Show* from 1961-1965.

From 1969 to 1971, she played Doris's best friend and co-worker, the humorous man-chaser Myrna Gibbons on *The Doris Day Show*. After the series changed its format in 1971, her role was written out of the series. Rose Marie continued working in film and television, appearing on *S.W.A.T.*, *The Hollywood Squares*, and the film, *Cheaper to Keep Her,* among others.

Myrna Gibbons first appeared in "Doris Gets a Job" and last appeared in "Skiing, Anyone?" Myrna Gibbons is a 40-something single gal who works at *today's world,* where she is Ron Harvey's secretary. She is also one of Doris Martin's closest friends, who loves to gossip and is always on the lookout for Mr. Right.

Myrna occasionally mentions a man named Marvin, who she's known for ten years and who we believe she is casually dating—until someone better comes along. He bowls three times a week and visits his mother often. Apparently their relationship is without commitment since Myrna hooked up with Mr. Singer of the accounting department at the 1969 office Christmas party, and had boyfriends, including Sidney who was "stingy with a buck."

But Myrna can be easily charmed by any man she finds attractive, for instance French movie star Claude LeMaire. She was flattered by Frenchman Jacques Giroux, who convinced her to add his name to the guest list of designer Montagne's second fashion show ("The Fashion Show").

Myrna once lost an earring in a man's apartment in order to get him to see her again, but he turned out to be a hippie and ended up wearing it himself. She is crazy about actor Steve McQueen and has an autographed picture of him in her apartment that she placed in a manila envelope for safekeeping. She once mistook Ron Harvey for McQueen when she went to Hollywood with Doris.

She is not the best secretary in the world. She does her nails during work hours, places and accepts personal phone calls during business hours, and takes more coffee breaks than is the norm. Mr. Harvey chides her for typing mistakes, and she once lost Ron Harvey's article on export versus imports at a Go-Go club.

She lied to Mr. Nicholson to get out of work and helped Doris move into her apartment, and said she speaks French in order to meet fashion designer Montagne. Myrna likes to do Jimmy Durante impersonations at office Christmas parties; dressed as a "floozy" to help rescue Doris from kidnappers; was on a banana diet for a while so that she'd get a figure like a banana; spent $32.50 on a jewelry box she gave Doris for Christmas; and sprained her ankle walking upstairs on a weekend skiing trip with Doris.

Myrna is a good friend to Doris, helping her whenever she asks. The pair worked at Leroy Simpson's gas station for a day; were instructors at Duke Farentino's dance studio for a week; and disguised themselves as society women to help convince a food critic to review Pallucci's restaurant—and then worked there for an evening as waitresses.

### Fran Ryan as Aggie, season 1 (opening title credit)

Fran Ryan was born in Los Angeles and is remembered for her portrayals of gruff, no-nonsense women. She was a familiar face due to her theatrical performances in the 1950s and appearances on *The Beverly Hillbillies* and *Green Acres*. Her first major television role on *The Doris Day Show* was as the opinionated and stubborn maid Aggie, an old friend of Doris Martin's from New York.

Although Ryan left the show halfway through the first season, she immediately replaced an ailing Barbara Pepper in the role of Doris Ziffel on *Green Acres*. She also appeared in various television works, including *Gunsmoke, Taxi, Charlie's Angels*, the daytime drama *General Hospital*, the Krofft Saturday morning show *Sigmund and the Sea Monsters* and in a commercial for Hungry Jack pancakes.

In addition, Ryan appeared in theatrical and television movies throughout her five-decade career. Among them are Disney's *The Apple Dumpling Gang* and *The Million Dollar Duck, Big Wednesday, Rocky II, Take This Job and Shove It, Pale Rider, Chances Are, Thanksgiving Day* and *Archie: To Riverdale and Back Again*. One of her more memorable roles is that of an uppity society dame who badgers cabdriver Bill Murray in the hit movie *Stripes*.

Aggie appeared in the first episode of *The Doris Day Show*, with her last being "The Camping Trip." She likes to talk on the phone for hours, having spent a record 2½ hours discussing *Gone With the Wind*. Her memory, however, is fading as she thought Clark Gable was killed falling from a horse in the film. Listening in on a receiver, Buck tells her it was Thomas Mitchell who was killed.

She lived in New York City at one point in her life and has known Doris Martin for several years. She's quick with a line, which is usually aimed at Buck. Strong, but kindhearted, Aggie ruled with an iron fist during the time she worked on the Webb farm.

**Paul Smith as Ron Harvey, seasons 2-3 (opening title credit season 3)**

A veteran of approximately 400 roles in motion pictures and television, Paul Smith's experience led to a guest spot on season one of *The Doris Day Show*. The following season, he was hired in another role as the "bumbling office Lothario" Ron Harvey on the series. Smith's popularity in the role as the charming skirt-chaser grew so much that in the series' third season, he received co-starring billing.

*The Doris Day Show* was Smith's fifth television series as a regular. Among his other credits were co-starring roles in *No Time for Sergeants, Mr. Terrific, Mrs. G Goes to College* (a.k.a. *The Gertrude Berg Show*) and *Fibber McGee & Molly*. Smith also appeared in several episodes of *Bewitched* prior to, during and after his stint on *The Doris Day Show*, and *Love, American Style*. Smith also guested on *Batman, McHale's Navy, The Andy Griffith Show, The Rookies* and *Police Story*.

Although he was a recognized face and talent on television, Smith had appeared in several movies. Three of his better-known works, however, were unbilled: Blake Edwards' *The Great Race, Exodus* and *All That Heaven Allows*.

Smith first appeared on *The Doris Day Show* in the episode "The Baby Sitter" as Hal Benson. His character Ron Harvey first appeared in "Doris Gets a Job," with his last appearance in "Doris Goes to Hollywood."

"I am to the secretaries what the motor club is to motorists," Ron says, which sums up his character and unabashed skirt-chasing activities. On Doris's first day of work at *today's world*, he asks Doris out for a date, but she declines. He later invites her to dinner and the theater. She declines at first, then later accepts. The date dissolves, however, when Ron leaves without Doris, after waiting a long time while tending to the boys' upset stomachs. Although he doesn't ask her out again, the two remain friends.

An associate editor at the magazine, Ron belongs to the country club. He tends to arrive at work with a hangover, smokes ten-cent cigars, and likes to take advantage of the expense account provided to him by the magazine, once spending $26 at the Clover Club.

One unnamed girlfriend is the hatcheck girl at La Petite Maison, arguably his favorite restaurant. The Bam Bam Club is another of Ron's hangouts as is The Colony, Joe's Topless Bar and Grill in Sausilito, and an unnamed Go-Go club in Northbeach.

Ron Harvey helped advance Doris's career at *today's world*. He gave Doris her first writing assignment [in "The Prizefighter and the Lady"] since he had a date with a stewardess. He also used Doris to acquire stories, including one on San Francisco Tigers' quarterback Joe Garrison. When Doris doesn't want to go with Ron to watch the football game, he cajoles her with foot-long hot dogs at the game.

With his secretary Myrna Gibbons, Ron lied to Mr. Nicholson to help Doris move into her San Francisco apartment; attempted to save Doris from kidnappers; and was a temporary dance instructor at Duke Farentino's studio when Doris asked him to help out. He also disguised himself as Rodney Alexander III in order to expose Duke's girlfriend Alison Otis Peabody as a fraud.

His ideas for stories include a boy finding a lost dog, hippies with short hair, a Go-Go dancer who's also a clinical psychologist, and a dog who finds his lost boy. All were turned down. Ron wrote an article on imports versus exports for the magazine's lead article and how it affects the average man. He got the idea at a bar when he ordered a scotch and learned 80 cents of the $1.10 tab went to tariffs and taxes.

Ron drives a two-seater and got lost on his first trip to the Webb farm; doesn't like confined spaces; tells terrible jokes (though he finds them amusing); played violin in school and did so again in the episode "Dinner for One" at Pallucci's. He also played a trumpet at Doris's 1970 Christmas party. He was born in Santa Ana, California. His real name is Rudolph Valentino Harvey, having been named after the silent film star.

**Tod Starke as Toby Martin, seasons 1–3 (opening title credit)**

Tod Starke made his acting debut when he was five years old on *The Second Hundred Years* television series. At a friend's suggestion, his mother had taken her daughter to an agent, and Tod went along. The agent heard Tod lisping through a missing front tooth and signed him on the spot. After doing some commercials, Tod won his first movie role as Dink in *Angel in My Pocket*, starring Andy Griffith, prior to the role of Toby Martin on *The Doris Day Show* when he was six years old.

Although he had little acting experience, his rapport with Doris, Denver Pyle and Philip Brown led to him winning the role of Toby Martin. Tod Starke played the youngest son, Toby, a very sensitive young man who looked up to his older brother and loved his mother and grandfather very much.

In 1971 Tod played Danny in the *Adam-12* episode, "Log 125: A Safe Job." Additional roles, however, did not follow. In 1983, Starke died at the age of 21 from injuries sustained in a motorcycle accident.

Toby Martin appeared on the first show of *The Doris Day Show* and last appeared on "The Father-Son Weekend." He is Doris Martin's youngest son, and is six years old in 1968. He is the bat boy for the Cotina Indian's Little League team, and is in Cub Scouts in 1969. When Toby helped Billy sell candy bars for the older scouts, protests from another scout's mother prevented him from selling additional bars. Doris softened his disappointment by explaining, "You're just a civilian." At times he was called "Buster" by Doris and "Skutter" by Buck.

Although the two argue on occasion, Toby is close to his older brother. When he came down with the measles, Toby gave them to Billy. Like Billy, he watches the TV show *Frogman*. He sold lemonade with Billy on the farm and in San Francisco. Toby once ate six chili dogs (to Billy's four) at Cubby Weaver's barbecue. The boys share the same bedroom, and Toby wears Billy's hand-me-down clothes. He confides in Billy, telling him he wasn't selected for the school choir. He plays checkers, football and Indians with Billy and their friends.

His responsibilities on the farm included cleaning out the chicken house with Billy. Toby leaves for school with Billy at 8:20 A.M., while living on the farm, riding his bicycle when not taking the school bus. In San Francisco, the boys left shortly before Doris, approximately the same time as in the country. He has snacks after school with Billy, one time having milk and freshly baked bread with sugar sprinkled on top. Toby is not a picky eater, but prefers cold to hot cereal for breakfast.

Toby likes to read *Snoopy* comics; was photographed with a candle in his ear at Billy's birthday party; and has a friend, Patty, who is the class dodgeball champ, but hates milk.

Toby earned an A in spelling and a gold star for attendance. At age eight, Toby ran away from home to the airport to try to get a ticket and join Doris in Greece because he missed her. At the San Francisco apartment, Toby accidentally ran into Mr. Jarvis—"Only because Billy was chasing me"—and broke his lamp.

Because he is smaller, Toby used two six packs of beer as a booster seat in a restaurant. "Isn't it cold?" Billy asked. "Yeah, it's crazy!" Toby answered. He loves his stuffed animals and wanted to take them with him on a camping trip. He also keeps his frog Harold in a shoebox under the nightstand by his bed

Toby went on a father-son weekend outing with Doris. There, the pair won gunny sack and wheelbarrow races, and presumed to have won an egg toss and fishing contest with eight catches. The two won the all-around competition and were awarded with a trophy.

### Naomi Stevens as Juanita, season 1 (opening title credit)

Originally from New Jersey, Naomi Stevens guested on several TV shows including *Have Gun, Will Travel, Hogan's Heroes, Dr. Kildare, The Man From U.N.C.L.E.* and *The Lawless Years*.

Prior to joining *The Doris Day Show* in 1968, Stevens was a regular on *The Flying Nun,* where she played Sister Teresa. As the warm and loving Juanita, Stevens played the second maid in the series' first season. At the time, she was one of a handful of Hispanic actors to appear as a regular performer on a television series

After *The Doris Day Show,* Stevens made appearances on many series like *The Partridge Family, Barney Miller, Cannon* and *Taxi,* and had a recurring role as Sgt. Bella Archer on the hit show *Vega$.*

Juanita was first seen in the "The Job" episode of *The Doris Day Show* and last appeared in the episode "The Relatives." She was the maid on the ranch after Aggie left and was a warm and loving woman. She never had a bad thing to say about anyone, even when she learned she was double-crossed when Doris set her up on a date. She once offered 300 pesos to Doris when she thought the family needed money (about $23), and she makes sure the family is well-taken care of. She helps Doris put Vapo-rub on the boys when they are sick, and her personal remedy for a bad cold is mustard plaster.

### McLean Stevenson as Mr. Michael Nicholson, seasons 2-3 (opening title credit)

The cousin of Democratic presidential candidate Adlai Stevenson and grandson of U.S. vice-president Adlei E. Stevenson, McLean Stevenson was born in Normal, Illinois in 1929 and served in the Navy then attended Northwestern University, where he received a bachelor's degree in theater arts.

After various jobs, from working in athletics to being press secretary for his cousin, Stevenson won a scholarship to the American Musical and Dramatic Academy in 1961. His summer stock and Broadway stage work include *The Music Man, Bye Bye Birdie* and *I'll Always Remember Miss What's Her Name.* Guest appearances on television in *Car 54, Where Are You?, The Defenders* and *That Girl* led to his regular role as frustrated boss Michael Nicholson on *The Doris Day Show.* Stevenson followed the series with his Emmy-nominated breakthrough performance on *M\*A\*S\*H.*

After three years on *M\*A\*S\*H*, Stevenson left to star in several short-lived series, including *In the Beginning*, *Hello, Larry* and *Condo*. He continued making guest appearances, including *The Golden Girls*, and was also the national spokesperson for the Children's Burn Foundation in Sherman Oaks, California until his death.

Stevenson's first appearance as Michael Nicholson was "Doris Gets a Job" and his final was "Skiing, Anyone?" Michael "Nick" Nicholson is the Editor-in-Chief of *today's world* in 1969 when he hires Doris Martin as his personal secretary. A single man, who is discreet with his playboy lifestyle, Nick was born in Bloomington, Illinois. He dated a woman named Rochelle, who had a deep sexy voice that Doris imitated to Myrna, and who lost her earring in his apartment. He also dated Karen Carruthers, who called him "Nicky." He last saw her in 1965 before she reappeared in 1969 in a fruitless attempt to reconcile.

Although there was never anything between them, it's apparent the working relationship between Mr. Nicholson and Doris Martin could have easily developed into something more. There is a mutual admiration, and he takes the opportunity to ask Doris to escort him to business meetings. He invited her to a business party because she's the "wholesome" type and would impress the hostess. He also asked Doris to "the biggest affair of the year" (the Magazine Guild Spring Dance), where there were four bands and continuous dancing until dawn.

Nick posted bail on Doris and Myrna when they were jailed for picketing without a permit. He also threatened to run a story on the utility company and its computer 1176B's errors in regard to Doris's paid bill. The mistake was resolved. And when Nick thought Doris was going to be taken advantage of by a suave bodybuilder, he sought her out in a rainstorm to "save" her.

Business-wise, Nick went to London for a publisher's convention with Col. Fairburn, gave a stockholder's report when Col. Fairburn was unable to do so, and fought to get Doris a ten-dollar raise.

## Lord Nelson as himself, seasons 1-3 (opening title credit season 1)

Lord Nelson was also known as Nelson and received billing in the series' first year [not even Benji received that distinction while on *Petticoat Junction*]. A sheepdog, Nelson appeared with Doris Day in her last film, 1968's *With Six You Get Eggroll*. Nelson gets the boys out of bed upon command and will deliver notes to people for a treat but wishes to be paid in advance.

Nelson, however, can be a nuisance, primarily because of his size. He gets into the way of people in practically every episode. He accidentally upsets a briefcase, but that act exposed a con man. He also knocks people down, including Doris once while she carried a large stack of empty egg cartons. Nelson likes cookies and helps himself unless reprimanded, like when he almost ate them off a platter in the first pair of Christmas episodes.

Nelson ran out of the apartment and into traffic after moving to San Francisco, for which he was scolded. Nelson doesn't steal, but retrieves, which he does several times after Mr. Jarvis moves next door to Doris in San Francisco. Nelson gets Jarvis's slipper two times, his hat, as well as his trousers.

## SELECT CREW CREDITS:
### Bruce Bilson

Directed many early and later episodes of the series then went on to work on other major television shows including *S.W.A.T.*, *The Rookies*, *The Six Million Dollar Man*, *Simon & Simon*, *Sledge Hammer!* and *Touched by an Angel*.

### James L. Brooks

Wrote "The Job" script for *The Doris Day Show*, which was referred to as the "guide" script which helped in the evolution of the Doris Martin character for the series' run. He went on to create or co-create the TV series *Room 222*, *The Mary Tyler Moore Show* and *Taxi* before winning three Academy Awards for his first feature film *Terms of Endearment* in 1983. He also helped bring *The Tracy Ullman Show* to Fox-TV from which *The Simpsons* was spun-off.

### Constance (Connie) Edney

Was the costume designer for the TV series *The Adventures of Ozzie & Harriet*, *Leave It to Beaver* and *The Virginian* before working with Doris on *With Six You Get Eggroll* and five seasons of *The Doris Day Show*. She also assisted designer Orry-Kelly in costuming Marilyn Monroe for the film *Some Like It Hot*.

### Jack Elinson and Norman Paul

Were producers and writers for *The Doris Day Show*. They also produced the series *Good Times*. They worked individually as well, as Elinson wrote for *The Danny Thomas Show* and *Get Smart*, and Paul did the same for *Hogan's Heroes*. As a team they also wrote scripts for *The Danny Thomas Hour* and *One Day at a Time*.

### Perry Ferguson II

Was the art director for *The Doris Day Show* and was responsible for the show's smart and stylish sets. His father, Perry Ferguson, was the art director for many films including Alfred Hitchcock's *Rope, The Best Years of Our Lives, Song of the South,* and was associate art director on *Citizen Kane*.

### James Fritzell

Was credited as creating *The Doris Day Show*. He was a writer for several TV series including *The Odd Couple, Goodyear Playhouse,* 29 episodes of *The Andy Griffith Show* and 24 episodes of *M\*A\*S\*H*. He also wrote the screenplays for *The Shakiest Gun in the West* and *Angel in My Pocket,* which featured Tod Starke.

### Jimmie Haskell

A three-time Grammy Award winner, Haskell served as the music composer, conductor and arranger for most of the series. Haskell had done the theme song to *The Adventures of Ozzie & Harriet* and worked on *Bewitched* and other series. He also worked on music for motion pictures including *Big, Spy Hard* and *The Color Purple*. In addition to rearranging several of Doris Day's recordings, including the theme song, Haskell wrote several pieces of original incidental music that were used in the series.

### Barbara Lampson

Was the hairstylist on *The Doris Day Show* and also worked with Doris on her films *Move Over, Darling, Send Me No Flowers, The Glass Bottom Boat, The Ballad of Josie, Caprice* and *With Six You Get Eggroll*. She then worked as the hairstylist for the films *A Star Is Born* (1976), *Footloose* and *Far and Away*.

### Harry Maret

Was a respected make-up artist for several years before *The Doris Day Show*. His movie work includes *Around the World in Eighty Days, The Big Country, Separate Tables,* and *Elmer Gantry* before becoming Doris's make-up man for her films *The Glass Bottom Boat, Caprice, Where Were You*

*When the Lights Went Out?* and *With Six You Get Eggroll.* In between the latter two, Maret did the make-up for *The Graduate.*

### Laurence Marks

Wrote several episodes for the series, as well as for many other television shows, including *Hogan's Heroes, The Flying Nun, My World and Welcome to It* and 25 episodes of *M\*A\*S\*H.*

### Richard L. Rawlings

Was the Director of Photography on *The Doris Day Show.* Rawlings' other work included the TV shows *The Alfred Hitchcock Hour, The Wild, Wild West, Scarecrow and Mrs. King, Kung Fu* and *Dynasty.*

### William Wiard

Helming several episodes of *The Doris Day Show,* Wiard also directed the shows *Barnaby Jones, The Streets of San Francisco, The Rockford Files,* six episodes of *M\*A\*S\*H* and eight episodes of *Bonanza.*

# Season One: 1968-1969
## "A Family Comes Together"

**1968-1969**

When *The Doris Day Show* premiered in September 1968, Day was cast as Doris Martin (nee Webb) who had freelanced as a writer for *Ladies' World* magazine in New York while having a family with her husband Steve. After Steve's death, Doris and her boys, Billy and Toby, and presumably Aggie, moved across the country to live with her father on the family ranch in California outside of San Francisco. There, she adjusted to rural life and helped on the ranch, along with her father Buck and Leroy the hired hand. In December 1968, Aggie left and was replaced by Juanita as the housekeeper.

The serenely beautiful opening credits of the first year's episodes showed Doris and the cast in the sun-sparkled outdoors. A new arrangement of "Qué Sera, Sera," with Doris and a choir of children, played on the soundtrack, which was similar to Doris's re-recording of the song on her album *With a Smile and a Song*.

There were three sponsors for the series the first season: Ralston-Purina, Bristol-Myers, and Proctor & Gamble. Doris made no commercials for the sponsors, but did a promotional short film for a Ralston-Purina convention. "Someone had written a script for me which I didn't understand, so I told them the only way I'd do it was my way," she told the *Los Angeles Times*' "TV Times" in 1968. Her way was to come on film and say she didn't understand the script, "but here's what they wanted me to read," and she read it. The *Times* reported: "Well, the whole thing went over like a house afire at the convention with everyone there loving Miss Day's candor."

"I can only do things I love to do," Doris said. "Then they don't possess me. I guess I really don't have any fear. That comes from ambition, anxiety and trepidation, which all lead to fear, don't they?"

The series was nominated for a Golden Globe Award for Best Television Comedy, and Doris Day also received a nod from the Hollywood Foreign Press for Best Actress for her work on the show.

**CBS PRESS RELEASE TO PROMOTE *THE DORIS DAY SHOW*:**

August 5, 1968

### Film Star Doris Day Makes Television Debut In New Comedy Series Starting September 24

Doris Day, one of the greatest box-office names in motion picture history, will make her television debut in "The Doris Day Show," new comedy series beginning Tuesday, Sept. 24 (9:30-10:00 P.M., EDT) in color on the CBS Television Network.

Sponsors of the program are Bristol-Myers Company, represented by Grey Advertising, Inc., and the Procter & Gamble Company.

Featured as Miss Day's father, Buck Webb, will be veteran character actor Denver Pyle. Fran Ryan will play the family's outspoken housekeeper, Aggie Thompson. James Hampton will appear as Leroy B. Simpson, a hired hand. The children will be played by Philip Brown, 10, as Billy, and Tod Starke, 6, as Toby.

Much of the action in the show will revolve around the family's adjustments from city to country life, the problems of a woman trying to be both mother and father to her sons, and how she handles the "generation gap" between the boys and their grandfather.

## THE EPISODES:

[Authors' note: We are presenting in this book, the chronological order of the series' storyline. MPI DVD presented the episodes in their original television airing dates, which were not always the scheduled air dates, let alone the ones filmed in sequence. You will find our order has very few differences, but are key in the telling of Doris Martin's evolution, as well as the introduction of characters in order of airdates, situations, and an actual final episode.]

**"Billy's Black Eye" [also known as "The Black Eye"]**
Production Dates: June 17-21, 24, 25, 1968
Original Airdate: November 26, 1968 [eighth episode to air]
Directed by: Bob Sweeney

This was the first filmed episode, and the official production starting date was June 3, 1968. The opening shows us the family home as Doris is playing outside with Nelson, the dog, and getting the mail from the mailbox. This takes us to the kitchen, where we meet the family for the first time, enjoying breakfast, and a letter to Billy will create the first intrigue.

Billy comes home from school with a black eye but won't tell Doris who gave it to him. The next day, Billy comes back with another black eye and refuses to say what happened. Under pressure, he admits to his grandfather that he did not fight back. Conflicts of generations arise between Doris and her father of how the situation should be handled. Doris decides to investigate and finds a young girl from the neighborhood named Jackie hiding on the ranch. Doris finds the bully to be a very lovely young lady in love with Billy.

Tod Starke and Philip Brown with Lord Nelson.

Written by: Ray Singer; Lisa Gerritsen as Jackie; Woodrow Parfrey as Maxwell Digby [Billy's teacher]

Groovy Day Facts:
Doris Martin's late husband Steve is mentioned.

Doris Day Movie Find!:
Robert Mersey, the music composer and conductor for this episode, also scored Doris's film *With Six You Get Eggroll.*
The family dog played by Lord Nelson was also in *With Six You Get Eggroll.*

Guest Star Mini-Bio:

This was the first of three appearances in the series by Lisa Gerritsen. She was a busy child actress in the late 1960s and 1970s. Perhaps her most famous role was as the smart and well-adjusted Bess Lindstrom, daughter of outrageous Phyllis (played by Cloris Leachman), on the series *The Mary Tyler Moore Show* for five years, followed by *Phyllis*.

**"Dinner for Mom"**
Production Dates: July 22-26, 1968
Original Airdate: September 24, 1968 [first episode to air]
Directed by: Bob Sweeney

Doris celebrates her birthday in a big way with a fancy dinner in a nightclub, a special present from Billy and Toby. They had saved all of their money and discovered this unusual place because of its neat ad in the phone book. Although Doris wishes her husband Steve was there to see this event, she is very happy to be joining her boys for dinner. Unfortunately, the place is quite below standards—it's a Roadhouse!—with an array of riff-raffs, a cigar, gum-chewing staff, and a few indiscreet houseflies ready to be swatted. Doris, of course, makes the best of it as her boys are completely enchanted with their discovery. They are seated at a center table, surrounded by smoke, noise, and seem to be interrupting a pool tournament. Doris and Billy are seated comfortably, while Toby is strategically boosted on top of two very cold six-packs. Doris soon finds that after their dinner order is made, that her wallet is missing. Well-intentioned Billy and Toby had taken it, making sure she wouldn't pay for dinner. The challenge becomes how will Doris take care of the $19.48 bill, not including a cake Billy had ordered.

Written by: Dick Bensfield, Perry Grant; Norm Alden as Roadhouse Manager; Leonard Stone as the Waiter

Groovy Day Facts:

Doris sings a few bars of "Que Sera, Sera."

Doris Martin's husband Steve is mentioned here for the last time.

The Martins ordered three Hopalong Cassidys—on the rocks—three filets with salad and baked potato, two sundaes, two milks, and coffee. They also got a birthday "pie."

With Tod Starke and Philip Brown.

Doris drives a Plymouth station wagon while living on the farm.

Doris Day Movie Find!:
    *Gone With the Wind*, with Doris's *Teacher's Pet* [1958] leading man Clark Gable, is mentioned throughout this episode.

**"The Uniform"**
Production Dates: August 13-16, 19, 20, 1968
Original Airdate: October 1, 1968
Directed by: Bruce Bilson

A lot of excitement at 32 Mill Valley Road as Doris and Aggie are about to find out if Billy will become the pitcher of his Little League team and receive his official uniform. To everyone's delight, he makes it. As Buck would say, "Of course, he's my grandson, isn't he?" The house is bursting with happiness over Billy's achievement. Toby suddenly feels completely left out and announces to his mom that he has also received a uniform as a member of his school choir. The excitement in the house is doubled. The next day, as Toby actually auditions for Mr. Digby, he painfully discovers that he can't sing "so good." To reward his grandsons, Buck gives them both brand-new bicycles. Toby never informs his mom and grandpa that he never made the choir, and is encompassed with guilt. Doris comes face to face with the fact that he was never in the choir and tries to convince Toby to admit the truth.

Written by: Sid Morse; Woodrow Parfrey as Maxwell Digby; Scott Crawford as Ben

Groovy Day Facts:
Buck is on Cotina's school board, and the school is completely integrated.

With Denver Pyle and Tod Starke.

ORIGINAL SONG:

Doris sings the song "Kemo Kimo":

> Kemo Kimo, stare a stare
> Ma high, ma ho,
> Ma rum a stick of pumpernickel
> Snoop bang, nip cap
> Polly met your cameo
> I love you [bis]
> Once a great magician taught me what to say.
> So now I use these magic words to steal your heart away.

Doris Day Movie Find!:
Aggie mentions the showman Florenz Ziegfeld. Doris, as Ruth Etting, worked for Mr. Ziegfeld in *Love Me or Leave Me* [1955] by appearing in the *Ziegfeld Follies*.

**"The Friend"**
Production Dates: July 29-August 2, 5, 1968
Original Airdate: October 8, 1968
Directed by: Bob Sweeney

It's a great day for milk in Cotina! Mr. Digby has been appointed as the faculty advisor for the milk fund drive. Actually the great news is that Doris Martin and her family have been chosen for a new milk ad. Via their participation, the school will receive 200 pints of milk a day for the children. Henry Pritchart, the owner of Sunnyvale Dairies, on the suggestion of Mr. Mitchell, his ad man from Phoenix, asks Doris to add two girls of her children's choice to complete the family portrait. Billy chooses his friend Jackie [episode "Billy's Black Eye"] and Toby chooses the dodgeball champion from class, Patty, who happens to be Black. The very nervous, chain-smoking Mr. Mitchell, who is worried about his job, refuses to take the picture, and wants to get rid of Patty. Doris's blood is boiling as she courageously confronts Mr. Pritchart into doing the right thing for all the right reasons.

Written by: E. Duke Vincent, Bruce Johnson. Woodrow Parfrey as Maxwell Digby, Peggy Rea as Grace Henley, George Morgan as Brig

Mitchell, Lisa Gerritsen as Jackie Clements, Cheri Grant as Patty, Raymond Kark as Harvey Miller, R. G. Armstrong as Henry R. Pritchart

Groovy Day Facts:
Peggy Rae makes her first appearance as Doris's friend Grace Henley. We learn how absentminded Leroy is when he loses the tractor in the barn. In 1968, the average U.S. family consisted of 3.8 children—2 boys and 1.8 girls.

Doris Day Movie Find!:
Doris faced some serious prejudice herself when she was killed by the Ku Klux Klan at the end of her 1951 film *Storm Warning*, starring with Ronald Reagan and Ginger Rogers. [On a personal note, Doris Day's father, William Kappelhoff, at age 62, fell in love with and married Luvenia Williams Bennett, a black woman who helped him run his bar and grill near Cincinnati.]

**"The Matchmakers"**
Production Dates: August 21-23, 26-28, 1968
Original Airdate: October 22, 1968
Directed by: Bruce Bilson

The great losers in a Cotina father and son competition are Toby, Billy and Buck. As they are beyond disappointed from this event, the boys feel desperate measures have to be taken and must get mom married ASAP to a good runner. Enter the very self-centered and unworldly Deputy Sheriff Ubbie Puckum, a former high school football player, who thinks he is the catch of every girl in town—a legend in his own mind. The boys bring him home to Doris and insist they marry right away, which Buck finds completely hilarious. Doris is trapped, but finds a clever way of getting rid of Deputy Puckum.

Written by: Richard Baer; Frank Maxwell as Sheriff Ben Anders, Carl Byrd as Deputy Dan Case, Noam Pitlik as Deputy Ubbie Puckum

Groovy Day Facts:
Cotina has a drive-in movie theater, and Benny's Eatery has the best French dip sandwiches.

Tod Starke, Doris Day, Philip Brown and Lord Nelson.

Buck will enter a fitness program, courtesy of his grandsons.

Doris works on a patchwork quilt like her mother did, according to Buck.

Doris Day Movie Find!:

Day's co-stars Rock Hudson [*Pillow Talk*, 1959; *Lover Come Back*, 1962; *Send Me No Flowers*, 1964] and Cary Grant [*That Touch of Mink*, 1962] are mentioned by Aggie as possible future husbands for Doris Martin.

**"The Songwriter"**
Production Dates: September 16-20, 1968
Original Airdate: October 29, 1968
Directed by: Gary Nelson

Country music takes center stage in the life of Leroy B. Simpson as he dreams of becoming Country's next gifted songwriter following in the footsteps of Country legend Ernest Tubb. Leroy enters his song, "Weeds in the Garden of My Heart," in a songwriting contest. And he wins.

Leroy beams with happiness, promising the entire family lavish gifts from his songwriting earnings. Doris and Buck discover Leroy has been fooled by racketeers who have been taking his money. Doris decides to play a trick on Leroy and writes a horrible song, "Your Love Is Like Butter Gone Rancid," sends it to the company, and it is immediately accepted in the same way his had been. Doris, who cares for him very much, hopes that Leroy will see that he's been taken advantage of by crooks.

Written by: Joseph Bonaduce; Jerry Hausner as the Mailman

Groovy Day Facts:
Pancakes are usually the order at breakfast time on the ranch, and in this episode, Doris prepares them.
Leroy says the Webbs are the only family he has—for now.
Joseph Bonaduce, father of Danny Bonaduce from *The Partridge Family*, wrote this episode.

Doris Day Music Find!:
Doris sings the song "Your Love Is Like Butter Gone Rancid"
Music and lyrics composed and sung by Doris Martin

> Your love is like butter gone rancid.
> It's no good now, it's starting to turn.
> I pray/think that it's just like the man said.
> You can't put it back in the churn.
> Can't put, can't put, can't put it back in the churn.
> Oh durn.
> You can't put it back in the churn. [bis]

[alternate ending:]
> You're gonna be sorry you're leaving,
> 'cause we're having cake and ice cream.
> You're gonna be sorry dear Grandpa,
> now that you're splittin' the scene.
> Cake and ice cream,
> We're having cake and ice cream,
> Oh boy!

Clockwise from bottom left: Tod Starke, Denver Pyle, James Hampton and Philip Brown.

**"The Antique"**
Production Dates: June 26-28, July 1-3, 1968
Original Airdate: November 12, 1968
Directed by: Bob Sweeney

As Doris, Buck and Aggie rummage through the attic for a White Elephant sale, Buck discovers a very valuable table that his grandmother brought across country when she moved west. He could have sold it many times for a lot of money but always kept it as it was to stay in the family. Later, when Billy and Toby use the table without permission for a lemonade stand, and it is bought by two spinster peddlers for $5 who plan to buy more from the Webb home. Doris gets into a "farm hick" character to trick the ladies into returning the table.

Written by: Dorothy Cooper Foote; Estelle Winwood as Gertrude, Maudie Prickett as Bertie

Groovy Day Facts:
Leroy has a date with Ms. Ann Harper, the "little red-headed beautician" from Cotina.

With Fran Ryan and Denver Pyle.

Doris Day Music Find!:

Doris sings a rendition of "Down by the Old Mill Stream," accompanied by Buck on the mandolin.

Guest Star Mini-Bio:

Estelle Winwood acted on the American and British stages with such works as *The Merry Wives of Windsor* and *The Importance of Being Ernest* for decades before agreeing to work in films and later television. She was 70 years old when she appeared in *The Glass Slipper* in 1955, followed by other films including *The Swan*, *The Misfits* and *The Producers* (1968), as well as guest spots on TV shows including three appearances on *The Doris Day Show*. Her last film was *Murder by Death* in 1976.

**"Leroy B. Simpson"**
Production Dates: July 11, 12, 15-19, 1968
Original Airdate: November 19, 1968
Directed by: Bob Sweeney

Doris and Aggie reminisce about the first time they met Leroy B. Simpson. Billy and Toby had kept Leroy hidden in the barn the entire day to slowly introduce him to Grandpa as a possible hired hand. When the meeting occurred, it was a catastrophe. Leroy, in trying to help, mis-

With James Hampton and Denver Pyle.

wired the electric pump and Buck was on the receiving end. Doris convinces her father to keep him on the ranch. Soon, jewelry starts disappearing from the house. Who is the culprit? Is it Leroy? Or is it bird?

Written by: Sid Morse

Groovy Day Facts:
Aggie previously lived in New York City where she will be returning very soon.
Doris had an off-screen date with a man named Matt.

## "The Librarian"
Production Dates: August 6-9, 12, 1968
Original Airdate: December 3, 1968
Directed by: Bob Sweeney

Leroy B. Simpson goes to the library for the very first time and falls madly in love with the librarian, Winifred Proxmire. Leroy tries literally everything to get her attention. When he overhears Winifred talking to Professor Travis Peabody about 19th-century English poetry, Leroy tells her he is a fan, too. He accepts an invitation to participate at the group's next meeting, even though his knowledge of poetry is "as much as a pig knows about soap." Doris comes to the rescue once again and saves Leroy from running away and coaches him forthwith on Shelley's poem "To a Skylark." But on the night of the poetry reading, Professor Peabody recites the poem that Leroy and Doris had so carefully prepared.

With James Hampton.

Written by: Harry Winkler; Ryan MacDonald as Dr. Travis Peabody, Kelly Jean Peters as Winifred Proxmire, Keith Taylor as Carl

Groovy Day Facts:
    Leroy had a dog named Winnie when he was a boy.
    Leroy ate 14 pancakes prepared by Aggie.
    Shelley's wife, Mary, created *Frankenstein*.

Doris Day Movie Find!:
    In the biopic *I'll See You in My Dreams* [1951], Doris's father is an English professor who loves quoting poets and their poems. He would inspire his daughter and her future husband, Gus Kahn, who became one of the best lyricists of all time. Kahn was touchingly played by TV legend Danny Thomas.

**"The Camping Trip"**
Production Dates: August 29, 30 September 3-6, 1968
Original Airdate: December 10, 1968
Directed by: Bruce Bilson

The most exciting day for Billy and Toby has arrived. They are going camping with their grandfather and his "Indian" friend of 40 years, Joe Whitecloud. The kids, being great fans of John Wayne and his movies, are thrilled to be living in the wild with a real "Indian." Buck has his own view on John Wayne and those "friendly Indians." As they arrive to the camping ground, Joe Whitecloud tells them he's going to show them things John Wayne never heard of, which ruins the entire trip and they quickly go back to the ranch. Doris finds a clever way of putting the trip back on schedule, using reliable Leroy B. Simpson as a ploy.

Written by: Jerry Devine; Harry Corden as Joe Whitecloud

Groovy Day Facts:
Helcher's Store in Cotina is mentioned for the first time.
Rialto is the walk-in theater in Cotina.
This is Aggie's last appearance in the series. We presume she moved back to New York.

Denver Pyle Movie Find!:
Denver Pyle co-starred in two of John Wayne's classics: *The Horse Soldiers* [1959] and *The Alamo* [1960].

Guest Star Mini-Bio:
Harry [Henry] Corden was born in Montreal, Quebec, Canada, and made his first of six appearances on *The Doris Day Show* in "The Camping Trip." By season five he would play recurring character Mr. Lohman. The well-loved character actor, who appeared in such great films as Cecil B. DeMille's *The Ten Commandments*, is best remembered for his many cartoon character voices, especially Fred Flintstone following Alan Reed's death.

[Note: The following episode, written by James L. Brooks, was pivotal to the later development of Doris Martin's character as a reporter. "The Job" introduced her as a well-rounded and qualified journalist.]

**"The Job"**
Production Dates: Ocotber 14-18, 21-23, 1968
Original Airdate: December 17, 1968
Directed by: Bob Sweeney

Doris gets an emergency telegram from New York that she is needed for a special assignment with *Ladies' World*, a magazine she used to freelance for. Doris refuses to go, so Maggie Wells, managing editor, decides to fly to the ranch on the West Coast and "drag" her back. Doris reluctantly goes and does an excellent job with the story, then is offered a permanent job with a marvelous salary, and an unlimited future. Doris is suddenly faced with a dilemma: very proud and satisfied with the assignment she's just completed, she is also a recent widow who is still adjusting her life. She may not be ready to start a new adventure quite yet. Determined career-woman Maggie Wells decides to go back to Cotina and convince the family that the move to New York would be the right thing to do.

Written by: James L. Brooks; Linda Watkins as Maggie, Jo Miya as Jo

Groovy Day Facts:
Doris and her family lived in New York City previously.
Doris and her family go to church every Sunday, although it is referred to only in this episode.
Doris wrote a similar story for the *Ladies' World* magazine two years earlier.
Cotina's telephone operator is Nell.
The first appearance of Juanita.
This episode, along with "Doris Leaves *today's world*," "Doris and the Doctor" and the special *Doris Day Today*, was selected as shows available for viewing at the Museum of Television and Radio.

Doris Day Movie Find!:
Doris lived in New York in a dozen of her films including *Lullaby of Broadway* [1951], *Lover Come Back* [1962] and *Where Were You When the Lights Went Out?* [1968]

**"Buck's Girl"**
Production Dates: September 23-27, 1968
Original Airdate: December 31, 1968
Directed by: Gary Nelson

Buck falls in love for the first time in a long time, but his best friend of 40 years, Doc Carpenter, the local veterinarian, falls in love with her as well. Verna McIntosh is the town's new manicurist who unintentionally causes the very first fight between the two old friends. Marriage is on the horizon for both men and is especially exciting for Doc Carpenter, who has never been married and never really had anyone in his life before. Doris visits Verna and helps Buck put things in perspective. In the end, Buck chooses between friendship and love.

Denver Pyle.

Written by: Carl Kleinschmitt; Walter Sande as Doc Carpenter; Kay Stewart as Verna McIntosh; Paul Barselow as the Barber

Groovy Day Facts:
Pizza Pagoda is a restaurant in Cotina.
Haleys is the barbershop in nearby town Greely.
Doc goes to Disneyland for his honeymoon.

Doris Day Movie Find!:
The series' hairstylist, Barbara Lampson, worked with Doris on many of her later films including *Move Over, Darling* [1963] and *With Six You Get Eggroll* [1968].

## "Love a Duck"
Production Dates: September 30-October 4, 7, 1968
Original Airdate: January 7, 1969
Directed by: Gary Nelson

The entire family is sick except for Doris and Juanita who are taking care of everyone. Not only is the family sick, but Sherman the duck has been hurt by buckshot. Leroy discovers that neighbor Tyrone Lovey is the poacher. Since hunting isn't allowed on grandpa's ranch, Doris is determined to stop him. She will go to great lengths to see that Lovey falls into a trap which will prevent him from future illegal hunting.

Written by: Jerry Devine; Strother Martin as Tyrone Lovey

Groovy Day Facts:
Doris insists on lots of fruit juice and applies Vapo-rub on the boys when they are ill, while Juanita's remedy is a mustard plaster.

Denver Pyle Movie Find!:
Strother Martin appeared in *The Horse Soldiers* [1959] with Denver.

## "Let Them Out of the Nest"
Production Dates: October 8-11, 1968
Original Airdate: January 21, 1969
Directed by: Bruce Bilson

Billy and Toby are ready for responsibilities and enter the job market—delivering eggs, that is. Taking over the route from one of Billy's friends, they throw themselves wholeheartedly into their new venture until Doris interferes. Doris not only interferes, but takes over the entire route and has one of the worst experiences of her life, including a chase with the paper boy. As she says, "All I know is everybody in the whole world should deliver eggs just once. It gives you humility."

Written by: Peggy Elliott, Ed Scharlach; Hal Smith as the Drunk, Barbara Pepper as the Woman, Raymond Kark as the Police Officer, Keith Huntley as the Paperboy, Robert Graham as Arthur

Groovy Day Facts:
Billy and Toby's menu for their self-prepared, 4:00 A.M. breakfast: pickles, spaghetti, strawberry jelly and root beer.
The boys have a pillow fight in their bedroom.

Doris Day Movie Find!:
Barbara Pepper appeared in Frank Sinatra and Day's film *Young at Heart* [1954]. She appeared in several movies and television shows, and was widely known as Arnold the Pig's mother, Mrs. Ziffel, on *Green Acres*. Pepper died in 1969 and her role on the series was then played by Fran Ryan (who played Aggie on *The Doris Day Show*).

## "The Clock"
Production Dates: October 31, November 1, 4-8, 11, 1968
Original Airdate: January 28, 1969
Directed by: Bruce Bilson

A completely exhausted Doris, who had stayed for two days and two nights helping deliver a calf, is now faced with a new challenge: how will she get some sleep? Doris immediately comes face to face with a new problem. She needs to complete a financial report for a women's committee. She soon receives a beautiful highboy for her room, which will be completed by a chiming clock given to her by Leroy. This clock will assure a few more sleepless nights for our heroine. Buck and Doris are faced with another new problem: How to get rid of the clock without hurting Leroy's feelings.

Written by: Joe Bonaduce; Strother Martin as Tyrone Lovey, Peggy Rea as Grace Henley

Groovy Day Facts:
The family has a cow named Alma.

With Philip Brown and Denver Pyle.

The differences between Mr. Lovey and the Webbs appeared to have been worked out.

The family purchased their oak kitchen table earlier from Mr. Lovey.

Doris Day Movie Find!:

Peggy Rae appeared with several of Doris's co-stars in films, including Cary Grant in *Walk, Don't Run* [1965], Rock Hudson in *Strange Bedfellows* [1965] and Tony Randall in *7 Faces of Dr. Lao* [1964].

**"The Buddy"**
Production Dates: November 12-15, 18,  1968
Original Airdate: February 4, 1969
Directed by: Gary Nelson

Doris gets a letter from Louise, who has just moved to Phoenix. She is about to have a baby, and is in dire need of help. She asks Doris to visit. Doris agrees after she is assured by her "menfolks" that they can take care of themselves as Juanita is gone as well. The house rapidly becomes...When Emma Flood, an old Marine buddy of Buck's, comes to the rescue and restores the house in tip-top shape, military style—and can stay permanently. Doris comes home and finds the marine has landed. When Juanita comes back, will Emma leave?

Written by: Harry Winkler; Mary Wickes as Emma Flood, Willis Bouchey as Col. Forsythe

Groovy Day Facts:

Buck was a sergeant in the Marines when he dated Emma—but he didn't have a beard back then.

Emma cooks a breakfast of chipped beef, waffles and sweet & sour sauce like the breakfast her and Buck had years earlier in Hong Kong.

Buck's favorite pie is blueberry.

Leroy's way to wash a load of clothes is to use an entire box of laundry detergent.

Guest Star Mini-Bio & Doris Day Movie Find!:

Mary Wickes appeared with Doris in four movies: *On Moonlight*

*Bay, By the Light of the Silvery Moon, I'll See You in My Dreams*, and *It Happened to Jane*. In the late 1990s, Mary Wickes appeared in a Turner Classic Movies short documentary narrated by Charlton Heston celebrating Doris Day. In addition, Wickes acted in dozens of films and television shows in her seven-decade career, including her comedic turns as nuns in 1966's *The Trouble with Angels* and in 1992's *Sister Act*—and their sequels. From *White Christmas* and *The Music Man*, to acting in live action and animated Disney works (*Snowball Express, 101 Dalmatians* and *The Hunchback of Notre Dame*), Wickes also appeared in several of Lucille Ball's TV shows as the two were close friends.

**"The Fly Boy"**
Production Dates: December 9-13, 1968
Original Airdate: February 11, 1969
Directed by: Gary Nelson

When a sonic boom from a military jet causes damage to the farm, an Air Force colonel personally comes to apologize and pay for the damages. When he sees Doris and finds that she is not married, he becomes determined to get her. Doris, amused by his advances, agrees to go on a date with him. Leroy discovers that the Colonel's intentions are not quite what they seem, and that a bet has been wagered with the military on his conquest. Doris gets this information and plots a plan. She arrives to the dance at the Officer's Club, stunningly beautiful, turning quite a few heads and puts her plan into action.

Written by: Howard Leeds; Frank Aletter as Col. Carson, Al Travis as Ben, Tom Curry as Charlie, James Truesdell as Al, Tom Falk as the Sergeant

Groovy Day Facts:
We learn that an Air Force base is located near the farm.

With Frank Aletter.

Doris Day Album Find!:
   Music from:
   "Summer Has Gone" from *Latin for Lovers* [1965]
   "Hold Me in Your Arms" from *Young at Heart* soundtrack [1955]

## "The Tournament"
Production Dates: November 19-22, 1968
Original Airdate: February 18, 1969
Directed by: Gary Nelson

The Cotina Annual Horseshoe Tournament is about to happen. Buck and Doc Carpenter have been practicing tirelessly, when Leroy accidentally injures Doc's pitching hand. Buck is mad, angry and upset over the loss of his partner. After calling everyone he knows, Buck finds no one to take Doc's place—until everyone discovers what an amazing horseshoe pitcher Leroy is. With Toby's help, anxiety creeps into Leroy and he develops a stiff arm, which could prevent him from entering the competition. Doris, using a little psychology, may solve his problem.

Written by Perry Grant, Dick Bensfield; Walter Sande as Doc Carpenter

Groovy Day Facts:
   Doris was a champion horseshoe thrower in the eighth grade.
   Doris tries to fix the broken toaster.

Doris Day Movie Find!:
   *Calamity Jane* [1953] is mentioned in this episode.

## "Love Thy Neighbor"
Production Dates: January 16, 17, 20-23, 1969
Original Airdate: March 4, 1969
Directed by: Harry Falk

The farm tractor is on the brink, and a new one needs to be purchased, which makes Buck take a second look at his financial situation. Buck, who has always been generous with everyone in town, is waiting for payments from friends and neighbors including two beautiful horses that were sold to Zeno Tugwell who lives way up in the hills. Doris's mission will be to go after him and collect payment. Zeno Tugwell has other plans for Buck Webb's daughter: getting her married to his son, rock-throwing champion Stonewall. Can Doris get the money or the horses without getting married?

Written by: Sid Morse; J. Pat O'Malley as Zeno Tugwell, Read Morgan as Stonewall Tugwell

Groovy Day Facts:
The old tractor, Henrietta, is a blue and white Ford. It is replaced with a 444 Red International model.
Buck tells Leroy that his head and his hands are complete strangers when it comes to mechanical things.
One of Buck's IOU's dates back to 1946, and in addition to Zeno Tugwell, neighbors Henderson, Henshaw, Miller and Applebee owe Buck money.
The Tugwells have a still in their barn which is used to make illegal liquor.

Jackie Joseph Movie Find!:
J. Pat O'Malley appeared in *The Cheyenne Social Club* [1970] with future *The Doris Day Show* alumnus Jackie Joseph. The film also co-starred James Stewart, Doris's leading man in *The Man Who Knew Too Much* [1956].

**"The Con Man"**
Production Dates: December 16-20, 1968
Original Airdate: March 11, 1969
Directed by: Bruce Bilson

Upon receiving several requests to stage events in Cotina, Doris coincidentally receives a letter from Mr. Roger Flanders, who is interested in building a community center. She invites him to spend a few days and showcase his proposal. Upon his arrival, he is welcomed with open arms, made completely comfortable, and almost part of the family. He gives a successful pitch to the committee with a great incentive program and sells his community center idea. Nelson uncovers his scheme to con the community. Now Doris and Buck find a way to point Mr. Flanders in the right direction.

On the farm set with James Hampton.

Written by: Si Rose; Joseph Campanella as Roger Flanders, Madge Blake as Mrs. Hardy, Bard Stevens as Committeeman, Peter Brocco as Jed Anslinger, James Millhollin as Horace Burkhart, Kay Stewart as Committeewoman #1, Evelyn King as Committeewoman #2, Dodie Warren as Committeewoman #3

Groovy Day Facts:
The combined community center, theater-in-the-round, concert auditorium and convention hall is budgeted at $210,000.

The Southwest Philharmonic Concert League, United Cattlemen's Association, and the Touring Theater Guild are among Flanders' fictitious organizations used to lure communities into building centers.

A scene from this episode was used in *Doris Day's Best Friends* with guest star Denver Pyle.

Doris Day Movie Find!:
Madge Blake is best known for the loving Aunt Harriet in the *Batman* TV series. A clip of that show was seen in Doris's super-spy *clin-deil, Caprice* [1967].

Guest Star Mini-Bio:

A veteran of more than 100 television, stage and movie roles, Tony-nominated Joseph Campanella appeared in the cult films *Ben* and *Meteor*; the TV series *Mannix*, *Dallas* and *The Colbys*; the daytime dramas *Days of Our Lives* and *The Bold and the Beautiful*; and voice-overs and narration for documentaries (*Italians in America*) and animated series (*Spider-Man*). Arguably, his most recognized character was Ed Cooper, the ex-husband of Ann Romano, on TV's *One Day at a Time*.

**"The Musical"**
Production Dates: January 8-15, 1969
Original Airdate: March 18, 1969
Directed by: Bruce Bilson

With Denver Pyle.

Bribed with Rocky Road ice cream, Buck commits Doris into directing a brand-new school musical. Doris, who clearly has theater background, creates an innovative and daring show depicting the change in generation and kids discovering who they are, which the principal, Mr. Ekstrom, finds appalling and controversial. After weeks of rehearsal, preparation and building of sets, he cancels the performance. Following a very disappointed company, Doris is very mad and goes shopping. Thinking things through, she convinces Buck to bring Mr. Ekstrom to reconsider his decision. Doris finds that Mr. Ekstrom had some generation challenge in his own life, and recreates a show showcasing his own time period. Will the principal find this acceptable?

Written by: Sid Morse; Ray Teal as Mr. Ekstrom, Gary Dubin as Freddie, Michele Tobin as Gloria

Groovy Day Facts:
   Doris and Buck eat ice cream from a Baskin Robbins container.
   Doris had earlier done the PTA Christmas pageant.
   Buck belongs to the Rotary Club.
   Proceeds from the show were to benefit the Traveling Library.

Mr. Ekstrom won the Black Bottom Contest at The Blue Moon in the 1920s

Musical budget: $7.50 to work with, including $2 and a little bit of elbow grease for the set. Costumes came from the attic at the ranch.

Doris Day Movie Find!:
Ray Teal appeared in *Lucky Me* [1954].

### "The Baby Sitter"
Production Dates: January 24, 27-31, 1969
Original Airdate: March 25, 1969
Directed by: Harry Falk

Doris is home alone as everyone has left to go bowling. She appreciates the silence and plans on listening to it all night. She suddenly gets a phone call from her good friend Dorothy Benson. Dorothy is about to have her new baby and needs someone to stay with her four kids, Elizabeth, Jenny, Adam and Rachel. Doris soon discovers that the quiet night she was hoping for has turned into a night of chaos and mayhem she'll never forget. The only place Doris can possibly find quiet could be the linen closet.

Written by: Bruce Howard; Paul Smith as Hal Benson, Peggy Rea as Dorothy Benson, Julie Reese as Elizabeth Benson, Jodie Foster as Jenny Benson, Ted Foulkes as Adam Benson, Lynnel Atkins as Rachel Benson, Hal Smith as Mr. Pebee

Groovy Day Facts:
After dinner, Buck usually takes a nap on the coach.

Denver Pyle Movie Find!:
Jodie Foster's film credits include *Maverick* [1994] with Denver Pyle.

### "The Still"
Production Dates: February 12-14, 17-19, 1969
Original Airdate: April 1, 1969
Directed by: Gary Nelson

Ben, local police sheriff, surprises Doris early in the morning with news that U.S. Treasury agents, with the alcohol and tax division, have just arrived in town. They are looking for the McGlinsey sisters, who they suspect of hiding a still and cooking up their own secret recipe for moonshine ["white lightning"], which they claim to use for only medicinal purposes "if they get the grip." Being old friends of the sisters since she was a little girl, Doris literally races to their rescue to the point of getting arrested to save those sweet and almost innocent old ladies. A race ensues [that will send shivers up your spine] and Doris puts pedal to the metal to find the infamous still has been disposed of at the ranch.

Written by: Lloyd Turner, Whitey Mitchell; Barney Phillips as Sheriff Ben Anders, Jesslyn Fax as Lydia, Florence Lake as Adelaide, Jeff DeBenning as Agent Bronson, Tom Falk as Agent Willoughby.

With Florence Lake.

Groovy Day Facts:

Saving the McGlinsey sisters really put Doris at risk by: speeding; reckless driving; hiding evidence; and possession of a controlled substance. This results in Doris being put in jail—in a private cell—for the first time in the series. It will not be the last. On the plus side, however, she did wear her seatbelt while driving.

The McGlinseys aren't the only ones in Mill Valley with a still. Zeno Tugwell in "Love Thy Neighbor" had one in a barn.

The McGlinsey Sisters' places to hide "White Lightning" in your home:

Inside a cut-out book

In the wall safe behind a picture

Inside a fake clock

Inside a fireplace

With Denver Pyle.

Inside a light fixture
Inside a bogus television set

Doris Day Movie Find!:
Barney Phillips played the doctor in *Julie* [1956]. While filming *Julie* on-location, Doris fell in love with Carmel, California.

**"The Gift"**
Production Dates: February 3-7, 10, 1969
Original Airdate: April 8, 1969
Directed by: Harry Falk

Doris sends notes to everyone in the family and orders a special meeting in the living room. Everyone fears the subject of the meeting will be one of them. Has Grandpa or Billy or Toby done something wrong? No. The meeting is about Leroy B. Simpson. It is his first year anniversary with the family and he has been chosen to receive a gift. But what gift? When all is said and done, a visit with his grandmother would make him the happiest. To prove that they can get along without Leroy for one week while he is gone, they each take over his chores. Leroy, feeling completely neglected and unneeded, runs away.

Written by: Arthur Alsberg, Don Nelson

Groovy Day Facts:
Doris's Aunt Lucille, "Lucy," lives in Kansas City.
There is a pillow fight in Leroy's room.
Doris always knew about mechanics. She was fixing the first cars [called "machines" then] at Hickey's Garage in *By the Light of the Silvery Moon* [1953], and worked on the pick-up truck's engine leak in this episode.
Doris sings "For He's a Jolly Good Fellow."

Doris Day Movie Find!:
On the bottom of Doris's notes, she writes: "This note will self-destruct in ten seconds," in an apparent homage to *Mission: Impossible*, starring Peter Graves. Doris co-starred with him in *The Ballad of Josie* [1968]. Graves narrated the two-hour A&E Biography of Doris Day called *It's Magic* [1998].

## "The Tiger"

Production Dates: March 3-7, 1969
Original Airdate: April 15, 1969
Directed by: Gary Nelson

Leroy does it again and gets fired for the nth time—and Buck wants to make it forever. No pleading from the family will help him. The only thing that could save Leroy at this point would be a tiger, of course, who stowaways to the ranch with Doris. The tiger has gotten away from Cooley's Country Carnival, and has become an instant family favorite drinking milk in the kitchen with the boys. The sheriff, the "army" and the canine corps come looking for him at the ranch, but Leroy inadvertently lets him get away, and the tiger heads straight for the hills. Doris and Leroy need to find him before the sheriff does, and bring it to safety. This could even help save Leroy's job.

Written by: Norman Katkov; Barney Phillips as Sheriff Ben Anders, Bard Stevens as Deputy Sheriff.

Groovy Day Facts:
Buck says the ranch has been in the family for three generations, and mentions an Aunt Bonnie.

Buck has 27 Holstein cows.

Buck says the B in Leroy B. Simpson stand for "Bumbler."

Doris Day Movie Find!:
The last time Doris worked with a tiger was in 1962's *Billy Rose's Jumbo*.

## "The Date"
Production Dates: October 24, 25, 28-30, 1968
Original Airdate: April 22, 1969
Directed by: Bruce Bilson

Doris is off on another date and feels bad that Juanita never goes out. Juanita works long hours and never gets the chance to meet anyone. Enter Doris, the matchmaker. She asks Frank Gorian as a very special favor to her to take Juanita out on a date. To her great surprise, Juanita gets a very special invitation. Juanita goes out with Frank and has the time of her life. Later, Juanita overhears Buck and Doris talking about the arrangement and planning of the date. She gets very upset and decides never to see Frank again. Doris decides to interfere one more time to hopefully save their new relationship.

Written by: E. Duke Vincent, Bruce Johnson; Joe De Santis as Frank Gorian

Groovy Day Facts:
   Frank owns a sporting goods store in Cotina.
   Spalding is a nearby town in the Mill Valley area.

Philip Brown Movie Find!:
   Philip Brown appeared with Dick Van Dyke in *Fitzwilly*. Van Dyke appeared in *The John Denver Special* with Doris Day in 1974.

## "The Five-Dollar Bill"
Production Dates: December 2-6, 1968
Original Airdate: April 29, 1969
Directed by: Gary Nelson

The state fair is opening and the boys are getting ready. Billy and his best friend, Alfred Loomis, are entering their pigs in a contest with special jeweled collars purchased by Alfred. n the midst of everything, Billy finds Alfred's mother's wallet and gives it to Doris right away. When Mrs. Loomis arrives to pick it up, she finds a five-dollar bill missing from her wallet and accuses Billy of stealing her money and Doris of harboring a juvenile delinquent. With Toby's help, Doris discovers that Alfred has

With Naomi Stevens.

been spending a tremendous amount of money on his friends for a long time. Where is his money coming from? Doris decides to have a heart-to-heart talk with Alfred in the hopes that he will admit the truth.

Written by: John McGreevey; Shirley Mitchell as Mrs. Loomis, Stuart Lee as Alfred Loomis, Jerry Hausner as Mr. Kibbler

Groovy Day Facts:
Doris reads in the newspaper that Henry Bink, who works at the post office, has accumulated 409 days of sick time.

Herman is the name of Billy's pig.

Stuart Lee was the second finalist to play Philip Brown's role of Billy Martin.

Naomi Stevens earlier played a housekeeper in the very messy *Peyton Place* TV series (what a relief to now work for Doris's family).

Doris Day Music Find!:

Shirley Mitchell was married to Jay Livingston, who co-wrote "Que Sera, Sera," *The Doris Day Show*'s theme song.

### "The Relatives"
Production Dates: March 10-14, 1969
Original Airdate: May 6, 1969
Directed by: Harry Falk

Buck, Leroy and the boys leave for a camping trip while Doris and Juanita stay home. They plan to overhaul the house, including wallpapering and painting, until an unexpected visit from three Simpsons, cousins of Leroy. A disappointed Doris informs them that he has gone for the

With Lord Nelson.

weekend, but invites them in for breakfast. To say thank you, they decide to help her overhaul the house in a very Simpson way.

Written by: Bruce Howard; Alan Sues as Edgar Simpson, Dennis Fimple as Herman Simpson, Robert Easton as Albert Simpson, J. P. Cranshaw as Ernie, Bard Stevens as Ben.

Groovy Day Facts:
Buck's favorite colors are "drab & dull."
The Simpsons come from Choctow County.
The last appearance of Juanita. Perhaps she and Frank Gorian married.

Doris Day Movie Find!:
Alan Sues appeared in Doris's film *Move Over, Darling* [1963].

Denver Pyle Movie Find!:
J.P. Cranshaw played a bankteller in *Bonnie and Clyde* [1967], which featured Denver.

**THE EPISODES THAT NEVER WERE...**
A handful of scripts were written for *The Doris Day Show* series which were not filmed.  Some were slated for production but never filmed since the production had fulfilled its contractual commitments.  These scripts from Season One include:

"The Shampoo" by Austin & Irma Kalish
"Romance and Rib Roast" and "The Building Fund" by Idelson & Miller
"The Cabellero (The Guest)" writer uknown

## THE WEBB FAMILY TREE

Although the Webb family was well known, well liked and respected in the Cotina area, there were surprisingly few of them mentioned in the series.

Buck (Buckley) Webb is a widower, but his wife's name was not divulged in the series. The couple apparently had only one child, that being Doris. She was married to Steve Martin and the couple had two sons, Billy (William) and Toby.

Doris calls sisters Lydia and Adelaide Lindsey her aunts. They live near the ranch and it was said Doris is the only person around they trust. Aunt Lucille (Lucy) lives in Kansas City. Buck remarks an Aunt Bonnie falls as much as a deputy sheriff in "The Tiger" episode.

There's an Aunt Edna, who lives in Pittsburgh, and Buck has a cousin named Vera June in Bald Knob, Arkansas. ["The minute she married that dentist," Buck remarked about the latter, "there was no more mingling on our side of the family."]

There was a Louise in Phoenix who had a baby. Doris visited her for a few days and she was probably a cousin.

April Tolliver Clarke is Doris's niece who moved to San Francisco and attended Berkeley for a year before contacting her aunt. April is related to Doris on her deceased husband's side as there was not any mention of Doris having any siblings, and she is probably her sister-in-law's daughter.

Doris has a cousin, Charlie Webb, who's been around the world and worked as a cook on a freighter and opened a tourist service in the South Pacific. He worked for a while in advertising sales at *today's world*, and does well securing

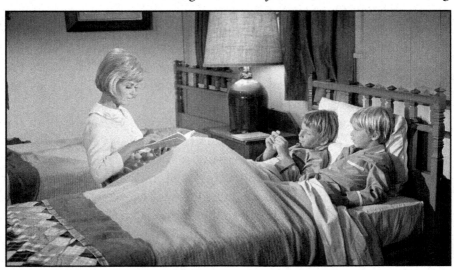

several accounts, including frozen turkeys and orthopedic shoes. But his tenure at the magazine is limited as he returns to his life traveling on freighters.

Doris's uncle (probably maternal), August von Kappelhoff, spent four years in prison for art forgery. He then uses Doris to obtain an original Vittorelli painting by switching it with a fake he has painted.

A few fictitious others were added to the family, although they were either jokes or disguises. When Doris introduces a government man investigating her as her Uncle Ed from Ohio, he really isn't and her co-workers are a bit confused, but take her word for it nonetheless. Another time, Doris's former boss, Maggie Wells, comes to visit and asks Doris for help on a story in New York. Buck introduces Leroy as Doris's oldest boy—for which he receives an elbow in the stomach from his daughter. Also, Mr. Nicholson is Doris's second husband for a day when he tries to shed an ex-girlfriend who he cannot get shake.

## *THE DORIS DAY SHOW* THEME SONG

### "Que Sera, Sera (Whatever Will Be, Will Be)"

Although Doris Day had 56 Top 40 hits, including the #1 recordings "Sentimental Journey" and "Secret Love," the song which is most closely identified with her is "Que Sera, Sera."

Composer Jay Livingston saw the film *The Barefoot Contessa* and noticed on a castle wall, an Italian phrase cut into the stone which read "Che Sera, Sera," which meant "what will be, will be." He wrote the words down thinking it may make a good song title. With Ray Evans, the two wrote the song.

Shortly thereafter, Alfred Hitchcock, who was preparing to film *The Man Who Knew Too Much* for Paramount, met with Livingston and his writing partner Ray Evans, who were under contract at the same studio. Since Doris Day was going to appear in the film, Paramount wanted her to sing in it despite the fact that Hitchcock was known as a non-musical film director. Hitchcock explained to the team that he needed a tune, but "I don't want a song." Hitchcock explained the storyline and that he wanted a song that Doris could sing to her little boy.

Original sheet music cover.

After the director left, they immediately knew "Che Sera, Sera" would work in the film; however, to make it appear the team was working hard on the song, they waited a couple weeks before presenting the piece. After playing it to Hitchcock, he replied, "I told you I didn't know what kind of song I wanted. *That's* the kind of song I wanted."

Livingston and Evans changed the Italian "Che" in the title to the Spanish "Que," feeling there would be a wider appeal since there are more Spanish-speaking people in the world. "However, the legal department wouldn't let us use that title," Livingston later said. "So we had to call it 'Whatever Will Be, Will Be,' with 'Que Sera, Sera' in parentheses." It later proved to be a wise decision since at the time, songs submitted for Oscar consideration had to have English titles.

Doris Day, however, did not like the song, but she felt it was fine where it was needed in the film, where it was sung twice: while tucking her son into bed and at the film's climax. Everyone else felt it would be a big hit, and Columbia Records asked her to record the song for the record-buying public. She reluctantly recorded it in one take and remarked to a person at the session, "That's the last time you'll ever hear that song."

Doris's recording of "Whatever Will Be, Will Be (Que Sera, Sera)" was released shortly after *The Man Who Knew Too Much* hit the screens. Both were big hits, with the film being one of top movies of the year. The single sold well over a million copies in the U.S., peaking at #2 for three weeks, and staying on the charts for more than half a year. In the U.K. and several other countries the song was a certified hit.

Livingston said Doris's remark was no reflection on him or Evans. "We've all been wrong in picking hits."

The song not only was nominated, but won the Academy Award for Best Song. This was a surprise to the composers. Livingston felt the Oscar-less Cole Porter would finally win with "True Love" from *High Society*. But, as Doris wrote in her memoirs, "Whatever Will Be, Will Be" was an overwhelming winner at the awards ceremony.

"I thought it would make a good record—for children. But I wouldn't buy it," Doris said forty years later. "I ate those words. Everybody bought it!" Doris eventually learned to love the song and she later sang it her films *Please Don't Eat the Daisies* and *The Glass Bottom Boat*. She also re-recorded it for her album, *With a Smile and a Song*.

From 1968 through 1973 it was the theme song to *The Doris Day Show* series with a different arrangement and vocal by Doris, furthering its identification with the star. The song was also heard at times in a couple episodes, including "Dinner for Mom," where Doris sings a few bars of it, and in "Doris Meets a Prince," where it is played on an accordion in a restaurant. In "A Woman's Intuition," while she is saying goodbye to a Cuban Major, and breaking the fourth wall between audience and actor, fiction and reality, Doris actually remarks "Que sera, sera!"

The public's recognition and fondness for the song has endured through the years. However, in a strange twist, most refer to and remember the song title as "Que Sera, Sera," rather than the official title. In addition, this title was the one used in the credits for *The Doris Day Show*.

## A VISIT WITH JAMES HAMPTON

*Was the character of Leroy B. Simpson difficult for you to play?*

I had come off of *F-Troop* and I had played that sort of character, though a bit more in-depth with Leroy. He was a likable "simpleton." It wasn't a lot to go for.

*What did the character contribute to* The Doris Day Show?

I liked Leroy a lot and I think he proved two things: one, he provided comedy for Denver because Denver was always exasperated over Leroy and how he was messing things up on the ranch, and it also gave Doris a character to be sympathetic to, one to help out and I think that made her very appealing.

*In one episode you sang a song to Billy and Toby about your Uncle Buster. Was that your voice?*

I sang. It was just part of that script. Of course, after they heard me sing, they knew it wasn't a very good idea. I mean, you have Doris Day on the show and you're going to have *me* sing? I don't think so.

*Then Leroy thought his talents may be as a lyricist in "The Songwriter."*

We had so much fun with that episode. Denver and I would sit around, making up song titles. He came up with "I'm Just a Caboose in Your Train of Thought" and I came up "I'm Lonsomer Than an Odd Sock in a Drawer Full of Pairs." But the writers wrote the songs used in the show.

*How difficult was it to do a show? Were you able to add your thoughts to a scene or was it strictly by the script?*

We were pretty loose, and you can be a little bit more with a single camera. We didn't film in front of an audience, and you didn't have a pack of writers and producers there making sure you've said everything exactly the way it was written. We were pretty free in how we could do it, but we stuck to the script pretty closely. We had kids on the show and things like that so you don't want to get too far [off the script].

*How many days did it take to shoot an episode the first year?*
We had a five-day schedule. It really wasn't an awful schedule—pretty normal. On *F-Troop* we had a little easier time of it. We came in on Monday and read the script, did a little bit of blocking and were done within an hour or two. And usually we'd get a rewrite and finish up on Thursday.

On *The Doris Day Show* we pretty much used up the five days. I don't remember any late working conditions, and part of that was because we had the kids on the show.

*What did you think of Philip Brown and Tod Starke on the show?*
I thought we had great kids on *Doris Day*. They seemed like real kids, very natural. And the show seemed very natural. When I watch something I'm in, I don't like to watch "acting." And they weren't.

*The director of photography, Richard Rawlings, really had a distinctive look with lighting and the use of colors. Do you recall his working with Doris?*
He was wonderful and worked well with Doris, who had a lot of freckles. She had to be lit a certain way. I thought they were cute, but they don't photograph that way—cute. So he was wonderful at making her film beautiful, and she was a beautiful woman, inside and out. A knockout.

*Which episodes are your favorites?*
I like the one with the tiger. I thought that was fun. But I liked the one where Leroy had a crush on the librarian, and so he wrote a poem and all that kind of stuff. It was sweet and there was a bit more depth other than chasing chickens around the yard. Kelly Jean Peters, the librarian, was a nice, nice actress. I don't know whatever became of her, but she was very sweet and fun to act with.

*Do you feel there was a problem with the first season?*
I don't think the show had enough bite to it, it didn't have enough edge, which they could have had much more of, a much more sophisticated comedy and so forth—wacky people around an office, that kind of thing. It was just too sweet, I think.

Basically, I was off the show after the first year, and I understood why. Basically, Doris had more confidence by the end of the first season, and for the first time, she could really have more control over her life. She had lost her manager and her husband, who took care of those things, but fortunately for her, her son came in and was very smart. And they made some good moves with the series. One was to get her off the farm and let her wear pretty clothes and have boyfriends and live in San Francisco. It was a much, much better idea. It wasn't a bad idea that Bob Sweeney came up with. It wasn't *The Egg and I*, but a more sophisticated comedy, and I think it was the right move.

*So when you learned you wouldn't be returning to the show...*
It was devastating to me because, basically, I was done, and I loved the people on the show and being on the show. And I liked Leroy, so I missed it. It wasn't anything personal. The only thing was, *TV Guide* had a little item in there that said that I had been "jettisoned"—I hate that verb because it's when the ship is sinking, you get rid of stuff. It was pretty inaccurate as far as I was concerned. But I had a good run and I had a lot fun.

*You were brought back for an episode in two seasons. First in "The Gas Station" and then "Lassoin' Leroy." It was not only nice of the powers-that-be to bring Leroy back, but the two episodes helped resolve what actually happened to the character. Why do you feel Leroy returned?*
I think probably it was in response to some letters asking, "What happened to Leroy?," that sort of thing, and giving closure to that character.

*What kind of letters did you get?*
Well, I mean, not *all* of the letters were from girls! But a lot of them were from grandmas who thought I was a nice boy and I was the type of young man a lot of the older ladies wanted their daughters to marry. But the good guy never gets the girl, you know that.

*Leroy competed in rodeos in his last appearance. Did you have any background working with horses?*
My brother was, in fact, a rodeo clown, and I grew up in Texas and we learned to ride very early. My father was a wonderful horseman and my younger brother was extremely good. They stopped where the horse began—very, very wonderful riders and cowboys. I did a little bit of cowboying.

I worked at the Tic Tac Toe Ranch one summer after college, and I like to be around horses. I think I entered one rodeo—bareback bucking horse—and I really thought there had to be a better way to make a living.

*What are your feelings about Doris Day?*
Doris was an amazing actress. When you watch her acting, it's not acting. She just "*is*." She believes in what she's doing, and was able to bring it on and on and on. I don't know how women can do it, but they can just puddle up those eyes.

I was just crazy about her. I think she was a much better actress than what she was given credit for.

# Season 2: 1969-1970
## "Doris Martin Rejoins the Publishing World"

**1969-1970**

The second season brought a change in format for *The Doris Day Show*. Feeling she should help with expenses on the ranch, Doris Martin finds a job in nearby San Francisco and begins a new life as a commuter, working at *today's world* magazine. The season's episodes alternated between both locations.

Doris Martin's job at *today's world* was as executive secretary to managing editor Michael Nicholson, played by McLean Stevenson. Paul Smith as Assistant Editor Ron Harvey was added, as was Rose Marie, who played single gal Myrna Gibbons, Mr. Harvey's secretary.

A new, hipper title credit opening was made for the second season, with Doris saying goodbye to her family on the ranch, then driving her red convertible into San Francisco. The theme song "Qué Sera, Sera" was replaced with a new version that was performed more upbeat and as a solo by Day.

**CBS PRESS RELEASES TO PROMOTE *THE DORIS DAY SHOW*:**

July 8, 1969

**Doris Becomes a Working Mother Next Season**

Doris Day will join the staff of a magazine headquartered in San Francisco when her popular situation comedy returns to the CBS Television Network on a new day and (with additions to the format), Monday, September 22 (9:30-10:00 PM, EDT) in color.

As a working mother, Miss Day will commute from her farm home outside San Francisco where she lives with her father and two children, portrayed by Denver Pyle, Philip Brown and Tod Starke, respectively.

*The Doris Day Show* is currently presented on the Network on Tuesdays (9:30-10:00 PM, EDT).

New additions to the cast will be Rose Marie, who won three Emmy nominations during her five years in the role of Sally on the long-running *Dick Van Dyke Show*, and McLean Stevenson, who appeared in the Broadway musicals *Bye Bye Birdie* and *Most Happy Fella* and wrote comedy for variety programs.

Rose Marie will play a secretary on the magazine staff and McLean will be seen as the magazine's managing editor and Miss Day's boss.

*The Doris Day Show* will be produced by Jack Elinson and Norman Paul. Terry Melcher is the executive producer.

Bristol-Myers Co., through Grey Advertising, Inc., is a sponsor of the series.

August 13, 1969

### 'The Doris Day Show': A New Look For the New Season

"I'm going to become a working mother this fall with a job on a San Francisco magazine," said Doris Day recently to a group of visiting television editors.

The vivacious actress was describing the changes to take place in her role as Doris Martin on *The Doris Day Show* when it begins its second season. "The new job will be only a 40-minute commuter drive from the ranch," continued Miss Day, "and we'll still keep the ranch in the show. I love it. I always wanted to live on a ranch."

Along with her new job on the magazine, Doris Martin will have a girlfriend played by Rose Marie, who is familiar to viewers as a result of her five-year role as Sally on *The Dick Van Dyke Show* and her numerous appearances on game shows. "Every girl needs a confidante, and she's perfect for me," says Miss Day.

Some of the other changes in the comedy series will include those in Doris Martin's wardrobe and social life. With the job in the city, she'll be able to trade off some of those jeans and gingham outfits for some new career-girl fashions to wear to the office.

As for romance in the series, Miss Day says: "I don't see any reason why Doris Martin can't find herself a man. Does a widow have to be a recluse?"

One of the new men in Doris Martin's life will be McLean Stevenson, who'll portray her boss, the magazine's managing editor.

"All in all, there are quite a few changes in the show," says Miss Day. "And, most importantly, they'll open up the show and give us more opportunity to do the best job we can—and that's what I want."

## CBS PROMOS / STATION BREAKS SPOTS

"Share one doll's delightful double life as a glamorous girl's new big-city job turns out to be just as fun-filled as life back on the ranch—on THE DORIS DAY SHOW, now (day) at (time)!"

"Enjoy a new lease on laughter when Doris, now a glamorous big city Girl Friday, adds sparkle to her role of widowed mom to two lively sprouts—at (time) tonight (tomorrow) on THE DORIS DAY SHOW!"

"What kind of day has it been for you? Good or bad, there's an even better one coming your way tonight (tomorrow) (this evening) on THE DORIS DAY SHOW. She's sparkle and sunshine…a touch wacky and occasionally way-out as she cuts copy capers as a staffer on 'Today's World' magazine. Join Doris and her friends in the center of everything—here at _____ on Channel _____."

"Her scene is today's scene. Her assignment: dig out the real story, and follow the exciting and adventurous people who make a story. But—the story behind the story for glamorous writer Doris Martin is often a lot more interesting than the one she's reporting. Make your own report of THE DORIS DAY SHOW fun—tonight (tomorrow) (Monday) at _____ on Channel _____."

"Now (day) nights are as bright as only a Day named Doris can make them! Yes, tonight (tomorrow) you'll find Doris—now commuting from the ranch to a glamorous career-girl job in San Francisco—entering a whole new world of comedy and romance. Make each (day) night laughter-bright with Doris and her new city friends Rose Marie and McLean Stevenson on THE DORIS DAY SHOW—at _____, in color!"

"Guess who's leading a delightful new double life? Doris Day, that's who! And you can share it tonight (tomorrow) when Doris—still harvesting a bumper crop of laughs home on the ranch—enters a new field of fun in the big city as a magazine's editor's glamorous Girl Friday. Enjoy the best of two worlds here on THE DORIS DAY SHOW—now (day) at (time)."

## THE EPISODES:

### "Doris Gets a Job"
Production Dates: June 16-19, 1969
Original Airdate: September 22, 1969
Directed by: Coby Ruskin

Doris is as nervous as a turkey on Thanksgiving as she prepares to go job hunting for the first time in twelve years. Finding something to wear, everything is either too big or too small, looking for her keys and getting the kids ready for school, she finally gets it all together and drives over the Golden Gate Bridge into San Francisco for her interviews.

Her first interview is with a law firm where she would be personal secretary to six attorneys, all at the same time. The next two are even worse. Finally, after reading an ad in the newspaper, she goes to *today's world* magazine in the heart of San Francisco. Doris is greeted warmly by secretary Myrna Gibbons, who explains to her the job qualifications. The only thing that may be a problem would be that Doris is a mother. She promises Myrna that she will not mention it as she is sent in for her interview. Mr. Michael Nicholson, managing editor of the magazine, likes her and hires her immediately. She soon meets Ron Harvey, who is the office playboy buffoon and promises to help her in any way he can with her new position. Doris spends the rest of the day avoiding calls from her family and covering up the fact that she has one until, at the end of the day, the family decides to join her for a surprise dinner in the city.

Written by: Jack Elinson, Norman Paul; Paul Smith as Ron Harvey, Carol Worthington as Miss Bennington, Eldon Quick as Mr. Willoughby, Joel Mell as Man #1, Larry Gelman as Man #2

Groovy Day Facts:
Billy takes piano lessons.

Jimmie Haskell was the series composer and conductor beginning with this episode and the remainder of the show's run.

The first appearance of Mr. Michael Nicholson, Myrna Gibbons and Ron Harvey.

*today's world* won an award for their series on Far Eastern Cults.

With Lord Nelson and McLean Stevenson.

*today's world* the now magazine Current Story:
"The Changing Ecology of California"

Doris Day Movie Find!:
In a reference to *With Six You Get Eggroll* [1968], the family finds a restaurant where with five people in your party you get eggroll.

### "A Frog Called Harold"
Production Dates: June 30-July 3, 1969
Original Airdate: September 29, 1969
Directed by: Coby Ruskin

Toby's frog Harold is on the loose and lost. The entire family is on the lookout. Where can Harold possibly be? After hours of searching, Doris is late for an important bank meeting with the magazine. There she discovers a frog in her purse. The frog literally causes havoc in the office, and could possibly prevent *today's world* from getting a major bank loan.

Written by: Budd Grossman; Paul Smith as Ron Harvey, Parley Baer as Mr. Thornby, David Manzy as Dave, Jack Garner as the Aide, Issa Arnal as Office Girl, Ralph Neff as Bank Guard, Ed McReady as Man in Restaurant

Groovy Day Facts:
Toby keeps Harold in a shoebox under the nightstand by his bed.
*today's world* the now magazine:
The magazine wants a $100,000 loan for a new high-speed printing press.
Dave is a worker at the magazine.

Doris Day Movie Find!:
Parley Baer was in *Where Were You When the Lights Out?* [1968], starring Doris.

**"Married for a Day"**
Production Dates: July 21-24, 1969
Original Airdate: October 6, 1969
Directed by: Earl Bellamy

As Doris and Mr. Nicholson are having a delicious lunch at Albertos, they see a woman, Karen Carruthers, walk in who has been relentlessly chasing him for years. In fear that she might see him, they quickly escape back to the office. After Karen learns he is there, Doris and Mr. Nicholson quickly go to Doris's ranch. With the help of Ron Harvey, the very push Karen goes to Doris's ranch to find Mr. Nicholson. The only option Mr. Nicholson has is to pretend that he is married to Doris. Will everyone in the family pretend as well? Will Karen ever leave?

Written by: Norman Paul, Jack Elinson; Julie Adams as Karen Carruthers, Paul Smith as Ron Harvey

*today's world* the now magazine:
"A Political Life."

Doris Day Movie Find!:
Doris appeared on *The Tonight Show* on November 26, 1973 with McLean Stevenson guest hosting that evening. They talked about her

With Julie Adams and McLean Stevenson.

film and television career, her campaign to save dogs and cats, and her difficulties in finding a "nice" man.

Denver Pyle Movie Find!:
Paul Smith appeared in *The Left Handed Gun* [1958] with Denver.

**"The Woman Hater"**
Production Dates: June 23-26, 1969
Original Airdate: October 13, 1969
Directed by: Coby Ruskin

Alex Rhinehart, the most important freelance writer at *today's world* magazine, has been very successful with his series about his negative point of view on women. Mr. Nicholson asks a very unwilling Doris to pick up the revision on the new article at Rhinehart's hotel. After meeting Doris, he finds her "the loveliest exception" and changes his point of view on women, which jeopardizes his *today's world* assignment. Doris sets a trap for him in a restaurant and plays the most obnoxious, talkative, annoying woman in the world to get him back hating women for the magazine.

Written by: Budd Grossman; Anthony Eisley as Alex Rhinehart, Luis de Cordova as Head Waiter, Johnny Collins III as Dave, Pete Kellett as Husband, Judy March as Wife, Julius Johnsen as Bartender

Groovy Day Facts:
Doris says she has an Aunt Edna who lives in Pittsburgh

*today's world* the now magazine:
"Women: The Unnecessary Sex"

Doris Day Movie Find!:
The title song to *Julie* [1956]
The title song to *Send Me No Flowers* [1964]

**"The Chocolate Bar War"**
Production Dates: July 7-10, 1969
Original Airdate: October 20, 1969
Directed by: Harry Falk

Bachelor Michael Nicholson is invited to a party at a very important client's house. Because of her "wholesomeness," he invites Doris to make a good impression. Meanwhile, at home, Billy and Toby, dedicated Boy Scouts, are competing in a contest selling chocolate bars. They were run off the supermarket by a woman and her son, so Doris takes them the next day to make sure that doesn't happen again. When she meets the lady, it's an all-out war to sell candy: charms, smiles, politeness—all ammunitions are allowed. Later that night, Doris goes to the party with Mr. Nicholson at Mr. Fletcher's house. When Doris sees the woman she met during the afternoon at the party, she panics. When she learns that it is Mrs. Fletcher, she hides in a closet.

Written by: Jack Elinson, Norman Paul; Max Showalter as Mr. Fletcher, Amzie Strickland as Mrs. Fletcher, Jane Aull as Woman #1 at Market, Howard Culver as Man #1 at Market, Brad Trumball as Man #2 at Market, Marshall Kent as Elderly Man at Market, Walter Mathews as Man #1 at Party, Tim Weldon as Jonathan Fletcher, Jan Arvan as Man #2 at Party, Lynn Wood as Woman at Party, Don G. Ross as Charlie

Groovy Day Facts:

Genson's Market is where the candy bar war takes place.

Toby can't help sell the candy because he's "just a civilian."

At the office, Doris is comp- limented on her coffee-making skills.

Doris drinks sherry at the party.

A scene from this episode was used to audition the role of Mr. Nicholson.

With McLean Stevenson.

*today's world* the now magazine: Entertaining a client for advertising.

Guest Star Mini-Bio & Doris Day Movie Find!:

Max Showalter [a.k.a. Casey Adams] appeared in Doris's *It Happened to Jane* [1959]. He appeared again with Doris in *Move Over, Darling* [1963]. His lists of credits also include *The Loretta Young Show* and the pilot for *Leave It to Beaver*. Showalter eventually moved to Chester, Connecticut (where he had filmed *It Happened to Jane*) and was later on the Board for the National Theater of the Deaf, which helped produce *The Christmas That Almost Wasn't* with Jackie Joseph.

## "The Health King"
Production Dates: August 19-22, 1969
Original Airdate: November 10, 1969
Directed by: Coby Ruskin

Mr. Nicholson is starting to realize Doris Martin's potential, even going as far as executive material. He sends her on an assignment of getting the rights to a new fitness book written by Bruce Saunders. Doris is confronted with Mr. Saunders' flexing and workout regiment, but does get invited to a health food restaurant to discuss the rights with him. On Mr. Nicholson's insistence, she accepts his dinner invitation and discovers a very different Mr. Saunders. Mr. Nicholson gets jealous and feels an urge to compete with "the Body Beautiful."

Written by: Budd Grossman; Michael Forest as Bruce Saunders, Ernest Harada as Ling, Lavina Dawson as Waitress, Joan Lemmo as Woman #1, Bunny Summers as Woman #2

Groovy Day Facts:
First time we see Myrna's apartment, as well as Mr. Nicholson's. Myrna's boyfriend is Sidney, who is "stingy with a buck."

*today's world* the now magazine:
A serialization of the book *How to Build a Better Body*.

Doris Day Movie Find!:
"You Make Me Want to Want You" from *With Six You Get Eggroll* [1968]

**"Doris, the Model"**
Original Airdate: November 17, 1969

[See the section "Doris—a la mode"]

**"Doris Strikes Out"**
Production Dates: August 26+, 1969
Original Airdate: November 24, 1969
Directed by: Coby Ruskin

French movie star Claude LeMaire is at *today's world* as the magazine will be covering the premiere of his new movie. He invites Doris to escort him to the premiere the following night. She accepts with great enthusiasm. When Doris arrives home that night, she lets the family know about the big event. The boys have exciting news of their own, as they prepare to play the most important Little League game of the season, which Grandpa has been chosen to umpire. The next day, Doris goes on a shopping spree with Myrna, returns to the ranch and finds Buck has injured his back and is bedridden. The boys have volunteered their mom to umpire the game. Doris races against the clock—with a few misguided decisions—to finish the game on time and make it to the premiere—where she falls asleep!

With McLean Stevenson and Jacques Bergerac.

Written by: Norman Paul, Jack Elinson; Jacques Bergerac as Claude LeMaire, James Chandler as Dr. Parker, Gordon Jump as Little League Manager, Darrell Rice as Joey, Alan DeWitt as the Hairdresser

Groovy Day Facts:
Billy's team is the Indians and Toby is the bat boy.
LeMaire's movie played on TV that evening is called *Strangers No More*.
Among other things, Doris calls strikes when the pitches are balls and calls an out with only two strikes. She also called ball five before telling the player to take first [four is all that is needed], and when the pitcher's ball hits Billy at home plate, Doris calls him out rather than letting the batter automatically take first base.

*today's world* the now magazine:
Feature story on Claude LeMaire's movie premiere in San Francisco.

Doris Day Movie Find!:
Jacques Bergerac was married at one time to Ginger Rogers, who starred in *Storm Warning* [1951]. He later became the head of Revlon's Paris office.
Buck mentions Brigitte Bardot in this episode. At the annual Genesis Award presented on the Animal Planet channel, the Doris Day Music Award is presented alongside the Brigitte Bardot Film Award. Bardot co-starred with James Stewart [*The Man Who Knew Too Much* (1956)] in her only American film called *Dear Brigitte* [1965] with "Lost in Space" star Billy Mumy.

**"Singles Only"**
Production Dates: September 15-18, 1969
Original Airdate: December 8, 1969
Directed by: William Wiard

After years of searching, going on horrible dates and a convenient boy-friend, Myrna has finally found the man of her dreams. Well, she knows where he lives—at Paradise Palms Apartments, the perfect swinging singles place, so owner Lou Lester's ad says. Without wasting any time, Doris helps her move in. Myrna soon discovers that not only does the man of her dreams *not* live there, but no one comes close. But she is stuck since she signed a year's lease which is as tight as a "set nail." It will take careful planning and help from Doris, Buck, Billy, Toby and especially Nelson, to get Myna out of the lease.

Written by: William Raynor, Myles Wilder; Sid Melton as Lou Lester, Ed Fury as Chet, Michael Lerner as the Fat Man, Joseph Perry as Harry Dumbrowski, Joe Ross as Virgil Praskins, Alice Backes as Agnes Albright, Ben Young as 2nd Handsome Man, Carol Worthington as Girl

Groovy Day Facts:
The Paradise Palms Apartments offers an Olympic-sized 50x100 swimming pool for mixed bathing; spacious recreation area with the official-sized ping-pong table ["For mixed doubles?" Doris asks]; his and hers laundry facilities; and a rooftop solarium for mixed sunning.

Myrna's apartment is a "one bedroom": one room that includes a living area, a kitchen that is in a closet, and a bathroom. The couch converts to a bed, and the coffee table also serves as her dresser. Her window view is a brick wall. "It's a real step saver," Myrna says.

Among the disappointed tenants who live there is Agnes Albright, who'd been there "four months, eight days, three hours and 17 minutes" when she met Myrna. Agnes lives in #212, while Harry Dumbroski— who likes broads and beer—is in #106, Virgil Praskins down the hall, and in #112, a larger man who asks Myrna for sunning lotion.

Doris Day Movie Find!:
Sid Melton appeared with Doris and Richard Widmark in *The Tunnel of Love* [1958]. This episode was his first of three appearances on the series. He recalls this episode: "It was a pretty sad looking place, wasn't it? It was a

With Rose Marie.

funny show and Doris was great. I love animals and Doris is a big, big animal lover, and they put that in the show—but it was a double who fell off the skateboard and then into the pool. That wasn't me! William Wiard was a terrific director who did that episode."

**"Togetherness"**
Production Dates: August 5-7, 1969
Original Airdate: December 15, 1969
Directed by: Alan Rafkin

An overworked Doris is anxious to spend the weekend with her family. She really feels that she has deserted them and wants the boys to feel they have a mother. Doris has a big weekend planned for the family, starting with an early breakfast, picnic, games, and a night of song and more games. The kids, on the other hand, have other plans, but not to disappoint their mom, they don't let her know until she finds out from Buck. On this, she lets the boys go to a sleep-over and she accepts a theater and dinner invitation from Ron Harvey. Ron drives to Mill Valley to pick up Doris as the boys return home, sick from overeating chili dogs. Can Doris take care of her boys and not disappoint Mr. Harvey?

Written by: William Raynor, Myles Wilder; Paul Smith as Ron Harvey, Karen Arthur as Gloria

Groovy Day Facts:
*How Deep Is the River* is the play Ron has tickets for.
This is the first time we see Ron Harvey's apartment.
Billy ate four chili dogs and Toby had six when they got sick at Cubby Weaver's sleep-over.

*today's world* the now magazine:
Ron Harvey makes up an assignment in Bulgaria

Doris Day Album Find!:
"Time to Say Goodnight" from *I Have Dreamed* [1961]

**"A Two Family Christmas"**
Original Airdate: December 22, 1969

[see "Doris's Christmas Present"]

**"You're as Old as You Feel"**
Production Dates: August 11-15, 1969
Original Airdate: December 29, 1969
Directed by: Larry Dobkin

Grandpa has a difficult time celebrating his birthday due to a serious toothache. Since he's never been to the dentist, he is petrified of having it checked out. After going and having the tooth removed, he feels that he is getting on in life, and retires permanently to his room, giving up everything including taking care of his ranch. Doris will do all she can to bring him back to normal and make him realize that he is as young as ever—even if it means hiring Buck's friend Merle to take charge of the ranch.

Written by: Norman Paul, Jack Elinson; Hal Smith as Merle, Herb Vigran as the Dentist

Doris Day Movie Find!:
  Bugs Bunny is mentioned in this episode. He appeared with Doris in *My Dream Is Yours* [1949] and was heard in *It's a Great Feeling* [1949].
  Herb Vigran appeared with Doris in *Lucky Me* [1954].

**"The Prizefighter and the Lady"**
Production Dates: October 6-9, 1969
Original Airdate: January 5, 1970
Directed by: Denver Pyle

Ron Harvey gives Doris a writing assignment to interview and follow Duke Farentino, middleweight boxing champion of the world. Doris tells him she is really not interested in boxing, but Ron forces her to do the story over the weekend. When Duke Farentino sees Doris for the first time, he cannot take his eyes off of her and gives her the assignment as the only journalist who will cover him during his training. Doris encounters jealousy from all of the other sports reporters there to cover the event. Doris discovers that Duke isn't interested in boxing. What he really wants to do is dance. She is then ordered out of the camp by his manager and advised never to return. Duke hides out in the trunk of her car and follows her home for more dancing. When he is retrieved for his bout, Duke does not fight well. Doris is then delivered by helicopter to the arena, hopefully to give Duke a boost before the end of the fight.

Written by: Budd Grossman; Larry Storch as Duke Farentino, Buddy Lester as Eddie, Jim Cross as Larry, Sidney Clute as Howard, Chick Casey as Herman, Gerald York as Pete, Lauro Salas as Garcia, Frankie Van as Referee, Paul Smith as Ron Harvey

Groovy Day Facts:
  The first appearance of Duke Farentino, who is known as "The Dancing Kid."
  Doris wears reading glasses for the first and only time.
  Duke opens Duke Farentino's Dance Studio—"for the young at feet."
  Billy and Toby are back at Cubby Weaver's where they recently had a bout with overeating chili dogs.

*today's world* the now magazine:
    "Duke: the Boxer"

Doris Day Movie Find!:
    Jim Cross played a photographer in Doris's *Love Me or Leave Me* [1955].

## "Doris Versus the Computer"
Production Dates: September 22-25, 1969
Original Airdate: January 12, 1970
Directed by: Denver Pyle

In the middle of a very busy day at *today's world* magazine, Doris gets a phone call from Buck. He tells her he received a letter from the electric company informing them the bill has not been paid and that their service will be terminated. During her lunch hour, Doris rushes to the electric company and meets for the first time Mr. Jarvis, who is in charge. He relies solely on the results of the company's computer and ensures Doris that her bill has not been paid, despite proof that she wrote a personal check. She goes home upset and frustrated, when the computer turns her electricity off. Doris and Myrna decide to fight back the next day and picket the electric company. But they get arrested and thrown in jail. Upset with this whole situation, Mr. Nicholson tries to resolve Doris's problem through the power of the press.

Written by: Arthur Alsberg, Don Nelson; Billy De Wolfe as Mr. Jarvis, Frank Corsentino as Hippie #1, Christina Dean as Hippie #2, Gregg Jakobson as Hippie #3, Jerry Jones as Policeman

Groovy Day Facts:
    The living room floor at the ranch is now covered with wall-to-wall carpeting.
    Billy and Toby like to watch the TV show *Frogman*.
    Mr. Jarvis thinks Doris is Hungarian and confesses Zsa Zsa Gabor is one of his favorite actresses.
    The computer causing the problem is 1176B.
    Doris Martin seen in a jail cell for the second time.
    Mr. Jarvis's first appearance in the series.

With Denver Pyle.

*today's world* the now magazine:
Possible story on the electric company and its computer—big business and the little people it affects.

Doris Day Movie Find!:
Doris and the counterculture: A group of hippies comes to Doris's rescue when they join her and Myrna in picketing the electric company. Another group also helped her out in *With Six You Get Eggroll* [1968].

**"Hot Dogs"**
Production Dates: October 27-30, 1969
Original Airdate: January 19, 1970
Directed by: Coby Ruskin

After just finishing a two-hour lunch, Doris and Myrna walk to the parking lot to get to their car. Doris notices a car full of beautiful French poodles who are locked inside with the windows rolled up and no water.

Doris decides to set them free even if it means breaking and entering into the car. With the help of a locksmith, she gets into the car and takes all of the dogs to *today's world* offices while Mr. Nicholson is meeting with a Supreme Court judge concerning his memoirs for the magazine. Doris does a great job of hiding the dogs until the poodle parlor owner arrives to retrieve them. Soon after, everyone is sent to court where Doris pleads her case with a little help from the Supreme Court.

Written by: Jack Elinson, Norman Paul, Don Genson; James Millhollin as Paul, Jerome Cowan as Justice William Forester, Paul Smith as Ron Harvey, Issa Arnal as Helen, Charles Lane as Judge Carter, Owen Bush as Locksmith

*today's world* the now magazine:
Supreme Court Justice William Forester's memoirs

Doris Day Movie Find!:
Charles Lane appeared with Doris in *Teacher's Pet* [1958].
Jerome Cowan acted with Doris in *Young Man With a Horn* and in *The West Point Story* [both from 1950].

**"*today's world* Catches the Measles"**
Production Dates: November 10-13, 1969
Original Airdate: January 26, 1970
Directed by: Fred de Cordova

The publisher of *today's world* in New York, Col. Fairburn, is very upset that the staff of the magazine is in a rut and not coming up with any new ideas for the next issue. Doris suggests to Mr. Nicholson and Ron Harvey that they go to her farm for the weekend so that they can come up with a fresh idea by the following Monday. They arrive the next day and everybody is there to greet them, except for Toby, who finally comes to say hello. They all have a great lunch, except for Toby who is not feeling well. Doris soon finds out that he has the measles. The house is suddenly quarantined by the County Medical Officer as everyone has been in contact with him. All will need to stay put and be patient, so the main operation of *today's world* is based out of Doris's house. Col. Fairburn makes a surprise visit to the magazine and discovers that everybody is at

With Rose Marie.

this "secretary's" house. Myrna takes him there and he surprises Mr. Nicholson, who is in the arms of the "secretary."

Written by: Jack Elinson, Norman Paul; Edward Andrews as Col. Fairburn, Walter Sande as Dr. Wagner, Paul Smith as Ron Harvey, Joe Hoover as Jack, Breland Rice as Phil, Issa Arnal as Helen, Geri Ewing as Secretary

Groovy Day Facts:
    Mr. Nicholson was born in Bloomington, Illinois
    Ron Harvey was born Rudolph Valentino Harvey in Santa Ana, California. His mother was a fan of the silent film star's *The Sheik*.
    Col. Fairburn was an ex-army officer and had German Measles.
    First appearance of Col. Fairburn in the series.

*today's world* the now magazine:
    Doc Wagner's memoirs, "The Country Doctor."

Doris Day Movie Find!:
    Edward Andrews was featured in Doris's *The Thrill of It All* [1963].

## "The Gas Station"

Production Dates: September 8-11, 1969
Original Airdate: February 2, 1970
Directed by: Hal Cooper

Doris spends a Saturday showing Myrna around Mill Valley, first by dropping Billy and Toby off at the movie theater and then introducing her to Leroy B. Simpson, now owner of his very own gas station. Leroy is preoccupied since his wife, Ellie, is in the hospital about to have their first child. Doris and Myrna take over the gas station so that he can go to the hospital, but he is too nervous to drive so Buck takes him. All of a sudden, Mill Valley becomes a detour as there are repairs being done on the main highway. The gas station is suddenly rushed with a huge number of drivers, including one who plans on robbing the station. Meanwhile, Leroy is delayed at the hospital as he is slowly becoming the father of triplets.

Written by: Jack Elinson, Norman Paul, Don Genson; Jim Hampton as Leroy B. Simpson, Tina Holland as Terry Tidy, John Carter as Hold Up Man, Bob Jellison as Smokey, Herman Griffith as Man #1,

Herb Weil as Sporty Guy, Virgil Frye as Motorcyclist, Charles Dugdale as Man #2, Martin Ashe as Man #3, Jon Kowal as Truck Driver, Eddie Quillan as Man #4, Eric Scott as Boy

Groovy Day Facts:
    Leroy's station is a Tidy Service franchise.
    A Tidy Oil lady makes a surprise visit to check on the station's appearance: In addition to demerits for untidy bathrooms and other things, she finds:
    General disrepair: 20 demerits
    Sloppy uniform: 10 demerits
    Arguing: 10 demerits

Doris Day Movie Find!:
    Eddie Quillan was in *Move Over, Darling* [1963] with Doris.

**"Kidnapped"**
Production Dates: November 17-20, 1969
Original Airdate: February 9, 1970
Directed by: Coby Ruskin

    Doris Martin, working for *today's world* magazine, is innocently picking up an article when she is kidnapped by members of organized crime. The article in question is an expose on Barney Moore, who is a cheap mobster who's "getting away with murder." Doris and the article's writer are taken to an undisclosed location. When Mr. Nicholson receives a phone call telling him what just happened, he conducts an investigation while Myrna and Ron do their own. Doris becomes friendly with the mobster's wife, who in return lets her try to get away.

    Written by: Doug Tibbles; Bruce Gordon as Barney Moore, Kaye Ballard as Flossie Moore, Avery Schreiber as Warren Coleman, Paul Smith as Ron Harvey, Hagen Smith as Lefty Watson, Gene Dynarski as Lefty Kretch, Scott Perry as Detective, Rico Cattani as Bartender

Groovy Day Facts:
   The hideout is in the back of the Mermaid Bar on the waterfront.
   Ron Harvey has bookmaker friends
   This is the first of several appearances by Kaye Ballard, who later
played the recurring role of Angie Pallucci.

*today's world* the now magazine:
   "Underworld Boss Exposed"

Doris Day Movie Find!:
   Doris portrayed Ruth Etting, who was married to real-life small-time
hood Marty Snyder, in *Love Me or Leave Me* [1955].

## "Buck's Portrait"
Production Dates: July 14-17, 1969
Original Airdate: February 16, 1970
Directed by: Earl Bellamy

Amanda Merriwether, one of America's best abstract artists, has been
hired to paint the pioneer cover for *today's world* magazine. The only thing
she really needs to get the job done is the right model. Doris takes her
through Mill Valley, Cotina, and just about everywhere, to look at people
in finding the right subject. When they take a break at Doris's house, Amanda
discovers Buck—who is perfect for the cover. Buck takes some convincing
from Doris, but eventually agrees to do it. As he poses day after day, he
starts to realize how widespread the issue will be, and can't wait to show the
cover to his friends from the lodge. When the cover of an abstract painting
is finished, it is a masterpiece. But where is Buck?

Written by: Doug Tibbles; Mabel Albertson as Amanda Merriwether,
Hal Smith as Merle, Charles Wagenheim as Edgar, Bob Jellison as Smokey,
Issa Arnal as Receptionist, J.P. Cranshaw as Farmer, Riza Royce as Woman
Farmer, Woodrow Parfrey as Barton Durston

Groovy Day Facts:
   We see the Buck's lodge for the first time.
   Buck likes onions and mushrooms with his filet mignon.
   Buck's cousin, Vera June, lives in Bald Knob, Arkansas.

A framed copy of the magazine cover replaces the "Home Sweet Home" wall hanging over the fireplace mantle.

Amanda says about Buck: "I'm painting a pioneer. Not a rural Rock Hudson."

Woodrow Parfrey and Hal Smith were in four episodes of the series from seasons one and two. Issa Arnal was seen in six episodes as the receptionist at *today's world*.

*today's world* the now magazine:
"The cover of the year!"

Doris Day Movie Find!:
Charles Wagenheim appeared with Doris in *The Tunnel of Love* [1958].

Guest Star Mini-Bio:
Mabel Albertson had a great opportunity in this episode to play something completely different: a blonde-haired avant-garde artiste who was well-dressed and determined, compared to the gray-haired mother-in-law with a "sick headache" [caused mainly by Endora] that she played to perfection on *Bewitched*, as well as Don Hollinger's mother in *That Girl*. She also appeared in the films *What's Up, Doc?*, *Barefoot in the Park*, *A Fine Madness* and *The Long, Hot Summer*.

**"Doris Hires a Millionaire"**
Original Airdates: February 23 and March 2, 1970

[see "Doris and the Millionaire" section]

**"A Woman's Intuition"**
Production Dates: December 1-4, 1969
Original Airdate: March 9, 1970
Directed by: Denver Pyle

Doris's intuition leads her on her very first trip with *today's world* magazine. Ed King, who became rich overnight with a hamburger chain, has agreed to do an in-person interview in Orlando, Florida for a five-part series in exchange for a cash payment of $20,000. On the way to Florida, the plane is highjacked to Havana, Cuba, where Doris and Mr. Nicholson fall into the hands of Fidel Castro's Major Laguinita. They are held there for several hours then are sent to Florida where they read in a newspaper that Ed King was just indicted on nine counts of income tax evasion.

Written by: Rick Mittleman; Bernie Kopell as Major Laguinita, Sandy Kenyon as Zeke Kraley, Carol Worthington as Stewardess, Gordon Jump as Ticket Agent, Ricco Cattani as Waiter, Perla Walter as Girl Soldier

Groovy Day Facts:
   While saying goodbye to the Major, Doris says "Que Sera, Sera."

*today's world* the now magazine:
   Interview with Joe Namath

Doris Day Music Find!:
   "Sorry" single [1967]

**"Doris Meets a Prince"**
Production Dates: December 15-18, 1969
Original Airdate: March 16, 1970
Directed by: Fred de Cordova

Ron Harvey and Doris are assigned to do an exclusive interview with the Crown Prince of Sadonia. The prince refuses, but when he sees Doris at the door, he not only accepts, but falls madly in love with her. She sweetly invites him to her house for dinner with her family, which he promptly accepts. The royal beef stew is served to the prince's delight, where he grows fond of Doris's family. He invites her to his hotel for dinner the following night where they dine on Sadonia's national deli-

With McLean Stevenson.

cacy, broiled locust legs. He follows the dinner with a marriage proposal, which astounds, surprises and shocks Doris and everyone at *today's world*. However, the throne is abolished in a revolution and the prince has lost everything before she gives him her answer.

Written by: Budd Grossman; Cesare Danova as Prince Carlos, Eric Mason as The Aide, Roy Roberts as Mr. Gilby, Luis de Cordova as Prime Minister, Paul Smith as Ron Harvey

Groovy Day Facts:
Typical American dinner according to Doris: beef stew, cold beer, popcorn and rhubarb pie.
Cesare Danova appeared two other times in the series, both as artist Carlo Benedetti.

*today's world* the now magazine:
Ron Harvey's interview "Prince Marries Secretary":
Q: "What was your first reaction when the prince asked you to be his wife?"
A: "I was dumbfounded. It was just overwhelming. Mr. Harvey, he's such a real person."
Q: "A real prince, huh?"

Doris Day Music Find!:
"Que Sera, Sera" is played on an accordion at Carlos' restaurant by the former Sadonian prime minister.

**"The Duke Returns"**
Production Dates: December 8-11, 1969
Original Airdate: March 23, 1970
Directed by: Denver Pyle

The Duke returns to visit Doris and to put an ad in the magazine for his new dancing school and invites her over to visit. It is a wonderful facility, full of clients and eager teachers who are about to get stolen by a rival dancing school that is moving into the same building. Poor Duke is left only with wonderful students, eager to learn how to dance. Good-hearted Doris comes to the rescue again and gets Myrna and Ron to help out until Duke finds replacements. Unfortunately, he works the trio to the point of complete exhaustion.

Written by: Norman Paul, Jack Elinson; Larry Storch as Duke, Michael Lerner as Mr. Murray, Paul Smith as Ron Harvey, George Dunn as Hillbilly, Margaret Wheeler as Mrs. Forbush

Groovy Day Facts:
Dances taught at Duke's school include The Bugaloo, The Fru, The Limbo, Shake Legs, The Fox Trot and The Cha-Cha.

*today's world* the now magazine:
A story on the smog situation in Los Angeles.
Ad for Duke Farentino's Dancing School

Doris Day Movie Find!:
"Au Revoir Is Goodbye With a Smile" from *Do Not Disturb* [1965]
"You Make Me Want You" from *With Six You Get Eggroll* [1968]

## "The Office Troubleshooter"
Production Dates: January 12-15, 1970
Original Airdate: March 30, 1970
Directed by: Coby Ruskin

Col. Fairburn hires Doris Martin's old nemesis from the electric company, Mr. Jarvis, as the efficiency expert for the *today's world* San Francisco office. Mr. Jarvis turns into a control freak: he constantly peeks over everyone's shoulders; measures pencils; re-bends paper clips; going through wastebaskets; bugging the offices; eavesdropping on personal conversations; and removing the coffee machine. Ron, Myrna and Doris attempt, after exhausting all possibilities, to beat Mr. Jarvis at his own inefficient game.

Written by: Budd Grossman; Billy De Wolfe as Mr. Jarvis, Edward Andrews as Col. Fairburn, Paul Smith as Ron Harvey

Groovy Day Facts:
Mr. Jarvis's list on improvements to make at *today's world*: set the office temperature at 66 degrees—the most efficient temperature to work

With Rose Marie.

in; remove the coffee machine to keep employees from standing around talking; all pencils should be at 1.5 inches or smaller before throwing away.

Mr. Jarvis introduces himself as Philip Jarvis to the receptionist, but in all the other episodes his first name is Willard.

Col. Fairburn is a golf fanatic, but wastes seven hours and 20 minutes according to Jarvis.

Doris types 85 words per minute.

Mr. Jarvis eventually moves to Alaska and Fairburn's Wood Pulp subsidiary.

Doris Day Movie Find!:

Edward Andrews was in *Send Me No Flowers* [1964] with Doris.

### Fun Day

## We Spend A Fun Day With Doris

What does a brilliant star like Doris Day do – in those long hours at the studio – when not facing a TV camera? We thought you'd never ask! And, confidentially, we were beginning to believe we might never get a chance tp show you... the bubbly blonde doesn't welcome visitors from "outside", and we couldn't help wondering: is that because it isn't half as much fun *making* a lighthearted comedy as it is *watching* it?

Now we bring-back-alive answers to both questions! Not posed shots taken on the same sets, in the same costumes, you see on *The Doris Day Show*... but a candid glimpse of a real "pro" at work and at play behind the scenes – in *non*-dress rehearsals, with sound engineers and other members of both cast and crew, laughing and joking with people she knows and trusts.

Doris learned most of show business the hard way... touring with bands before her first hit records, singing on radio before she became a big "box office" movie star... but she learned to love TV through Martin Melcher, her late husband. here, in the show Marty had created especially for her, she is most *herself*, as only her close friends usually see her. Here, she is truly "at home" – and enjoying every moment of it!

*Work can be fun??? You find it's true, sitting in with us on the first "run-though" of a Doris Day script. Her infectious laugh (right) and famous double-take (above) are guaranteed to banish those early-morning doldrums!*

A visit to the set.

## "Colonel Fairburn Takes Over"
Production Dates: January 5-8, 1970
Original Airdate: April 6, 1970
Directed by: Coby Ruskin

Col. Fairburn makes another surprise visit to the magazine and decides to make his GHQ (General Headquarters) in San Francisco for the time being, taking over Mr. Nicholson's office and his secretary. Mr. Nicholson now moves into Ron's office. Col. Fairburn now has room to work on crossword puzzles, throw darts and practice his golf. But most of all, he develops a very strong interest in Doris and takes her out to long lunches, buys her expensive presents, even offers her a promotion. Doris, who thinks of him more as a father, is surprised and a little confused by his advances. She finally accepts a dinner date with him and asks him to take her to a disco, where he surprisingly meets his daughter and her new husband. He takes her home and Doris sweetly helps him realize that their relationship is a friendship.

Written by: Rick Mittleman, Don Genson; Edward Andrews as Col. Fairburn, Fredericka Myers as Sharon Fairburn, Paul Smith as Ron Harvey, Scott Perry as Jim, De De Young as Helen, Titus Moody as Messenger

Groovy Day Facts:
Col. Norton Fairburn is at this time a widower with two children, Junior and Sharon.
With Col. Fairburn's permission, Doris eats candy and works on crossword puzzles at her desk.

*today's world* the now magazine:
*today's world* is a monthly magazine, and Mr. Nicholson noted its circulation increased 18.5 percent from the previous month.

Doris Day Album Find!:
"I Believe in Dreams" from *I Have Dreamed* [1961]

**THE BARRACUDA**
Throughout the series, the Chrysler Corporation provided automobiles for use in the series. Of all of them, the most memorable was the car Doris Martin used for her commute to San Francisco. It was not a family-type vehicle like the green station wagon from the first season, but what was called a pony car: a compact, affordable, highly-styled automobile with a sporty look. It was a candy-apple red Plymouth Barracuda convertible that she was first seen driving in the season two opening credits of *The Doris Day Show*.

Doris drives to her *today's world* office at 650 California Street in San Francisco.

The Barracuda was first introduced to buyers in 1964 by Chrysler and was spun-off of the existing Valient series to appeal to a sportier market. It is considered the first pony car as it was introduced in April, two weeks before Ford unveiled its Mustang model. As the pony cars became more popular, Plymouth revised the Barracuda in 1967 to a more sportier look, and its engine options resembled its Road Runner line more so than its Valient series.

Doris's first 'Cuda, as it was called, was the two-door 1969 model with a beige interior. Of the 32,000 produced that year, only 1,442 were convertibles. This is the type Doris drove in season two through five opening credits.

New models were provided for the season's episodes, each red in color, but with different grills, headlights and taillights depending on the year. Only 635 'Cuda convertibles were made in 1970, and 374 in 1971. However, in the last season of *The Doris Day Show*, Doris's car had a black interior and was a hardtop as the convertible option was dropped in 1972.

In time, the car's sales lagged behind the wildly popular Ford Mustang and the Camaro/Firebird, but the Barracuda would make a name for itself in 1970 when a more powerful engine called the Hemi was made available.

Despite promotions, including its product placement in *The Doris Day Show*, the 1970-74 generation of Barracudas was considered a "marketplace failure" and it never successfully competed with its rivals. Colors, such as Go Mango, Panther Pink and Plum Crazy, as well as hood modifications, decal sets and the fact that the engines were easy to modify slightly, were offered to entice buyers.

Still, the 'Cuda could not make a comeback, and 1974 was the last year for the car when only 4,989 of them were manufactured. In fact, production ended ten years to the day after it had begun. One reason was the oil crisis that occurred at the time, and another was stricter emission laws and safety regulations which altered its performance and look respectively. Today, however, the 'Cuda is a highly sought after by car collectors because of its history, its look, and the fact that far fewer of them were produced compared to other pony cars.

## SOCIAL ISSUES AND CENSORSHIP

Although *The Doris Day Show* was described as a sitcom (situation comedy), those close to the series feel it was more of a dramedy (drama and comedy), and that it was not necessarily a series in which a problem arose each week that was solved in half an hour. Many times the ending remained unresolved, especially in regard to Doris Martin's boyfriends.

While most of CBS's more popular comedies at the time tended to make a strong social comment with each episode, *The Doris Day Show* was more subtle in its approach in doing the same. At times the episodes asked us to take a look at ourselves and how we the viewer treat others, or how we are treated. Others were more direct in their messages. Among *The Doris Day Show*'s social issues were:

Environment ["Doris Versus Pollution"]
Medical Costs ["Doris and the Doctor"]
Homeless and the Downtrodden ["Who's Got the Trench Coat"]
Racism ["The Friend"]
Poaching ["Love a Duck"]
Fraud ["The Con Man," "Charity Begins in the Office," "The Hoax"]

Sexism ["The Woman Hater"]

Swinging ["Singles Only"]

Technology ["Doris Versus the Computer," "A Fine Romance"]

Organized Crime ["Kidnapped," "Wings of an Angel," "Jimmy the Gent," "Follow That Dog"]

Retirement ["Buck Visits the Big City," "The Last Huzzah"]

Pre-Marital Relationships ["Forgive and Forget," "No More Advice...Please," "The Music Man," "Family Magazine"]

Women's Lib ["The Feminist"]

Health ["The Health King," "A Weighty Problem"]

Counterculture ["Col. Fairburn, Jr."]

Animal Rights ["Hot Dogs," "It's a Dog's Life"]

"Real Women Wear Fake Fur"

The latter issue was very strong to Doris Day, and its message of animal rights were very clear when brought up in the series. Her public push for animal rights exploded during the run of *The Doris Day Show*, and she appeared with Amanda Blake, Jayne Meadows, Angie Dickinson and Mary Tyler Moore in an advertisement that appeared in several magazines.

In terms of censorship, CBS seemed more lenient with *The Doris Day Show*'s subject matters than with other series on the network at the time. Was it because they felt "Doris Day" would not do anything distasteful or controversial and did not need to be watched? Or did they allow things simply because it was Doris Day's show and they trusted in her taste?

More than a decade later, however, when the series was rebroadcast on CBN in the 1980s, *The Doris Day Show* did run into a few minor problems that resulted in censorship. The words "damn" and "hell" were removed from the episodes that contained them. It was said that some episodes were initially not shown on CBN due to the channel's criteria. These included "The Office Troubleshooter" (probable reason: getting Mr. Jarvis drunk); "The Albatross" (possibly because of the flirtatious restaurant scene); and "Lost and Found" (perhaps because Doris auditions to be a Go-Go dancer in a strip club).

## *MAD* MAGAZINE and DORIS DAY

*MAD* is one of the most influential magazines of all time, even being featured in a 2006 edition of *The Wall Street Journal*. Its social satire of the very best in news, films, and television poked fun at culture and social mores.

It became so well known and popular for its humorous takes on current movies and television series that it was an honor to be spoofed by the magazine. And so in its 140th issue, the January 1971 edition, the inevitable happened: *The Doris Day Show*'s second season was satirized as *The Doris Daze Show*. It was drawn by one the best comic book artists, Angelo Torres.

NUMBER 140          JANUARY 1971

# MAD

"THE DORIS DAZE SHOW" (A MAD TV SATIRE) Pg. 43

### FRECKLES AND HER FRIENDS DEPT.

Why are most weekly series TV shows pretty awful? Because some hack Writer comes up with a trite idea, an incompetent Producer puts it on, and an inept Director moves around the no-talent Star! That's why most weekly series TV shows are pretty awful! Now...what happens when the Star of a weekly TV show is also the Producer and has all the power on the show? What happens when the Star makes all the decisions and signs all the checks? It'll probably come out looking remarkably like...

# THE DORIS DAZE SHOW

ARTIST: ANGELO TORRES          WRITER: STAN HART

## A TALK WITH ROSE MARIE

*How did it come about that you joined the series?*

My understanding was that Doris asked if I was available to do her show. I went to meet her and we clicked immediately and I did the show for three years.

*Myrna and Doris had a fun camaraderie. Was that a reflection of your real-life friendship with Doris Day?*

Doris had just lost her husband, so I sort of felt a kinship based on that alone. She was wonderful to work with and we became very good friends. She's so good that people take her for granted, as far as her talent is concerned. She's really very, very professional and she knows what she's doing, plus she's got a way about her that you just like her immediately. We worked well together.

*There's a story that you're a late riser in the morning...*

Oh yes. I would make fun of her that she always got up so early. She's a morning person and I'm a night person; when I would go to work, it was dark, and the CBS gate man would always say, "Good morning," and I would always say, "Looks like last night," and he would always laugh. I used to tell Doris, "I'm going around shaking trees so no birds will sleep." She'd laugh and say, "Oh, *you.*"

*Although she was the star of the show, Doris wasn't its producer until its last year. How much say did Doris have about things in the years you were on the series?*

Doris knows what's good and what's not. And I love anybody who knows his or her craft, and Doris is one of the best. We would get different directors and she could size them up the first day. She'd say to me,

"Watch." She'd say to the director, "I think this should be a two-shot," and if the director said, "Oh yes, sure dear, whatever you want, dear," she'd say to me, "Oops"—but not in front of the director or whoever. But she would lose respect for him. If the director agreed with her and said, "If you want a two-shot, fine, but I was going to do two close-ups," she'd say, "He knows what he's doing." I learned a lot from her too, and I'm forever grateful.

*It's obvious Doris also respected your opinions about the series.*
She'd always ask me if I had seen the show on the night it was on, and I always had. I told her what I thought of the show and she'd say, "I know I can always count on you for an honest answer."

*We recall hearing about an incident with you and a leather purse you used in a show. Wasn't it an alligator bag?*
One day I carried my alligator bag in a scene. She noticed it and said, "I sure hope that's not real alligator." I said, "For what I paid for it, it better be." She looked at me as if I had killed it personally.
Then I said to her, "Did you know that the female alligator lays 300 eggs at a time and that the male alligator eats 275 of those 300 eggs?" She said, "Really?" "Yeah. And if the male alligator didn't eat 275 of those 300 eggs, then you'd be up to your ass in alligators." She looked at me and said, "Oh *you*."

*With the scripts, it seemed you were given the spoken joke while Doris was given the physical joke.*
What they wrote for the two of us, it was wonderful.

*Did you have any input with the scripts?*
During rehearsal if we'd come up with something, Doris would say leave it in, you know? We did a model show ["Doris the Model"] where we were supposed to be guarding the models, and we did the scene and nobody said cut. So we kept going. And I looked at her and I said, "Do you want a baloney sandwich?" She said, "Baloney gives me gas." And I said, "Everything gives you gas!" We started to laugh and Doris asked, "Is anyone gonna yell cut?" It was cute. So yes, there *were* ad-libs. It was a lot of fun doing her show.

*Did you work with Billy De Wolfe before the series?*

Yes, I worked with him on the *Van Dyke Show*. He was a doll. He was a professional to work with.

*Kaye Ballard?*

Kaye and I were friends from a long way back.

*McLean Stevenson?*

He was funny as hell. He used to make us laugh all the time. He was wonderful—a cut-up.

*Denver Pyle?*

You're talking about an honest-to-God all-time talent. He was great, and he did a *Van Dyke Show* too. He played Uncle George. I remember Lew Ayres too. He played the millionaire. He was a doll, a doll. A wonderful man.

*Philip Brown?*

Yes, but I don't see him. The kids were wonderful working with on the show. We were a nice, big family. I know that's a cliché that everybody uses, but it was true because Doris was a very easygoing kind of person. There were no tantrums, no temperamental things. And if the kids had any problems with their lines or whatever, they'd go to Doris or come to me. It was a very good working group.

*What were the dressing rooms like?*

Doris had a bungalow, and every day she'd come down to the set with two or three dogs. She had 20 at the time, I think. But she would take two or three different ones every day. And I had just lost my dog, and she dogged me—excuse the expression—so I got another one. And she became the godmother to my dog Scruffy.

*Do you recall making the episode "Doris Goes to Hollywood," with Henry Fonda, and was it on-location?*

That was at the studio. At CBS—Studio City. That was a fun one to do because everybody loves Doris and everybody respects her, and it was wonderful.

*For season four in 1971, your character and others were gone from the show. Were you surprised?*

Well, they figured they wanted to change the whole concept of everything. It's just like anything else. You're not on and you're on, or you're on and you're not on.

*So it was nothing personal, just one of those things. What are your feelings about Doris Day the person and the actress?*

I loved her. First of all, she's the most underrated talent in the business today. She's so wonderful and so brilliantly talented. Everybody takes her for granted. It was wonderful to work with her. She was such a professional. So great to work with. We still write to one another, we call one another. Christmas cards, birthdays, everything.

*And Rose Marie's favorite* Doris Day Show *episodes? "The Gas Station" and "The Ski-Trip."*

# Season Three: 1970-1971

## "San Francisco has cable cars, the Golden Gate Bridge and best of all, the radiant Doris Day" [CBS promo]

**1970-1971**

The third season found Doris Martin and her sons moving off the ranch and into an apartment above Pallucci's Italian restaurant in San Francisco. The Palluccis (played by Kaye Ballard and Bernie Kopell), as well as nemesis Mr. Jarvis (Billy De Wolfe), joined the cast as her neighbors. Doris continued working at *today's world*.

In hindsight, it was perhaps a wise decision to relocate Doris Martin to the city. In 1971, CBS canceled many of its highly-rated comedies, including *The Beverly Hillbillies, Green Acres, Mayberry, R.F.D.* and others, because they did not fit into the demographics their advertisers wanted to reach. In other words, CBS felt a majority of these series' viewers were people who lived in rural areas who did not purchase a large number of the products being advertised [however, one would need a large number of urban viewers for shows to place in the upper echelon of the ratings]. It was also said CBS did not wish to be called "the Country Network" since it had been known for years as "the Tiffany Network." A few years later, CBS fell to last place of the three networks. It could only have wished it had half the number of hits it already canceled.

A new opening credits sequence for *The Doris Day Show* was made this season to usher in its new look and location. Doris ran down the spiral stairway of her apartment in the first shot, while scenes of her in San Francisco and the main cast were featured. The theme song was rearranged as well. The opening was fashionable with split second, zoom-in repeat cuts unlike anything seen before—or since.

137

This season the series was up against ABC's *Monday Night Football*, which the network felt would draw a larger audience. *TV Guide* predicted football would prevail over America's Sweetheart in an article entitled "Pro Football Tackles Doris Day." But such was not the case and *The Doris Day Show* continued to win its ratings slot over its competition.

"Doris has a very brilliant antic quality that I dig," Coby Ruskin, who directed some of the series' episodes, told *TV Guide*, "and I get particular relish in seeing her fulfilled in that direction. She's great with clutter and bits of business, [and] we don't argue about comedy style."

## THE EPISODES:

### "Doris Finds an Apartment"

Production Dates: June 29-July 2, 1970
Original Airdate: September 14, 1970
Directed by: Denver Pyle

Doris, exhausted with her commute from the ranch to the city, decides to make a move over the bridge. She spends her lunch hour with Myrna looking for an apartment, but Doris has difficulty finding one that will accept kids and dogs. While driving on Jasper Street, she comes to the corner of Parkway and sees an apartment-for-rent sign on a restaurant front called Pallucci's. Something tells her that this is it. She and Myrna go into the restaurant and meet the Palluccis. Mr. and Mrs. Pallucci are on a cooking frenzy, but Mrs. Pallucci takes them upstairs and shows

With Rose Marie, Carol Worthington, Paul Smith, Kaye Ballard and Bernie Kopell.

them the apartment, which is bare and colorless, to say the least. Doris envisions every room in her own style. Without any hesitation, she tells Mrs. Pallucci she'll take it. Mrs. Pallucci is thrilled to have two "girls" moving in, but Doris explains that it will be her, her two boys, and her big, shaggy dog. Mrs. Pallucci is shocked at first, but says yes. Now if she can only convince her husband.

Written by: Jack Elinson, Norman Paul; Kaye Ballard as Angie Pallucci, Bernie Kopell as Louie Pallucci, Gene Dynarski as the Moving Man #1, Jon Kowal as the Moving Man #2, Carol Worthington as the Welcome Lady, Gordon Jump as the Captain, Joe Hoover as Co-Pilot

Groovy Day Facts:
    The Palluccis bought the building with Angie's father's money.
    A stewardess named Judy once lived in the apartment.
    Nelson runs away during moving day.
    The Welcome Wagon Lady—more than likely—is Ethel, who sits for Doris later in the season.
    The first appearance of Louie and Angie Pallucci.

Doris Day Movie Find!:

Doris experienced moving day in several of her films, including *On Moonlight Bay* [1951], *Please Don't Eat the Daisies* [1960] and *Do Not Disturb* [1965].

## "The Feminist"

Production Dates: July 20-23, 1970
Original Airdate: September 21, 1970
Directed by: Denver Pyle

While parking his car, famous race car driver David Cowley bumps into Doris's car. They exchange information, and he makes a date with her later that evening, just to make sure she doesn't have whiplash. Back at *today's world*, Ron Harvey is failing miserably on getting the serialization rights to hard-core feminist Harriet Henderson's book. Doris is asked to confront Ms. Henderson and to commit her to *today's world* magazine. Doris makes a quick change into a masculine suit and eventually meets up with an entire feminist group in Ms. Henderson's hotel room, where she is almost assured of getting the rights for the magazine. Later that night, on her romantic date with David Cowley, she comes face-to-face with Harriet Henderson and her date, the editor of *Newsmonth*.

Written by: Norman Paul, Jack Elinson; Jason Evers as David Cowley, Elvia Allman as Harriet Henderson, Lavina Dawson as Clara, Robert Shayne as Andrew McIntyre, Ralph Montgomery as Waiter

Groovy Day Facts:

*today's world* has no women in its executive areas—at the moment.

Doris smokes a cigar—with difficulty.

The feminist cause is called the San Francisco Movement and Doris says her target is the YMCA: demanding equal rights for use of their pool.

Doris likes beef short-ends and asparagus with hollandaise sauce.

Doris changes her appearance under the table.

Doris says daisies are her favorite flower.

A clip of Doris walking down the stairs in a black dress was later used in seven episodes of the series' last season.

*today's world* the now magazine:
The serialization of Harriet Henderson's book.

Doris Day Movie Find!:
"You Make Me Want You" from the film *With Six You Get Eggroll* [1968].

**"How Can I Ignore the Man Next Door?"**
Production Dates: July 13-16, 1970
Original Airdate: September 28, 1970
Directed by: Denver Pyle

A new neighbor moves in next door to Doris. He is off to a bad start when Toby accidentally runs into the man and breaks the man's lamp. They run back into their home, and when Doris arrives, they tell her what happened. Doris doesn't get mad because they were honest with her. She goes next door to apologize and meet the new neighbor with welcome tokens. She knocks on the door and who is on the other side? Doris's old nemesis, Mr. Jarvis. For now, and the next several years, Doris will do everything she can to be nice, caring and friendly to him. Mr. Jarvis will do everything in his power to avoid her. As Mr. Jarvis would say time and time again: "Ne-vah touch!...Ne-vah touch!"

Written by: Budd Grossman; Billy De Wolfe as Mr. Jarvis

Groovy Day Facts:
Mr. Jarvis is now, more than likely, divorced as he is now single.
Doris takes bread, salt and sugar to welcome Mr. Jarvis to the neighborhood.
Mr. Jarvis likes to watch nightly cello concerts on public television.
Billy and Toby like the TV show *The Winding Trail.*
Doris helps the boys with their homework.
In a clip from season one's "The Fly Boy," Doris Day—looking stunningly beautiful—appears on the TV screen as herself. Mr. Jarvis sees her and says, "Can't stand that woman!"

Mr. Jarvis's list of unfortunate incidents:
Nelson takes his slipper.
Drenched with water from the hose, as well as his *Wall Street Journal,* and weakened his tea.

A reception problem from the Martin's TV interferes with his set.
Jarvis accidentally pokes himself in the foot
Nelson takes his hat.
TV set breaks after Doris has the remote repaired.
Doris puts icing from a cake on Mr. Jarvis' sweater.
Doris pulls the buttons off his sweater.
Takes, leaps and falls on Billy's skateboard.
Breaks his back after Doris attempts to put it in line.
Is squeezed inside his hospital bed.
Nelson takes Mr. Jarvis' pants.

Doris Day Movie Find!:
   Billy De Wolfe was featured with Doris in *Lullaby of Broadway* [1951].

With Billy De Wolfe.

**"Dinner for One"**
Production Dates: July 6-9, 1970
Original Airdate: October 5, 1970
Directed by: Denver Pyle

Pallucci's Restaurant is struggling to get customers in even though "it is the best restaurant in town [and] Louie is greatest cook there is." Doris makes it her mission to try to get people to dine there and experience this wonderful food. She first tries her friends in the office, and convinces Myrna to go to San Francisco's best-known restaurant critic and get him to review Pallucci's. With the help of Mr. Nicholson, Doris and Myrna as restaurant servers and Mr. Harvey as a musician, they are ready for Mr. Grey, the incognito food critic, who promises to dine at Pallucci's. When a panhandler walks into the restaurant, they mistake him for Mr. Grey and give him the best food he's ever eaten.

Written by: Jack Elinson, Normal Paul; Kaye Ballard as Angie Pallucci, Bernie Kopell as Louie Pallucci, Stubby Kaye as the Panhandler, Robert Emhardt as Dudley Grey, Ellon Quick as Perry Ferguson, Martin Ashe as the Chauffeur

Groovy Day Facts:
"Grey's Gourmet Guide" column by Dudley Grey:
"Among the restaurants your culinary correspondent intends to check out this week is a little place called Pallucci's. Word has reached these ears that even though it's out of the way, it's becoming in. Sunday's column will let you know if it's worth the trip."
Dudley Grey critiques on Friday nights and wears a white carnation in his lapel. His favorite restaurant is Four Winds, which Doris feels is overrated.
Myrna's on a banana diet where she eats nothing else so that she'll "have a shape like a banana."
Dudley Grey's assistant is named Perry Ferguson in tribute to the show's art director.

Denver Pyle Movie Find!:
Series music director and arranger Jimmie Haskell played in the orchestral recording for *The Alamo* [1960], which featured Denver.

With Rose Marie and Bernie Kopell.

**"Doris Leaves *today's world*"**
Original Airdates: October 12 & 19, 1970

[see "Doris and the Millionaire" section]

**"The Fashion Show"**
Original Airdate: October 26, 1970

[see "Doris—a la mode" section]

**"Lost and Found"**
Production Dates: August 24-27, 1970
Original Airdate: November 2, 1970
Directed by: William Wiard

Myrna is procrastinating over typing Ron Harvey's first lead story for *today's world*. It is late Friday and she has only typed the title and first paragraph. She finishes it by five o'clock but, in typical Myrna fashion, it is full of mistakes. Myrna convinces Ron to let her take it home to work on it over the weekend. He agrees on the condition that Doris go to Myrna's and proofreads the article before it is turned into Mr. Nicholson on Monday. Doris arrives at Myrna's on Sunday, but Myrna has lost the article, as well as the notes on it. It was actually lost at the Clover Club where Myrna had gone clubbing the night before. They both decide to go to the club early Monday morning to try to retrieve the article. The club is in the middle of auditioning new Go-Go dancers, and Doris, taking the name of "Peanut Brittle," is forced to audition while Myrna looks for the important documents.

Written by: Norman Paul, Jack Elinson; Buddy Lewis as Mr. Vincent, Jerry Crews as Stage Manager, Jade Manhatten as Girl #1, Kitty Malone Girl #2

Groovy Day Facts:
Myrna is crazy about Steve McQueen and has photographs of him on the walls of her bedroom. She also has an autographed picture of McQueen that she keeps in a manila envelope.
Marvin, Myrna's boyfriend on the side, took her out on Saturday night—first to his mother's house, then to the Clover Club.
Doris auditions under the name Peanut Brittle alongside Lemon Drop, Honey Dew, Cinnamon Apple and Candy Stick. She says she worked at the Grand Casino in Baltimore and her dance specialties are the bump, grind and the twist. "Whatever the cops allow," Candy Stick says. "Yeah, whatev-ev-ever," she replies.
The costume for the Go-Go dancers is a sheer scarf.

*today's world* the now magazine:
An article on imports versus exports, and how international trade affects the average guy on the street.

Doris Day Movie Find!:
Ron Harvey suggests his article could be turned into a movie with Rock Hudson, Doris's co-star in three films.

## "Duke the Performer"
Production Dates: September 8-11, 1970
Original Airdate: November 9, 1970
Directed by: William Wiard

Duke Farentino is having a difficult time with his dancing school and creates for himself a nightclub act in the hope of generating some publicity to increase business. He invites his friends from *today's world* to see his act. His first performance at the Hi Jinx Club is a disaster and he immediately gets fired from the nightclub. Doris, always wanting to help Duke, stages a new act with his dancing, his singing and his delivery until he is perfectly ready to go onstage again. But will it be good enough for the owner of the club? The owner relents—but only if Doris joins Duke onstage.

Written by: Fred S. Fox, Seaman Jacobs; Larry Storch as Duke Farentino, Norman Alden as Nicky Burke, Marie Roe as Duchess #1, Dean Myles as Duchess #2, Chick Casey as Waiter

Groovy Day Facts:
Duke's act is performed at the Hi Jinx Club at North Beach. The Kit Kat Klub is right across the street and is mentioned in other episodes.

Doris worked with Duke a whole month perfecting his act.

Doris has laryngitis before going on-stage—"It comes and it goes!"

Doris Day Movie Find!:
James Cagney, who co-starred with Doris in three movies including *Love Me or Leave Me* [1955], and Cary Grant, who co-starred with Doris in *That Touch of Mink* [1962], are impersonated by Duke during his act.

Doris Day Music Find!:
Doris sings "Shine on Harvest Moon."

**"Doris the Spy"**
Production Dates: September 21-24, 1970
Original Airdate: November 16, 1970
Directed by: Reza Badiyi

Doris flies in from Portland where she just completed an assignment acquiring Mrs. McDougal's secret recipes for *today's world*. Myrna is at the airport to pick up Doris and her attaché case. After using a payphone, Doris rushes out, taking with her the wrong attaché case, which happens to hold a homing device. She is suddenly pursued by nine secret government agents who end up at her home and breaking her door down to get their secret attaché case back. Doris will now be under 24-hour surveillance by their top man, who moves in with her.

Written by: Budd Grossman; John McGiver as Chief, Estelle Winwood as Mrs. McDougal, Carol Worthington as Ethel, James Sikking as Bowers, John Kroger as Nelson, B.J. Mason as Foster, Bernie Kuby as Lab Man, Kaye Stewart as Emma

Groovy Day Facts:
Under hypnosis, Doris admits to having done one secret thing in her life: when she was 13 she was invited to her first school dance, but was so embarrassed with her freckles. She ordered a freckle cream remover, applied it and broke out in a rash, which prevented her from going to the dance.
The Chief poses as Doris's Uncle Ed.
Doris makes great short eggs.
The agency changes its plans for the air command's underground emergency installation to Long Peak, Vermont.

*today's world* the now magazine:
The secret recipes of Mrs. McDougal.

Doris Day Movie Find!:
This episode is a wonderful tribute to Frank Tashlin's *The Glass Bottom Boat* [1966] and *Caprice* [1967], starring Doris Day. It includes Sodium

Pentothal (truth serum), used in *Caprice,* and actor John McGiver, who pursued Doris in *The Glass Bottom Boat*, convinced she was a spy for a foreign government. McGiver says in the episode, "This woman is either completely innocent or the greatest spy since Mata Hari"—who Doris spoofs in the latter film.

### "Tony Bennett Is Eating Here"
Production Dates: September 14-17, 1970
Original Airdate: November 23, 1970
Directed by: Reza Badiyi

It is early in the morning and Doris is on her way to a very important assignment: her first big celebrity interview. Angie is getting back from Fisherman's Wharf getting fresh fish for the restaurant, and Doris tells her she is about to interview Tony Bennett—who happens to be Angie's favorite singer. Doris arrives to Tony Bennett's hotel room for the interview. She is nervous, excited and thrilled to be there with him—but he ends up interviewing her. He makes her feel very comfortable and invites her to have lunch with him that he just ordered. The fettuccini is just terrible so Doris invites him to the very best Italian restaurant where everything is extremely fresh—Pallucci's—which he accepts. Doris goes to the restaurant and tells Louie and Angie that Bennett will be there in a

With Bernie Kopell, Kaye Ballard and Tony Bennett.

With Tony Bennett.

few hours. They are beyond excited and Angie makes a promise to Doris that she will not tell a soul. But can Angie keep that promise?

Written by: Jack Elinson, Norman Paul; Tony Bennett as Himself, Kaye Ballard as Angie Pallucci, Bernie Kopell as Louie Pallucci, Jerome Guardino as Man, Joan Lemmo as Woman #1, Bunny Summers as Woman #2, Lou Massad as Waiter

Groovy Day Facts:
   Doris remarks her boys sold lemonade and rides on Nelson.
   Tony Bennett autographed a pizza for a fan.
   Louie wears his blue ribbon for cooking while serving Bennett.
   Tony Bennett would later appear on *Doris Day's Best Friends*.

*today's world* the now magazine:
   An interview with Tony Bennett

Doris Day Music Find!:
   Doris sings a portion of "I Left My Heart in San Francisco" with Tony Bennett. He also solos with the song "Just in Time."

Guest Star Mini-Bio:

Although he made guest appearances on television and acted in a few films, Tony Bennett was a multiple Grammy Award winner and became a successful album artist in later years with *Perfectly Frank* and *Steppin' Out*. His 1994 album, *Unplugged,* not only hit #1 on the charts and went platinum, but won the Grammy Award for Album of the Year. Bennett paid tribute to Doris with his album *Here's to the Ladies*: "She's gifted in a way that makes everything she does work. She's a Hollywood producer's dream. She has beauty. She's a great actress and wonderful singer—putting it simply, she has it all."

## "Cousin Charlie"
Production Dates: September 28-October 1, 1970
Original Airdate: November 30, 1970
Directed by: William Wiard

Cousin Charlie Webb makes a visit. He first stops by to visit Buck at the ranch, who tells him that Doris and the boys are living in San Francisco. After not seeing Doris and the boys for four years, he makes a surprise visit as he's just returned from Samoa and may stay in San Francisco for a while. Doris discovers his talent for sales and convinces him to settle down. She gets him a job interview at *today's world*, and Charlie starts working right away with instant success. The advertising sales for the magazine are skyrocketing. All of a sudden, Charlie starts getting impatient, spending a lot of money, taking pills, and feeling a tremendous amount of pressure from his new job, taking it out on Doris and the kids before realizing his mistake.

Written by: Budd Grossman; Van Johnson as Charlie Webb, Read Morgan as the Policeman, Peter Hobbs as Mr. Donovan, Henry Hunter as Mr. Williams

Groovy Day Facts:

Toby likes to read about Snoopy in the comics.

The strive to succeed leads Charlie to take blood pressure pills.

Doris runs a stop sign while driving around San Francisco with Charlie. She is stopped by an officer, but Charlie talks him out of giving her a ticket.

Billy and Toby miss school for a baseball game

*today's world* the now magazine:

Charlie's sales for the magazine include accounts with:

Corn, Carp & Flugger; Twitwiller & Miller Frozen Turkey; Canmostovitz & Frtiz Orthopedic shoes; Williams, Williams & Williams

Doris Day Movie Find!:

Charlie gets another cooking job on a freighter, but after the first meal, the ship was turned around and he was deposited at Catalina. Doris's *The Glass Bottom Boat* [1966] was filmed in Avalon, Catalina.

With Van Johnson.

Guest Star Mini-Bio:

Van Johnson appeared in a few small roles before landing a contract with MGM, where he appeared in such classic films as *Madame Curie, A Guy Named Joe, The White Cliffs of Dover, Thirty Seconds Over Tokyo* and *In the Good Old Summertime.* One of his best remembered roles was in *The Caine Mutiny.* Throughout the years, Johnson continued acting on the stage and guesting on television shows, as well as an occasional movie, including Woody Allen's *The Purple Rose of Cairo.* He and Doris were friends for years and she wrote about their friendship while he was at the Cannes Film Festival and she was filming *The Man Who Knew Too Much.*

**"Love Makes the Pizza Go Round"**
Production Dates: October 12-15, 1970
Original Airdate: December 7, 1970
Directed by: William Wiard

Doris and Ron Harvey have spent a long day investing psychics. They are hungry and, of course, they go to Pallucci's for a bite. The kitchen is not only closed, but it is spotless. Angie offers baked rigatoni and half a bottle of Chianti left from a beautiful young couple in love.

With Kaye Ballard and Bernie Kopell.

And how does Angie miss those early days clam-digging at Pismo Beach with Louie. Doris feels Angie and Louie are in a rut, so she gives Angie a bit of advice that will help Louie see her in a different way and bring some excitement back into their marriage. But Louie becomes jealous and thinks Angie is having an affair with Mr. Harvey.

Written by: Budd Grossman; Kaye Ballard as Angie Pallucci, Bernie Kopell as Louie Pallucci, Charles Circillo as Mario, Paula Victor as the Fortune Teller

Groovy Day Facts:

Although Doris's perfume of choice was a potpourri in "The Prize-fighter and the Lady," it is now Fascination.

Angie wears a long, flannel nightgown to bed—and one with short sleeves that's "sexier."

The Palluccis have been married ten years, and they met while clam-digging at Pismo Beach.

Angie spends $35 on a wig to make herself more attractive. When that fails, she says she can give the wig to a bird who can use it for a nest.

Paula Victor appeared in three episodes of *The Doris Day Show*, and in *Rhoda*, she played Rhoda's mother-in-law.

*today's world* the now magazine:
A story about fortune tellers.

Doris Day Movie Find!:
Doris was a bit familiar with the situation of this episode in that she tried really hard to bring her parents together in the film *By the Light of the Silvery Moon* [1953].

## "Buck Visits the Big City"
Production Dates: October 5-8, 1970
Original Airdate: December 14, 1970
Directed by: William Wiard

Buck is in San Francisco on his weekly Sunday visit with Doris and the kids. Doris tries to convince him that it's time for him to sell the farm and move in with them. Buck completely refuses, but Doris talks him into staying for a week to experience San Francisco, one of the exciting cities in the world where there are a million things to do. Buck experiences a week of complete boredom with nothing to do, to the point of getting arrested at 5:00 A.M. for walking on the street. Doris decides to give him a party and introduces him to George Stoner, who is recently retired from *today's world's* accounting department. Her hope is that he can convince Buck to retire and enjoy the city.

Written by: Budd Grossman; Denver Pyle as Buck, King Moody as Policeman, John Gallaudet as George Stoner, Iris Adrian as Roxie, Sylvia Hayes as Woman, Geraldine Ewing as Helen

Groovy Day Facts:
Lunch at *today's world* starts at noon.
On his Sunday visits, Buck brings fresh produce from the farm.
Billy has baseball practice after school and Toby watches him.
A party without Ron is one in which you need half as much booze. "I spill a lot," he says.
Ron brings a woman to introduce to Buck at the party, but Doris and Myrna think the woman is actually Ron's date.
Buck enjoys freshwater fishing and play pinochle.

While he is in San Francisco, Buck:
    Is unable to wake Nelson up for a 4:30 A.M. walk, so he goes alone.
    Paints the front door red.
    Encounters less-than-friendly people.
    Goes to the park where he pulls weeds out of a flower bed.

Doris Day Movie Find!:
    John Gallaudet was in Doris's *Julie* [1957].

## "It's Christmas Time in the City"
Original Airdate: December 21, 1970

    [see "Doris's Christmas Present" section]

## "Doris Versus Pollution"
Production Dates: November 2-5, 1970
Original Airdate: December 28, 1970
Directed by: Denver Pyle

    While Mr. Nicholson is away at a European conference, Col. Fairburn takes over command. He informs Doris that he's just been elected chairman of the board of Amalgamated Ltd. At home, Doris is worried about her plants that were brought in from Mill Valley. They don't seem to be very healthy. She brings in a man from a nursery who informs her that they are being affected by sulfur in the air. Doris makes it her mission to get rid of sulfur in San Francisco. Doris and Myrna investigate and discovers the sulfur is coming from Federson Sulfur Company, which is part of Amalgamated Ltd.

    Written by: Jack Elinson, Norman Paul; Edward Andrews as Col. Fairburn, Carol Worthington as Ethel, James Sikking as Mr. Sutton, Kay Kuter as Nursery Man, Jerome Guarding as Cab Driver, Owen Bush as Serviceman, Eddie Baker as Driver, Donald Newsome as Man

Groovy Day Facts:
    Ethel took a year of Botany in college, but flunked.
    Ethel and the boys dance The Funky Chicken, Moonwalk and The Flea
    Ron Harvey is claustrophobic and afraid of heights.

*today's world* the now magazine:
Industrial Pollution

Denver Pyle Movie Find!:
Owen Bush appeared in *Bonnie and Clyde* [1967] with Denver.

**"The Forward Pass"**
Production Dates: November 9-12, 1970
Original Airdate: January 11, 1971
Directed by: William Wiard

Ron Harvey, always trying to impress his boss, Mr. Nicholson, promises him an exclusive interview with Joe Garrison, the "lover boy of professional football." To achieve this interview, he will desperately need Doris's help. When Joe Garrison sees Doris, he tries to go forward for a pass. There is a scrimmage with Doris [a good running back] at his apartment where Garrison breaks his leg as he attempts to tackle her. Doris ultimately gets the ball and the interview.

Written by: Budd Grossman; Dick Gautier as Joe Garrison, Gordon Jump as Man #2, Tony Giorgio as Maitre d', Gavin Mooney as 1st Reporter, Tom Stewart as 2nd Reporter, Vern Rowe as Hawker, Michael Michaelian as Man #1, Paula Warner as 1st Girl, Beverly Ralston as 2nd Girl, Marty Koppenhafer as 3rd Girl, Karen Bouchard as 4th Girl, Carollyn DeVore as 5th Girl

Groovy Day Facts:
Doris goes to the football game—for the food. At the game she orders:
Foot-long hot dogs with mustard, relish, onion, followed by salted peanuts and a root beer. She then orders ice cream, but when there is no Rocky Road, she decides not to have any. When she dines with Ron and Garrison after the game, she orders vanilla, strawberry and chocolate ice cream, with hot fudge sauce, marshmallow and pineapple topping, whip cream, nuts and a cherry. Ron asks, "Why don't you have a Banana Split?" "I'll have one," she says.
A painting of Ron Harvey in his military uniform hangs in his apartment. He also smokes cheap cigars.
Doris takes candy and a copy of Bruce Saunders' book *How to Build a Better Body* [from the episode "The Health King"].

*today's world* the now magazine:
An article on Joe Garrison, the lover boy of football.

Doris Day Movie Find!:
In a wink to Doris's *Pillow Talk* [1959], Joe Garrison has a musical couch similar to Brad Allen's in the film.

## "Duke's Girlfriend"
Production Dates: November 16-19, 1970
Original Airdate: January 18, 1971
Directed by: Peter Baldwin

Duke arranges to meet Doris at a very expensive jewelry store downtown. When she arrives, he breaks the news to her that he plans to get betrothed. His wife-to-be calls herself Alison Otis Peabody, from one of San Francisco's so-called leading families—Nob Hill all the way. To make Alison really happy and before proposing, Duke buys her a $2,200 broach, which Doris finds a little excessive and somewhat suspicious. But she goes long with it until she meets Alison for the first time at dinner with Duke. With Ron's and Myrna's help, Doris discovers that Alison is a genuine 14-carat phony. Doris discusses the situation with Myrna and Ron and asks Ron to bait Alison and play the part of Rodney Alexander III and convince her to go out with him. She immediately accepts and cancels her date with Duke. To catch Alison with another man, Doris makes a date with Duke at the same place, La Parisienne. When the two couples meet, Duke finally discovers who Alison really is, but a catfight ensues between Doris and Alison…

Written by: Jack Elinson, Norman Paul; Larry Storch as Duke Farentino, Charlene Polite as Alison Otis Peabody, Alan DeWitt a Salesman, Lou Massad as Waiter, Karen Bouchard as Cigarette Girl

Groovy Day Facts:
Ron, as Rodney Alexander III, is referred to as the world's wealthiest and most eligible bachelor in the effort to expose Alison.

After receiving the broach, it is returned to Steven's Jewelry for more diamonds to be added—at Alison's suggestion.

We learn Marvin, Myrna's boyfriend on the side [until-someone-better-comes-along], and she have known each other ten years.

The exposing of Alison takes place at La Parisienne, one of Ron Harvey's favorite dining places.

When Duke and Doris talk on the telephone, he tells her Alison canceled their date. Doris says she's sorry. Duke replies that he's disappointed, but "like that lady on television says, 'que saea sera.'" The last appearance of Duke Farentino.

Larry Storch mentions that he was "hit by cupid's arrow" in this episode. He later played cupid in the 1990 Valentines' Day episode of *Another World,* seen on cable's Soapnet.

Doris Day Movie Find!:
>    The title song to *Send Me No Flowers* [1964]
>    "Au Revoir Is Goodbye With a Smile" from *Do Not Disturb* [1965]

Guest Star Mini-Bio:
>    A four-time guest star on the series as Duke Farentino, Larry Storch is a gifted impressionist who started his career as a teenager in vaudeville houses. He has appeared on stage, nightclubs, radio, movies and television as both an onscreen and a voice-over performer. His first break was in 1946 when he substituted for Frank Morgan on *The Kraft Music Hall* radio show. He went on to do musical theater with *You Never Know* and *The Tender Trap,* as well as starring in his own television series in 1953. Film roles, including *Who Was That Lady?* and *Sex and the Single Girl,* led to his most famous role of Corporal Agarn on TV's *F-Troop* in the 1960s.

**"Jarvis' Uncle"**
Production Dates: December 1-4, 1970
Original Airdate: January 25, 1971
Directed by: Reza Badiyi

Mr. Jarvis, Doris's unfriendly neighbor, brings a list of rules for her and her family to observe while his uncle, Mr. Randolph Jarvis, will be visiting from Florida so that he will not be disturbed in any way, shape or form. When Randolph arrives the next day, Mr. Jarvis isn't home so Doris invites him in and finds him sweet, charming and entertaining, the complete opposite of her neighbor. Randolph spends all his time during the week with Doris and her friends, infuriating Doris's neighbor one more time.

Written by: Budd Grossman; Billy De Wolfe as Mr. Jarvis /Uncle Randolph "Randy" Jarvis, Sylvia Hayes as the Waitress

Groovy Day Facts:

Mr. Jarvis's list of rules for the Martins to follow during his uncle's visit include:

No loud door closing.

No television after 8:00 P.M.

No vacuuming near open windows

No humming in the halls

Marvin, Myrna's boyfriend, bowls three times a week.

At Hamburger Harold's, Doris, Myrna and Randolph order a super-duper #4 Hamburger Harold's special deluxe with mayonnaise, mustard, pickles, relish, onion and tomatoes.

Mr. Jarvis orders salt for his watercress sandwich.

Doris dances the Funky Chicken with Randolph. Mr. Jarvis dances it at the end.

Doris Day Movie Find!:

"Au Revoir Is Goodbye With a Smile" from *Do Not Disturb* [1965]

**"Lassoin' Leroy"**
Production Dates: November 20-25, 1970
Original Airdate: February 1, 1971
Directed by: Peter Baldwin

Leroy B. Simpson makes a welcomed visit to *today's world* and invites Doris and Myrna to the rodeo finals at San Francisco's Cow Palace where he is competing to win the grand prize. It's a chance for him to buy his own ranch for his wife, Ellie, and their triplets. After riding a horse called Jezebel, Leroy wins the grand first prize of $20,000—enough money to get his ranch and settle down. Unfortunately, with his big heart, Leroy keeps lending and giving his money away to different rodeo competitors, and then starts spending money everywhere. Doris decides to take his money until he leaves for the ranch so he will not spend any more. Doris hides the money carefully in a broken toaster. But Billy gives the toaster away for a library fund-raiser.

Written by Jack Elinson, Norman Paul; Jim Hampton as Leroy B. Simpson, Carol Worthington as Ethel, Paul Sorenson as John Wilkinson, Winifred Coffin as Clara Bixby, Dan Scott as Tex Bradshaw, Vern Rowe as Waiter, Roland "Rusty" Loudermilk as Red Davis, Jane Aull as Woman, De De Young as Girl Photographer, Kitty Malone as Souvenir Girl

Groovy Day Facts:
Doris says she's late for work and Myrna is early—both for the first time.
Leroy has moved to Montana after leaving Mill Valley to work on a farm and started riding horses in rodeos to make more money. This seemed inevitable since he had a rodeo poster hung in his bedroom when he lived at the Webb ranch.
Toby imitates Ethel at the rodeo when he yells "Suu-per!"
Leroy spends approximately $700 before Doris intervenes.
When Ethel arrives to collect items for the library fund sale, the boys give her the broken toaster holding Leroy's winning. At the sale, Doris gets into a bidding war with another woman and spends $100 to get the toaster back.
This is the last series appearance of Leroy B. Simpson.

Doris Day Movie Find!:

Winifred Coffin is credited as playing Clara Bixby in this episode. Clara Bixby was a name that Billy De Wolfe had given to Doris when he saw an article where Clara Bixby was speaking at UCLA in Westwood, California. He said to Doris that she looked like a Clara Bixby, and from then on he always called her Clara.

## "Colonel Fairburn, Jr."
Production Dates: December 14-17, 1970
Original Airdate: February 8, 1971
Directed by: Lee Philips

Col. Fairburn and Mr. Nicholson fly to London for a publisher's convention. Instead of Ron Harvey taking over in their absence, Col. Fairburn Jr. has been put in this position. During introductions, Col. "Clifford" Fairburn Jr. appears very conservative. He says he plans to stand "shoulder to shoulder" with the troops. Doris arrives on schedule the next morning to a drumbeat heard through the entire floor of the magazine. She walks office to office and finally gets to Clifford's, which he's completely redone overnight into a perfect hippie pad. Clifford's hair has "miraculously" grown. Clifford changes the magazine completely. He adds poetry, art and a Miss *today's world* centerfold, plus gives it a young, mod, wild, cosmic look. But for how long?

Written by: Budd Grossman, Don Genson; Edward Andrews as Col. Fairburn, Rick Ely as Clifford Fairburn, Larry Gelman as Terry Madden, Nancy Kerby as Girl #1, Karen Specht as Girl #2, Annette Molen as Girl #3, Murray Polluck as Man, Louise Lane as Woman

Groovy Day Facts:

Clifford attended a military academy followed by Carruther's College of Business Administration where he was the top of his class.

Clifford calls Doris "Chickie" and everyone else "Peeps."

Clifford's revamping of the magazine includes an exclusive on Terry Madden's artwork, which are simply triangles, as they are "what's happening. Last year was rectangles, but this year they are square." Madden is paid $10,000 for the rights.

Another idea is a Miss *today's world* centerfold, with finalists Miss Hawaii 1969, Miss Florida 1968 and Miss New York 34-23-34.

Mr. Nicholson's office is redecorated with the latest in mod furnishings and wall coverings, including posters of "Peace," "Stop Your Motor," "Life," "Don't Miss It," "Love," and "Gentleman" spelled out in every language.

Clifford asks Doris to join the editorial staff of his new magazine, but she declines.

*today's world* the now magazine:

Stories on "The Grand Old Families of San Francisco" & "Inflation versus Unemployment" are thrown out by Clifford and are replaced by:

An in-depth story on Mama and the Bulldogs singing group
"Group Therapy While Skydiving"
An Interview with poet Alan Kaplan
Alan Kaplan's Poem [publication cost: $5,000]:
"Life is love.
Love is life.
The morning never follows the afternoon.
The wave that engulfs a guppy
may someday be bath water for your toes."

Doris Day Movie Find!:

Edward Andrews co-starred with Doris in *The Glass Bottom Boat* [1966].

**"Billy's First Date"**
Production Dates: December 18-23, 1970
Original Airdate: February 15, 1971
Directed by: Reza Badiyi

Toby let the cat out of the bag: Billy has his first official girlfriend. So he tells his mom all about her. The problem is, Billy hasn't formally introduced himself to her. So Doris suggests that after school, even though it's a little old-fashioned, he offers to carry her books, enticing him to compete for her. Later that day, after school, Billy walks Sue Ann home, sits on the steps in front of her house and talks and talks for more than an hour. He even asks her for a date to the school dance. The problem is, they need a chaperone and Billy volunteers Doris, who already has a date of her own that night. Sue Ann's father has the same problem, so Doris decides to discuss the problem with him and work out a solution. So amicable is the solution that Doris and Sue Ann's father start double-dating with their children.

Written by: Jack Elinson, Norman Paul; Ricardo Montalban as Richard Cordavan, Lisa Gerritsen as Sue Ann Cordavan, Alene Towne as Mrs. Gessford, Carol Worthington as Ethel, Ceil Cabot as Hostess

Groovy Day Facts:
Doris meets Sue Ann's father, architect Richard Cordovan, at Beanies Coffee Shop on Market Street.
Richard is a widower.
Doris drinks coffee with cream.
Doris starts to call Billy "William."
Last appearance of Ethel in the series, where she stays with the kids while Doris goes out with Richard.
Toby imitates Ethel's "Suu-per!" saying just as he does in "Lassoin' Leroy."

Sue Ann's Games:
Movie Star—give their initials and guess their name
Countries—take the last letter of the name of a country and take the last letter to name another country

Guest Star Mini-Bio & Denver Pyle Movie Find!:
Ricardo Montalban, who was in *Cheyenne Autumn* [1964] with Denver, appeared on Broadway and in Mexican films before signing with MGM in 1947. He appeared in such movies as *Sayonara, Neptune's Daughter, Let No Man Write My Epitaph, The Singing Nun, Sweet Charity, Escape from the Planet of the Apes* and *Conquest of the Planet of the Apes*, as well as guesting on many television shows. To some, he is best remembered as Mr. Rourke on TV's *Fantasy Island*; however, to others he is Khan from the *Star Trek* TV series and the movie, *Star Trek: The Wrath of Khan*.

**"Doris Goes to Hollywood"**
Production Dates: December 7-10, 1970
Original Airdate: February 22, 1971
Directed by: William Wiard

In Hollywood, Harry Maret, publicity man for mega-boxoffice and recording star Doris Day, has organized a special Doris Day lookalike contest. Entries come from all over the world, including one from two boys, Billy and Toby Martin from San Francisco. They entered their mother without telling her because they didn't want her to be too disappointed if she didn't win. Weeks go by, and Billy and Toby are beyond excited, jumping on the couch that their mom has won this Doris Day contest. Doris does not believe it and doesn't really want to go.

The very next day at the office, Mr. Nicholson convinces her accept the prize to get a behind-the-scenes look and an exclusive interview with #1 star Doris Day. He sends Ron as a photographer and lets Myrna go to accompany her.

They arrive at the Globe Studios to find nothing that was promised is there. No limousine, no food—and where is Doris Day? After a long walk through 13 soundstages, they arrive at the office of Mr. Conroy where they wait an hour only to get the runaround from Harry Maret. Along their journey, Doris and Myrna encounter many people who think Doris is Doris Day, including Doris Martin's favorite star Henry Fonda. But director Otto Von Braunstein mistakes her not as the star but for the little Kappelhoff girl from Cincinnati who lived next door to him. He and her father used to send out for pitchers of beer. More encounters and missteps follow as Doris and Myrna bide their time touring the studio.

Finally, at the end of the day, as Doris Day exits her Rolls-Royce, she comes face to face with Doris Martin. Ron then captures the moment for *today's world* magazine.

Written by: Jack Elinson, Norman Paul, Don Genson; Henry Fonda as Himself; Oscar Beregi as Otto Von Braunstein, Joey Forman as Harry Maret, Paula Victor as Secretary, William Tregoe as Mr. Conroy, Ralph Montgomery as Security Policeman, Bill Martel as Guard, Eddie Baker as Indian

Groovy Day Facts:

There is a lot of mistaken identity: Henry Fonda, Conroy's secretary and the security man all mistake Doris Martin for Doris Day. Myrna, on the other hand, confuses an incognito Ron Harvey for Steve McQueen, her favorite movie star. Harry Maret, however, asks Doris and Myrna which of them was selected as the winner of the lookalike contest.

Pictures of famous celebrities grace the wall of the studio head's reception area—Lucille Ball, Bob Crane, Mike Connors and Doris Day—all whom had or were presently starring in CBS shows.

The true-life Doris Day was from Cincinnati and her real name was Kappelhoff.

Harry Maret was the actual makeup man on the series.

This episode marks the last appearance of both Billy Martin and Ron Harvey.

*today's world* the now magazine:

The lead story on Doris Martin's adventures at the movie studio.

With Rose Marie and Paul Smith.

Doris Day Movie Find!:
Of course, Doris Day appeared in 39 motion pictures.

Guest Star Mini-Bio:
One of the greatest movie actors, with one of the longest acting careers of all time, Henry Fonda appeared in dozens of films, including *The Grapes of Wrath, The Lady Eve, My Darling Clementine, The Ox-Bow Incident, Mister Roberts* (which he first played on the stage), *The Best Man* and *On Golden Pond,* for which he won the Academy Award a few months before his death in 1981. He also starred in two short-lived TV series: *The Deputy* [1959-61] and *The Smith Family* [1971-72], as well as guest-starring on several TV shows, including *Maude,* in which she unsuccessfully tried to convince him to run for President of the U.S.A.

**"Skiing Anyone?"**
Production Dates: January 5-8, 1971
Original Airdate: March 1, 1971
Directed by: Reza Badiyi

Myrna convinces Doris to go to Bear Valley Inn for a ski weekend. She hopes to meet French Olympic champion Jacques DuBois. But first, since neither can ski, they decide to practice in the office. When arriving to the ski resort, Myrna twists her ankle going up the stairs. She is forced by Dr. Jeffrey Forbes to stay in bed for the entire weekend. Doris tries to make the best of it, and spends a lot of time with Dr. Forbes, dining and taking skiing lessons from him. All the while, feeling guilt for leaving Myrna alone. Dr. Forbes invites Jacques DuBois and a few

With Rose Marie.

With John Gavin.

friends for a night of *je ne se quoi*. By the end of the weekend, Doris breaks her leg stepping out of a sleigh.

Written by: Jack Elinson, Norman Paul; John Gavin as Dr. Jeffrey Forbes, Miguel Landa as Jacques DuBois, Bob Kenneally as Room Clerk, Robert Shayne as Mr. Gilroy, Michael Sterns as Bellhop, Scott Perry as Bill Walley, Harper Carter as Jerry Clark

Groovy Day Facts:

Myrna finds the inn has a weekend package special—two people for $89.95.

Marvin, Myrna's boyfriend on the side, took her bowling the Saturday night before the skiing weekend.

Doris plays gin rummy and drinks hot-buttered rum during the weekend getaway.

Last appearance of Michael Nicholson and Myrna Gibbons on the series.

Doris Day Movie Find!:

In the episode, Dr. Jeffrey Forbes says his patient is Gene Kelly. Kelly directed Doris in *The Tunnel of Love* [1958].

Guest Star Mini-Bio & Doris Day Movie Find!:

John Gavin was Doris's leading man in *Midnight Lace* [1960]. Gavin's films include *Imitation of Life* (1959), *Spartacus*, Alfred Hitchcock's *Psycho*, *Back Street* (1961) and the musical *Thoroughly Modern Millie*. He served as president of the Screen Actors Guild from 1971-73, and was the U.S. Ambassador to Mexico during Ronald Reagan's presidential administration.

**"The Father-Son Weekend"**
Production Dates: January 19-22, 1971
Original Airdate: March 8, 1971
Directed by: Reza Badiyi

Toby is finally old enough to go on his first YMCA father-and-son weekend. The problem is that grandpa is away at a meeting in San Jose. So he tries to borrow a father, starting with his teacher, Mr. Simpson. Doris decides to take him herself. The challenge will be convincing the camp counselors to let them be part of the campout. Once that's accomplished—other than putting up their tent—they become hard competitors for all the other fathers and sons. After all, a trophy is at stake.

Written by: Budd Grossman; John Astin as Jim Keatley, John Lupton as Charles Rogers, Richard Steele as Bradley Keatley, Ted Foulkes as Dean Rogers, H.M. Wynant as Gary Hansen, Billy McMickle as Chris Hansen

Groovy Day Facts:

Doris brings along food and supplies, including an outdoor stove to cook meals, which comes in handy after a rainstorm has dampened the firewood.

Doris and Toby came in first place in the gunny sack race, the wheelbarrow race, first or second in the egg toss, and presumably first in the fishing contest.

Mother and son caught eight fish using sausage links as bait since Buck always said it's better bait than worms.

Doris sings "Row, Row, Row Your Boat" in a camp singalong.

The last appearance of Toby Martin in the series.

Doris Day Movie Find!:

Richard Steele played Doris's youngest son in *With Six You Get Eggroll* [1968].

Guest Star Mini-Bio & Doris Day Movie Find!:

John Astin appeared with Doris in both *That Touch of Mink* [1962] and *Move Over, Darling* [1963]. He guested on many TV shows, including *Batman*, *Ben Casey*, *Hazel*, *The Odd Couple*, *Route 66* and *The Nanny*. His most famous role was that of Gomez Addams in TV's *The Addams Family*, followed by other memorable roles in *Night Court* and *Eerie, Indiana*.

**"Young Love"**
**[a.k.a. "Generation" and "The Best Laid Plans"]**
Production Dates: January 11-15, 1971
Original Airdate: March 15, 1971
Directed by: Norman Tokar

It is 2:00 A.M. and someone is ringing Doris's doorbell. It is her niece, April Tolliver Clark, who she hasn't seen since she moved to Berkley. Recently married, she is having problems with her husband Peter and decides to confide in Doris. After listening to her carefully for more than an hour, Doris tells her: "April, this isn't advice, it's just experience: that the older you get, the more you're going to realize that nothing ever stays the same. Everything in life just keeps changing all of the time, you know, sometimes for the better, which makes us happy. And sometimes for the worse, which makes us grow. But nothing, nothing ever stays the same."

Written by: Bob Sand, Bruce Bilson; Meredith Baxter as April, Michael Burns as Peter, Bobby Griffin as Coleman, Brenda Sykes as Dulcie, Abbi Henderson as Erica, Dick Van Patton as April's father

Groovy Day Facts:

April is the daughter of Doris's late husband's sister.

This was a pilot for a possible series that was not picked up by the network and had several names while it was being produced. The pilot was changed and integrated into the last episode of season three of *The*

*Doris Day Show* by filming new wraparounds with Meredith Baxter and Doris and then by trimming the pilot because the pilot actually ran long. The pilot did air independently in the 1973-74 season under the title "The Young Love Generation." It was presented as it was originally shot, which did not include the scenes with Doris and Meredith Baxter. Jim Pierson of MPI Home Video says the episode "was actually like a cross between *Room 222* and *Love, American Style* because it has a kind of early '70s youth drive to it. But it didn't have the jubilance of *Love, American Style*. It has a much more serious tone."

Guest Star Mini-Bio:

This pilot was designed for Meredith Baxter and produced by Doris's company Arwin. Baxter would follow this in 1972 with her own successful, but short-lived series, *Bridget Loves Bernie*. She continued with the acclaimed drama *Family*, and, of course, as the mother of Michael J. Fox in the comedies *Family Ties* and *Spin City*.

## THE EPISODE THAT NEVER WAS...

According to the season three production status report, "Roller Derby" was slated as an episode. No information is available on this script other than it was written by Seaman Jacobs and Fred Fox who had written the episode "Duke the Perfomer".

## DORIS MARTIN'S MARRIAGE PROPOSALS

While many men became enamored with Doris, she was not asked for her hand in marriage in every episode. Nor did she charm every male she came into contact [witness Mr. Jarvis]. But there was a handful of proposals and near-proposals in the series:

—Prince Carlos of Sadonia, who proposed but then withdrew his proposal after a revolution abolished the throne and he became penniless. He ended up opening a restaurant in San Francisco.

—Sir Robert Kingsley proposed to Doris when she traveled to England to purchase the serialization rights to his book *After Normandy*. Although she turned him down, he still sold the rights for $100,000.

—Green shipping tycoon Nicholas Kavros romanced and almost asked Doris to marry him, but then he learned she is "almost engaged" to Dr. Peter Lawrence.

—Rising singer Johnny Reb announced his and Doris's engagement before asking her. She told him she loved him, but that he was moving too fast. He was never seen or heard from again.

—Jonathon Rusk asked Doris to marry him in the hospital where she and Cy await the birth of possible septuplets [quadruplets arrived instead]. Jonathon and Doris put their wedding on hold until they decide what to do with their careers.

And once Doris Martin turned the tables by scaring a man out of a future with her. That distinction belonged to Cotina's Deputy Ubbie Puckum, who wanted to date Doris, but did not want a commitment. Doris was not interested in him, and as soon as she and her family started talking about marriage, Puckum ran off soon after.

## A CONVERSATION WITH PHILIP BROWN

*Around 1985, I was working at a t-shirt store in Westwood and you walked in and I recognized you. And we talked about the show.*
That was in '85?

*Yes, '85, '86. And you were with a very cute blonde. I don't remember her name.*
Hmm.

*By the way I heard you just got married. Congratulations.*
Oh thank you.

*You worked on the series for three seasons—longer than most of the show's other stars. Do you recall your first day on the set of* The Doris Day Show? *Were you nervous or excited to work with Doris Day?*
I wasn't that nervous because I had already been in show business for four years and I had shot a movie with Dick Van Dyke and Barbara Feldon called *Fitzwilly*, and I had done numerous commercials, so it was really just another adventure for me. It was something I really enjoyed, and when you're a little kid, you know, people like Doris Day—I didn't really know her background or her history. It was just going to work.

*Doris started the show just a few weeks after her husband's death. Do you recall her grieving or upset?*
She never let that show. She was always like a mother to us. She was just a wonderful, loving woman.

*Your relationship on screen with Denver Pyle seemed real.*
Denver was always right there for us. Always ready to teach us something, as well as James Hampton. It was a fun group to be around. Always a great mood and a fun set to be on. Everybody was very professional, but everybody also had a lot of fun.

*And then you got to work with Denver later on* The Dukes of Hazzard.
Yes, and it was nice to be with him again. It gave us time to catch up. He was a nice, nice man.

Doris Day, Philip Brown and Tod Starke.

*Did you keep in touch with any of the cast members?*

I see James Hampton every now and then, although he's recently moved, and I used to run into Fran Ryan at the market, and Doris, we'd talk once in a while on the phone. Rose Marie, now, I don't think I've had contact with her since the show ended. But then there wasn't any reason to—we didn't have many scenes together, and I think there were four or so episodes we were in with her.

*There was the episode with you and Rose Marie where she moved into a new apartment* ["Singles Only"]. *That looked like a lot of fun.*

Yes, we did. It was a blast. It was in the neighborhood where I grew up. So it was a lot of fun. It was done at an actual apartment that's still in North Hollywood.

*You and Tod Starke played Doris's sons on the show for three seasons, and you really acted like brothers. What memories do you have of working with him?*

Well, you know, Tod is not alive anymore. He was killed in a motorcycle accident. I do miss him. He was a lot of fun and did look up to me. He was like the brother I never had. We used to have a lot of fun.

We used to go to school for three hours on the set, and our first teacher was Shirley Decker and had a lot of fun with her. She was the type of woman where we had our school on this big soundstage. It was just Tod and I. We had a swing set and we had bicycles. And we'd just get into a lot of mischief. Sometimes we'd hide from her, and when the three hours were up, school was over with. There was hardly any discipline with her. The next year she was replaced, and the teacher was Marian Fife. We just knew by her vibes that we couldn't get away anything so we never tried to.

But Tod was a lot of fun. We used to ride all over the backlot and have lunch together. My family would visit his family once in awhile. I would spend the night at his place or he'd spend the night at my place once in awhile.

*Did you have any brothers or sisters yourself?*
I have six brothers and sisters. Half brothers and sisters, yeah.

*Did Tod have any brothers or sisters?*
He had an older sister. I believe her name was Jean.

*Billy was sports-oriented. Were you as well?*
Yes, I grew up playing soccer. Very competitive at soccer and I loved baseball as well. They did an episode and there was a baseball game. It was a lot of fun, with a lot of kids I'd hang around with playing baseball were at the field playing in it, so that was nice.

*Lisa Gerritsen made a few appearances as your girlfriend, and one of the last episodes you were in was "Billy's First Date," co-starring her.*
Yeah. I really liked her and she was a lot of fun. She was cool. We did three or four episodes together. I haven't kept in touch with her and I wonder what she's been doing.

*What was it like working with Kaye Ballard and Bernie Kopell?*
You know, we rarely did scenes with them so I really don't know them.

*You were in several with Billy De Wolfe, though.*
We enjoyed working with Billy De Wolfe. He was a blast—very funny, very friendly. He always had that line—"Ne-vah touch!"

*You got to sing with Doris in "The Songwriter" and the Christmas episodes. Were the vocals prerecorded?*
That was live, right there. That was a lot of fun. You could tell how much fun it was.

Philip Brown with Tod Starke.

*How much input did you have in the scripts?*

None. Basically in the third season, we weren't really in there. It was "Hi, Mom. Bye, Mom." Except for that episode with Lisa Gerritsen, the rest were very, very limited with lines.

*I heard a story about you and Doris. Once you saw Doris…*

Naked. Yes. It was a real simple deal where I was riding my bike around the soundstage and she was in her dressing room. She had this big trailer on the set and its door just came unhinged and she just happened to be changing. I looked over and I saw her—and she was the most beautiful woman I'd ever seen. But I looked away and I drove my bike off the set. I think it was on a Friday and that whole weekend I was really sick because I thought if she saw me riding my bike away she'd think that I was spying on her or something. And I just got really sick to my stomach because I loved Doris so much.

So that Monday on the set, it was a read-through, and as soon as I saw her I asked if I could talk to her in private. She said, 'Sure, honey,' and we walked over to where no one else could hear us and I said, 'On Friday I was riding my bike and your dressing room door came unhinged. And I saw you. With no clothes on. And I just wanted you to know I wasn't spying on you or anything.' And she said, 'Oh honey, don't worry about it. That door comes unhinged all the time. I'm going to have to fix that.' She just put me at ease right away. I was just sick about it and she was so cool. She just made life so easy for everybody.

*There is some footage we saw in the blooper reel where we hear a director yelling and screaming at you. Whoever it was seemed to be horrible to do that to you.*
You know what? I really loved that man, actually. He's the man who hired me for the show and his name is Bob Sweeney. He'd done a lot of directing before with *The Andy Griffith Show*, and he'd been around for years as a character actor. He'd been on *The Rifleman* and he had done a lot of shows. He demanded that we work hard. He wasn't playing around, and we knew that. And we tried to give him our best. But, yeah, my reaction was 'It's his [Tod's] line!' It wasn't as cruel as it sounded. Bob Sweeney kept us on our toes and we couldn't fool around. If we fooled around, he let us know that he was not happy.

I do remember this one episode and the director was Coby Ruskin, who had done a lot of *The Andy Griffith Show*s and he had been around for years. I'm sure he started his career, probably in the '40s, maybe doing radio, I don't know, but he was an old director. For whatever reason, he walked up to me on the set, and he grabbed me by the hair, and he took my head and he hit right me against the wall. Out of nowhere. I wasn't doing anything wrong. I told Doris, and she fired him. She was protective of us.

*This was during the shooting of an episode?*
Yes.

*And they had to bring in another director?*
I guess. That's how I remember it. She let him go. We were like her kids.

*Did you recall any script changes while you were on the set?*
If there was, that was all Doris's deal. We were just kids there to do whatever we were supposed to do. If Doris did not like a scene, she would definitely change it or just cross it out. No else could do that.

*There were many animals—both on and off the set. These also included Doris's dogs.*

She had a lot of dogs on the set and we loved playing with them. And we got to work with tigers once. That wasn't the easiest thing. When you're a little kid and you're right there, the same height as the tiger, they see children as food. And one of the tigers was standing next to me and he growled and he looked right through me. It sent a rush of adrenaline through my body like I've never felt before. And I'll never forget that. He was bolted down to the floor, and I remember the chain and the bolt, but he could have gotten through that easy. That was a scary episode. They're scary animals. I was only ten years old.

*Of course there was Lord Nelson. What was he like?*
He was smart and cool. We played with him like he was our dog.

*And all the chickens and ducks and pigs on the farm…*
It was a great atmosphere for a child to grow up in.

*You changed shooting locations each season.*
Yes, we started out at the Golden West Studios on Sunset and then we went to CBS, and then after the third season she was a single woman.

*Well, she was always a single woman. In the last two seasons, you weren't on the show. Some assumed you went to your grandfather's ranch to help him out.*
Well, I'm glad you assumed it 'cause I sure didn't! (laugh)

*There was another thought as to what happened to your character: That the series "jumped" six or seven years ahead and Billy and Toby had left the nest.*
But she never mentioned her children again, either. Really what happened was, there was more stuff for her to do as a single woman than as one with children. They were running out of ideas. They had really done everything they could, I thought, with us. So it was like, 'let's just pretend she never really had any, and we'll start the fourth season as really, a different show.' I actually called her up when I heard I wasn't returning and I asked her, 'Doris, what happened?' She said, 'Well, honey, you know the executive producers decided to go a different way.' And then I later found out *she* was an executive producer.

*Yes, she was in the fifth season, but not before. I asked her about that change with the cast and she said, 'Pierre, I had nothing to do with those changes.' And looking back, there were a lot of shows with single, working women and it seemed like the thing to do. Perhaps it was a decision— collectively with the network—to make that happen.*

It's possible, yes. But nonetheless, here I am in the seventh grade, the whole school is teasing me, and I cannot wait to go back to work. And then to find out you're not going back to work and I have to stay in this public school that I haven't been in since the fourth grade. It was torture, and plus I loved to work.

*You were fortunate in that you were able to continue to work.*
Yes, I did a lot work in my teens and twenties and in my thirties.

*I remember you in the series* The City, *where you played a bartender...*
Yes, and *Loving* before that.

*And* The City *was a sequel to* Loving.
The people who weren't killed moved to New York City. I loved doing it and working with the cast members. It was one of the best jobs I ever had.

*Have you watched any of* The Doris Day Show *episodes on DVD?*
Yes, and they look great. They really do. Do you remember the episode ["The Gift"] where we're washing the car and I sprayed Tod? I'm like, 'Give me that!' and Tod looks like a fish out of water and he looked like he's ready to drown. I can watch that over and over. Funny.

*There was the episode "Doris the Spy," where a group of government agents breaks into the apartment. You and Tod come out of your room but Doris tries to get you to leave and tells you to go watch television. But then you tell her, "This is much better than what's on television!"*
That's funny. She was always trying to get rid of us!

*The series is almost ageless, isn't it?*
It really is. And look how good Doris looks in her outfits. She was ahead of her time with her clothing.

What a fun show, especially in the flavor of the first year. In the kitchen and the barn, it had such a nice feel to it. Very uncomplicated, very simple.

*Doris recently said you and Tod Starke were like her own.*
I absolutely love Doris Day and I've always... oh boy... she was such an influential person in my life.

# Season Four: 1971-1972
## "Associate Editor Doris Martin Takes Charge"

**1971-1972**

The fourth season saw the fourth and final format change in the series. Doris Martin was promoted to associate editor at *today's world*, working for city editor Cyril (Cy) Bennett (played by John Dehner). Jackie Joseph came aboard as Mr. Bennett's secretary, Jackie Parker. Doris was still a single working woman, but whose children was not referred to or seen.

As for the unresolved absence of characters, there are a couple theories as to where they went. One is they were still around but simply not seen in any of the episodes. The workers at *today's world* worked in a different area of the magazine, and the boys spent a lot of time at Buck's farm. Another theory is that the story simply moved a few years ahead: the boys have grown up and are living on their own, probably in college, Ron Harvey and Myrna Gibbons left the magazine, and Mr. Nicholson moved to another job in the journalism field. Whatever the actual reason was not resolved—however, none of these characters were ever mentioned in the remaining episodes of the series.

"It's just one of those things," Doris Day said of the change in 1971. "CBS wanted to go in another direction."

Ed Feldman was brought in as producer for the fourth season and several changes were made. One was with the character of Doris Martin, as well the addition of new characters and the eliminating of some previous ones. The producer and star shared their feelings with writer Morton Moss:

Doris Day: "We want to show some spice and variety. Ladies should have some romance. Each year, I think, there should be something different for viewers of the series. There should be an extra little shock of change.

"TV is opening up. The concept of what you can and can't do on television is changing. I'm an associate editor. It gets me out of the office. It gives them a way to go with me.

"…Now this is 1971. Why does a widow have to go home and be asleep at nine? There will be more romance, more guys. Why not? Widows and divorcees would agree with me. You don't just fold up. I work so hard at putting this TV program together that I go home and fall into bed at nine. But why should we put that up on the screen?"

Ed Feldman: "Now, as a writer and editor, she's in a position to be the protagonist. She won't be taking care of other people. She'll be right out there in it all the time. She'll be involved with mystery and romance and exposés.

"I don't think we'll refer to the kids. They simply won't be around. If we mentioned in the first episode that they were at school, we'd have to mention where they were in the other episodes, too.

"The same kind of thing with her being a widow. What would be the point of bringing it up? Women don't go around telling everybody that they're widows. I really don't see any reason to mention either of these matters unless it happens to be to our advantage."

The pair reiterated the changes to Paul Henninger of the *Los Angeles Times* shortly before the new season aired:

"When you have such a standout performer as Doris you want to take advantage of it," Feldman said. "This year we will involve her more in stories, rather than involve her with other people. The approach we're taking is that if there's a problem or attitude it's Doris's. I have a feeling the public will like that better than what they've had from Doris before in the series."

When asked if she felt the series would have an "adult feeling," Doris replied: "Yes, I think so because it isn't the secretary-boss relationship anymore. Now it's associate editor and boss level. If you're a secretary, it's 'Yes, sir. No, sir. May I have the day off, sir?' But now I can enter his office and blow off steam; get in sharper dialog and have some fun with it.

"They seem to be taking a lot of the family shows off. I guess that's why I lost my kids. But if a real good story comes along involving them, they may be back. Nothing is ruled out.

"It's really difficult to figure what people want these days. But we all know now that because of *All in the Family*...my goodness, if they can get by on TV with the things they say, we know we're growing up."

After learning of another change in format, Donald K. Epstein and Dick DeBartolo suggested a *Doris Day Show* ten-year plan before the series' fourth season. In a September 9, 1971 *New York Times* article, their ideas included that Doris:

1972-73:   gets a job as wardrobe mistress at Radio City Music Hall, in which Doris becomes a Rockette

1973-74:   moves from New York to Africa as a tour guide, where she goes on a blind date with an elephant and accidentally uses a cobra as an extension cord

Doris Day and Friends--From Left: Rudy, Bubbles, Daisy and Bambi

1974-75:   becomes a coal miner

1975-76:   moves to Tokyo and is a geisha

1976-77:   the pilot of a Super Jumbo Jet

1977-78:   is elected President of the U.S. and is chased by a young, cute senator around her desk and inadvertently sets off a nuclear holocaust

1978-79:   is chosen as the first woman astronaut in which she asks astronauts from other nations not to leave their beer cans on the moon

1979-80:   joins the New York police force and tangles with a jaywalker, a litterbug and man walking his dog without a leash

1980-81:   becomes captain of the *Queen Elizabeth II*, in which she allows an ex-submarine captain to take the wheel which causes the ship to go under.

Another change was in the presentation of each episode. The show did not begin with the opening credits as in previous seasons, but with a "bumper." This consisted of the title against a San Francisco trolley car scene that lasted onscreen for a few seconds, which identified the series. It was followed by a "teaser": a short scene, lasting a minute or two, that usually set-up the episode. The opening credits then rolled and at last the episode itself. This technique continued through season five of the series as well.

**THE EPISODES:**
[Note: In the chronology of the Doris Martin story, "Mr. & Mrs. Raffles" is the first episode of season four. This episode introduces Doris's new boss Cy Bennett, and her new best friend, his secretary Jackie Parker.]

**"Mr. & Mrs. Raffles"**
Production Dates: June 28-July 1, 1971
Original Airdate: September 20, 1971
Directed by: Norman Tokar

It is a late, rainy night in San Francisco and Mr. Jarvis has reluctantly agreed to walk Doris to the mailbox so that she can mail an overdue traffic ticket. On the way there, they notice the door of the Dauphine et Cie Fine Jewelers store is open, but it is after business hours. Always cautious, Mr. Jarvis closes the door, which causes an alarm to go off. The police are there in seconds and Doris and Mr. Jarvis are arrested and thrown into jail. They are released on bail by Cy Bennett, Doris's grouchy new boss. At the office the next day ,while Doris is discussing all of this with her friend and Cy's secretary Jackie Parker, Mrs. Jarvis walks in with a pocketful of jewels. Through a series of incidents, they try to find the true criminals who did the heist.

Written by: Arthur Julian; Billy De Wolfe as Mr. Jarvis, Ken Lynch as Detective Broder, H.M. Wynant as Rodney, Lynnette Mettey as Dolly

Groovy Day Facts:
Cyril Bennett plays golf and likes to gamble.
Mr. Jarvis has an unnamed sister who he says is a "stunning brunette."
Mr. Jarvis is mistaken for Doris's father while at the jewelry store.
Doris got a traffic ticket and if she doesn't have payment postmarked by midnight, there will be a warrant out for her arrest.
Doris says she's left her rubber plant to Mr. Jarvis in her will.
Doris Martin's third appearance in a jail cell.

*today's world* the now magazine:
An investigative series on jewelry heists.

Doris Day Movie Find!:
Jackie Joseph appeared with Doris in *With Six You Get Eggroll* [1968].

**"And Here's...Doris"**
Production Dates: July 13-16, 1971
Original Airdate: September 13, 1971
Directed by: Norman Tokar

Doris has been given an assignment to interview Bob Carter, popular late-night talk-show host. If successful with this story, Doris is promised by Cy, a very comfortable new office. But Cy desperately wants to be a guest on the show which, in his own mind, could lead to a television news anchor job. After pleading and begging from Doris, Bob Carter agrees to put Cy on the show, but only with her as well. Two minutes before airtime, Cy becomes paralyzed with fright with the thought of facing a huge audience.

Written by: Laurence Marks; Bob Crane as Bob Carter, Jack Wells as Jim, Joseph Mell as Jacob Berns, Alan DeWitt as Professor Frisbee

Groovy Day Facts:
First appearance of Cy Bennett and Jackie Parker
Cy Bennett has "trenchcoat, will travel" and was a foreign correspondent in China. His dream is to be a television news reporter.
Guests on *The Bob Carter Show* include Doris Martin and Cy Bennett from *today's world* magazine, Professor Malcolm Frisbee and his priceless glassware, and Jacob Berns, who plays his Stradivarius violin.
The new office Doris is given is painted gray [later red], with two file cabinets, desk and two chairs, a typewriter on a stand, and a window with a view. The walls are decorated with various pieces of framed artwork, including an L'ermitage poster.

*today's world* the now magazine:
"Bob Carter late-night great" interview

Doris Day Movie Find!:
Joseph Mell was in Doris's *Pillow Talk* [1959].

Guest Star Mini-Bio:
Although he loved jazz and big band music, Bob Crane began his professional career in radio as a disc jockey and had a hugely successful radio program in Los Angeles. His dream, however, was to act. He began

making guest appearances on television shows, including *The Dick Van Dyke Show* and *The Twilight Zone*, as well as small parts in a few movies, including *Return to Peyton Place*. In 1963 he was signed as a regular on *The Donna Reed Show*, which led to starring in CBS's *Hogan's Heroes*. After the series was abruptly canceled in 1971 (as part of the network's cleaning house of older, but still popular shows), Crane continued acting in movies, television and stage. His 1978 homicide remains unsolved and his life was made into the film *Auto Focus* (2002).

**"When in Rome, Don't"**
Production Dates: July 20-23, 1971
Original Airdate: September 27, 1971
Directed by: Jerry London

Jackie wins a wild weekend in Rome and decides to take her mother. At the last minute, her mother's dog gets sick and Doris, who drove Jackie to the airport, goes along for the trip. In Italy, Jackie meets an old friend Albert, from John Marshall High School. She takes off with him and tours Rome. At the same time, Doris meets, unknowingly, famous artist Carlo Benedetti, whose art she dislikes. He presents himself to her as a tour guide and they see the sites of Rome. Meanwhile, *today's world* is planning a huge

With Jackie Joseph.

story on Carlo Benedetti. Following a series of crazy events, Doris breaks up with Carlo, makes up again; sees Cy and doesn't; takes the flight back to San Francisco with Carlo and Cy, and doesn't know they're there.

Written by: Richard M. Powell; Cesare Danova as Carlo Benedetti, Dick Patterson as Albert, Lew Palter as Pietro, Ryan MacDonald as Clerk

Groovy Day Facts:
In Rome, Doris phones Brett at her answering service, and asks her to call Angie Pallucci to turn off the water she left running on her geraniums.
Doris and Jackie fly to Rome on Wide World Airlines and return on a TWA jet.
Like her onscreen character, Jackie Joseph attended John Marshall High School.
Jackie and Albert agree to a second date—at their 50th class reunion. However, they meet again in "The Wings of an Angel."

*today's world* the now magazine:
Cy appreciates Benedetti's artwork for *today's world* and theorizes different aspects of them, but Doris explains the pieces need to be cleaned-up:
Brown stain symbolizes corruption [it is really from spilled coffee]
Circles connecting words with pictures [from the bottom of wine glasses]
Small rippled area [her tears from when Carlo left]
and a red blotch [she ate a hamburger and some ketchup spilled from it]

Doris Day Movie Find!:
The title song to *Midnight Lace* [1960]

**"Charity Begins in the Office"**
Production Dates: August 2-5, 1971
Original Airdate: October 4, 1971
Directed by: William Wiard

Jackie is helping Doris prepare for her vacation in Mexico City. Cy Bennett arrives and demands her to postpone her trip and do a special favor for Colonel Fairburn's sister. Doris is furious but negotiates an extended vacation. She is off to assist Mrs. Fairburn with the annual charity ball. She soon discovers that Roger Sidney, who is in charge of the budget for the ball, is exceeding normal costs. She starts investigating and discovers that Roger has been extremely dishonest, and for years has been ripping off Mrs. Fairburn's charitable organization; from photographers, to musicians, to caterers, Roger has lied from the very beginning. At the end of the ball, the net results are very disappointing, but Doris has a surprise and puts Roger on the spot.

Written by: Phil Sharp; Elvia Allman as Mrs. Fairburn, Joey Forman as Roger Sidney, Estelle Winwood as Rhoda, Will B. Abel as Gordon, Winifred Coffin as Agnes

Groovy Day Facts:
Charity cost breakdown:
After investigating Roger's price quotes for the ball, Doris reveals he was pocketing money intended for charity. The ball event to raise money for the orphanage's playground equipment only raised $4,300. However, Doris reveals that the photographer reduced from $460 to $100, and the orchestra as well, from $4,000 to $1,800. With additional "reduced" fees from others who supplied their services [from flowers to the caterer], the final total raised from the ball was $11,553.
The charity ball the previous year was for an animal shelter.
Photo of Cy Bennett is on the wall of the photography studio.
Cy gives Doris an additional week of vacation for helping with the ball.

Doris Day Music Find!:
While discussing Asian Beetles, Doris makes an off-reference to The Beatles music group in this episode. In their recording "Dig It," John Lennon yells out "Doris Day" and Doris recorded their song "Ob-la-di, Ob-la-da" for her first variety special. Years later, she met with Paul McCartney. He recalled after their visit: "For many years I have thought of Doris as a great singer and actress. Classic films as varied as *Calamity Jane* and *Pillow Talk* illustrate this point clearly. When Heather and I recently had the pleasure of meeting Doris, we were delighted to find out that she also was a charming person and perhaps the ultimate animal lover. Suffice it to say, we are huge fans of this wonderful lady." [from *Doris Day: Her Life in Music, 1940-1966*. Sony Music]

Kaye Ballard and Bernie Kopell.

### "A Weighty Problem"
Production Dates: August 16-19, 1971
Original Airdate: October 11, 1971
Directed by: Bruce Bilson

Doris is on her way to a special assignment at the ladies-only MeadowBrook health spa in San Diego. She is there to instigate an interview with Mrs. Miggins, whose husband is about to be released from jail after stealing $2 million. As Doris is about to leave, Angie Pallucci walks in. She has just left her husband, Louie, because he called her "Fatso." Doris decides she cannot go on the assignment and abandon her friend in her hour of need. Doris offers Angie to go with her to relax and do mud packs while she works on her assignment. And off they go. At the health spa, Doris gets the room next to Mrs. Miggins so that she can try to eavesdrop on her conversation. While Angie is put on a strict diet regime, Doris is put in a group for weight gainers. Doris meets Mrs. Miggins at the gym, and discusses her husband's release. She tells Doris she never wants to see him again, but Doris later hears through the walls that Mrs. Miggins is planning a secret escape to South America. With the help of Angie's nose, Doris plans to find the money and prevent them from leaving.

Written by: Arthur Julian; Kaye Ballard as Angie Pallucci, Iris Adrian as Mrs. Miggins, Rob Hathaway as Bellboy

Groovy Day Facts:
Angie and Louie have been together for 22 years—which means they knew each other for around a dozen years before they married.
When Angie smuggles food into the spa, Doris asks her how could she do such a thing. "The devil made me do it!" she replies, in homage to *The Flip Wilson Show.*
Cy sneaks in to the women-only MeadowBrook health spa as a waiter and then as a gardener.
Angie loses one-and-a-half pounds at the spa.

*today's world* the now magazine:
    An interview with Mrs. Miggins

Doris Day Movie Find!:
    Iris Adrian appeared in Doris's *My Dream Is Yours* [1949].

**"The People's Choice"**
Production Dates: August 9-12, 1971
Original Airdate: October 18, 1971
Directed by: Jerry London

There is a scandal brewing in Doris's neighborhood launderette. Cy and Doris go to investigate. Not only do they find Mr. Jarvis doing his laundry but an illegal bookmaking ring run by popular city councilman Sam Appleton. Cy and Doris convince Mr. Jarvis to run against Appleton as a write-in candidate in the upcoming election, and with the support Doris and Jackie and *today's world*, it could be an easy victory for him. Appleton will do everything he can to stop Mr. Jarvis from gaining political ground, even if it means stopping speeches, beating up his team, and sending a beautiful brown-eyed blonde to entice Mr. Jarvis into an uncompromising situation. As election day approaches, it is a very tight race. Can Mr. Jarvis actually win?

Written by: Arthur Julian; Billy De Wolfe as Mr. Jarvis, Harold Peary as Sam Appleton, June Wilkinson as Laura, Russell Gossett as Man

Groovy Day Facts:
    Mr. Jarvis's campaign slogan was "Jarvis: His Heart Beats for You" and then changed to "Smiling Sam Appleton Has Given Your District a Black Eye."
    *The San Francisco Dispatch* ran the page one headline: "Councilman Caught In Love Nest."

*today's world* the now magazine:
    San Francisco's illegal bookmaking scandal

Doris Day Album Find!:
    "Summer Has Gone" from *Latin for Lovers* [1965]

**"A Fine Romance"**
Production Dates: June 21-24, 1971
Original Airdate: October 25, 1971
Directed by: Norman Tokar

Cy assigns Doris to a computer dating story. Doris goes undercover in the world of programmed blind dates with Couples Incorporated. Her first date is with Harvey Krantz, a very nice, lonely man looking for companionship. Feeling guilty leading him on, she quits the story. Cy forces Doris to date Krantz once again, to his great surprise and suspicions. Krantz goes to the police and informs them that this beautiful, intelligent lady is after him and possibly his money. Going undercover as a computer dating client, a policeman begins to investigate Doris. And

With Robert Lansing.

now the two undercover investigators are dating and liking each other, not knowing the other's true identity.

Written by: Laurence Marks; Robert Lansing as Sgt. Bill Winston, John Fiedler as Harvey Krantz, Bunny Summers as Lucy, Michael Fox as Captain Mallory, Gordon Jump as Mr. Robinson, David Frank as Harry, Larry McCormick as Jim

Groovy Day Facts:
Doris goes bowling with George Roberts [Bill Winston] and isn't very good; she makes up for it by being a good dancer.
Cy acts as Doris's favorite uncle Cyril in order to get photographs for the story.
Walter Cronkite was the then-nightly news anchor on the *CBS Evening News*.

*today's world* the now magazine:
"Are Monkeys People?" story possibility
Computer Dating story

Memo: to Cy Bennett:
"Additional notes—computer dating story. Paragraph. Yesterday I had two phone calls. One from Mr. Robinson with Couples Incorporated—and he shouldn't have his own card in the computer. The other from a man named Krantz, spelling: K-R-A-N-T-Z, like in 'leader.' Anyway, he's coming by tonight which explains the four Cheese Danish, two chocolate eu clairs and two Napoleons on my expense account, Mr. Bennett."

Doris Day Movie Find!:
John Fielder was in Doris's *That Touch of Mink* [1962] and *The Ballad of Josie* [1967].

Guest Star Mini-Bio:
Gordon Jump appeared in four other episodes of *The Doris Day Show*, and acted in many television shows, including *Here Comes the Brides*, *The Mary Tyler Moore Show*, *The Golden Girls*, *Baywatch*, *The Brady Bunch* and *The Partridge Family*. He played the recurring roles of Chief of Po-

lice Tinkler on *Soap* and the National Editor on *Lou Grant*. His most famous role was that of Arthur Carlson on *WKRP in Cincinnati*.

**"The Albatross"**
Production Dates: September 13-16, 1971
Original Airdate: November 1, 1971
Directed by: Irving J. Moore

Cousin Charlie is back from Columbo, Ceylon, for another visit with Doris. They meet at a bar by the pier, and when the bartender hears Charlie is back, he shows him an elephant model from Ceylon and gives

With Van Johnson.

it to Doris. Although the elephant has its trunk down and is considered bad luck, Doris takes it home with her. When he learns how much Doris loves the elephant, Charlie hides a microfilm in it that needs to be delivered to U.S. government agents. Doris brings the elephant to the office and gives it to Cy. He then hides it and all of a sudden, everyone—foreign spies, Jackie, Doris and cousin Charlie—are looking for the elephant. They must find it before it falls into enemy hands.

Written by: Arthur Julian; Van Johnson as Charlie Webb, Felice Orlandi as Antoine, Rico Cattani as Boris, Sabrina Scharf as Valerie Becker, Howard Curtis as Hans, Paul Sorenson as Bartender

Groovy Day Facts:
Doris is not superstitious: she walks under ladders, loves black cats, and goes out on Friday the 13th.
After the elephant appears, a few mishaps occur, such as Doris's favorite vase breaking, Jackie's typewriter flying off her desk, Cy locking his necktie in his desk drawer, an art piece falling off the lobby wall at *today's world*, and a fishing net dropping onto Doris and Charlie.
Cy buys his date, Valerie Baker, a gift of Midnight Madness perfume—at $2.50 a bottle.
During the elevator races to escape from three agents after the microfilm, Doris gets in on the fights, hitting the enemies with her purse.

*today's world* the now magazine:
A story about offshore drilling.

Jackie Joseph Movie Find!:
Howard Curtis was in *The Split* [1968] with Jackie.

## "Have I Got a Fellow for You"
Production Dates: September 20-23, 1971
Original Airdate: November 8, 1971
Directed by: William Wiard

Angie Pallucci is on a matchmaking frenzy. All of a sudden she is determined to find Doris a husband, introducing her to plumbers from out of town to Italian pilots from out of town. Meanwhile, two killers have escaped from prison and Cy desperately needs Doris for a background story. After sitting through a shootout, enjoying scampi with one of the killer's wives, Angie makes a visit to the scene and discovers Lt. Tim Walker is single. She attempts to match him up with Doris as they all wait patiently for the killers to come out. Finally, Angie succeeds in setting up a dinner at her restaurant with Doris's favorite match.

Written by: Arthur Julian; Kaye Ballard as Angie Pallucci, Alan Hale, Jr. as Charlie, Nico Minardos as Nico, John Stephenson as Tim, Barbara Nichols as Mrs. Hollister, with Tony Cristino

Groovy Day Facts:
When Cy fails to introduce Doris to the lieutenant at the stakeout, Doris presents herself as infamous gangster Ma Barker.
The feather in Angie's cap is actually shot at after she arrives to the stakeout.
Referring to Angie's nonstop efforts to hook Doris up on blind dates, Doris asks, "What am I playing? *The Dating Game*?," a then-popular TV game show.

*today's world* the now magazine:
A story on the jail escape.

Doris Day Movie Find!:
Barbara Nichols was featured with Doris in *The Pajama Game* [1957].

Guest Star Mini-Bio & Doris Day Movie Find!:
Alan Hale, Jr. appeared with Doris in *The West Point Story* [1950] and *Young at Heart* [1954]. He was also in several films, including the Western classic *Hang 'em High*. Hale was a frequent guest on many television shows, including *The Wild, Wild West*, *Batman*, *Here Comes the Brides* and *Here's Lucy*, but is best remembered as the Skipper on *Gilligan's Island*.

**"To England With Doris"**
Production Dates: September 27-30, 1971
Original Airdate: November 15, 1971
Directed by: Lee Philips

Doris Martin is on her way to London to acquire the serialization rights to Sir Robert Kingsley's novel *After Normandy* for *today's world*. After a very long flight and an introductory meeting, Doris makes a horrible first impression. She goes back to her hotel completely defeated and calls Cy to give him the bad news. Later, she receives a phone call from an apologetic Sir Robert, who admits to her that he was "rather beastly," even more, "beastly rotten." He invites her to dinner and Doris promptly accepts. After taking Doris to The Happy Dog pub, in a complete turn of events, the next day he brings her home to meet his parents. On the way back to her hotel, he asks her to marry him and become Lady Doris. Doris, of course, is completely flattered and shocked by his proposal. She does like Sir Robert very much and certainly does not want to hurt his feelings. Cy arrives to London and comes up with a crazy idea that they could tell Sir Robert that he and Doris are engaged, which would allow her to decline his proposal while still getting the deal for the magazine.

Written by: Laurence Marks; Jon Cypher as Sir Robert Kingsley, Diana Chesney as Mother, Laurie Main as Father, Dick Wilson as Callahan, Towyna Thomas as Maid

Groovy Day Facts:
   *today's world* is now a weekly magazine, whereas in the previous two seasons it was a monthly periodical
   The furniture used as props in the scene of Sir Robert's parent's home were actual pieces from Doris Day's dressing room.
   Sir Robert Kingsley is paid $100,000 for the serialization rights to *After Normandy*.

*today's world* the now magazine:
   The serialization of *After Normandy* by Sir Robert Kingsley

Doris Day Movie Find!:
   Dick Wilson was in Doris's *Caprice* [1967].

## "The Sheik of Araby"
Production Dates: October 4-7, 1971
Original Airdate: November 22, 1971
Directed by: Richard Kinon

In a special ceremony honoring the King and Queen of Kurdaman, Cy sends Doris to do an interview with the Queen. She follows the Queen to her room, dressed in a Kurdaman costume, when she is suddenly mistaken for the Queen and taken hostage by the Kurdaman People's Liberation Freedom Fighters Militant Activists Democratic Popular Front Army and flown to Kurdaman. She soon finds out that the group is only looking for freedom and the right to handle their country their own way. While Kurdaman is rich in oil, the people suffer. Cy comes to the rescue but is unable to do anything. However, Doris finds a way of freeing the people of Kurdaman, herself and Cy at the same time.

Written by: Arthur Julian; Dick Gautier as Omar, Richard Angarola as Ben Ali, Vanda Barra as the Queen, Henry Corden as the King, James Lemp as Guard #2, Joe Lo Presti as Guard #1

Groovy Day Facts:
Her Serene Highness was the former Shirley Kaminski from Jersey City, New Jersey, where she waited on tables at her father's delicatessen.
The pickled tarantula dish that Doris says is "So crunchy, I just love them," is a common Kurdaman specialty that is made by Omar's mama. Her recipe calls for:

> 4 cups vinegar
> 2 onions sliced thin
> 4 dill pickles sliced thin
> a pinch of salt
> 1 lb. tarantulas

*today's world* the now magazine:
A story on the revolution.

John Dehner Movie Find!:
Former *Doris Day Show* co-star Denver Pyle appeared in *Top Gun* [1955] with John.

Guest Star Mini-Bio:

A veteran of many television shows, Dick (Richard) Gautier was well known to TV audiences as Hymie on *Get Smart*. Not only was he an actor, but an author, singer artist and composer. Some of his compositions include "Like Our Love," "Quiet Place" and "Lonely River." He was also nominated for a Tony Award as Best Supporting or Featured Actor (Musical) for 1961's *Bye Bye Birdie*. Most recently he has done voice-over work for several television animated series.

**"Doris and the Doctor"**
Production Dates: August 20, 31, September 1, 2, 1971
Original Airdate: November 29, 1971
Directed by: William Wiard

Hypochondriac Cy is home in bed when Doris arrives to pick up some work. He is waiting for the doctor to come at any moment. When the doctor arrives, he meets Doris first and a certain chemistry ignites between the two. Dr. Peter Lawrence instantly describes his personal symptoms to Doris. They are chronic hunger and severe loneliness. The cure for that is dinner for two and Doris's phone number, and this is the beginning of a long and interesting relationship. Doris and Peter start seeing more and more of each other, and one day Cy receives his bill from Dr. Peter Lawrence and realizes that he really couldn't afford to be sick. He asks Doris to do a thorough investigation of doctors and their fees. Doris agrees only to prove to Cy that he is wrong.

Written by: Laurence Marks; Peter Lawford as Dr. Peter Lawrence, Paula Victor as Lady Patient, Lew Palter as Luigi

Groovy Day Facts:

First appearance of Dr. Peter Lawrence

Cy does not sleep with his money belt on.

When Peter Lawrence first meets Doris, he asks if she is Mrs. Bennett. Doris answers, "Never."

When Cy receives his medical bill, he says, "For this I could have gotten Marcus Welby *and* Florence Nightingale!"

Doris has food sent up from Pallucci's on her dumbwaiter and she and Peter dine at the restaurant as well.

With Peter Lawford.

Doris faints while preparing for surgery
Peter calls Doris "Ralph Nader in basic black."

*today's world* the now magazine:
The high cost of medical services

Doris Day Movie Find!:
"Au Revoir Is Goodbye With a Smile" from *Do Not Disturb* [1965]

**"Happiness Is Not Being Fired"**
Production Dates: August 23-26, 1971
Original Airdate: December 6, 1971
Directed by: Irving J. Moore

Doris gets fired for writing a story on a housing development scandal of which Col. Fairburn was a major investor. An angry Doris, who was about to do a story on famous Italian artist Cellini, decides to do the story anyway and sell it to another magazine. Luckily, it is Doris's good friend Angie Pallucci's cousin Vito who is doing the exhibit of the Cellini collection. The pair venture to the gallery, where they discover an impostor is playing the part of Vito. Doris and Angie are in hot pursuit of the real Vito. They learn he has just been abducted by kidnappers who plan to steal the works of art, and they encounter several twists while in the building's parking garage.

Written by: Arthur Julian; Kaye Ballard as Angie Pallucci, Bruce Kirby as Vito, Joe Ruskin as Harry, Lou Krugman as Phony Vito, Richard Hurst as Mechanic, Donald Newsome as Policeman

Groovy Day Facts:
Doris gets her job back at *today's world*, as well as a raise, the key to the powder room, and an open account at Trader Vic's.
Vito calls his cousin Angelina.
Doris and Vito eat at Pallucci's, where Cy plants his wallet in Doris's purse to frame her in order to get the story.
With the help of Doris and Angie, Cy's car is accidentally destroyed.

*today's world* the now magazine:
A story on Tokyo Trade Show, having already done one on Japanese Massage Parlors.

Doris Day Movie Find!:
Lou Krugman was in Doris's *The Man Who Knew Too Much* [1956].

## "Whodunnit, Doris?"
Original Airdate: December 13, 1971

[See "Doris's Christmas Present" Section]

## "The Wings of an Angel"
Production Dates: October 11-14, 1971
Original Airdate: December 27, 1971
Directed by: Richard Kinon

Frankie Fury, head of "the Family" and one of the biggest crooks in the country, has been sitting in prison for years. He is a big fan of Doris Martins' reporting for *today's world*, including her nonexistent aunt Gertrude. He is now dying and wants to dictate his memoirs on tape to Doris for *today's world*, which could be one of the biggest stories the magazine has ever published. Doris attempts to get this done over and over again, and finally gets it accomplished. But then the tape disappears. Later, Frankie Fury gets released and brings Doris a tape that should contain everything. But does it?

Written by: Richard M. Powell; Marc Lawrence as Frankie Fury, David Doyle as Warden McPherson, Jack Griffin as Guard, Dick Patterson as Albert

Groovy Day Facts:
Albert Gramas, who Jackie ran into in Rome, makes his second appearance in the series not as a tourist but as a hotel employee where Doris and Jackie are staying.
Warner's State Prison was the home to Frankie Fury, inmate #49179. Doris Day was signed to a seven-year movie contract with the studio Warner Brothers.
Warden McPherson remarks that his commander is the governor of the state, who at the time was Ronald Reagan. He co-starred with Doris in two films, *Storm Warning* and *The Winning Team*.

*today's world* the now magazine:
Doris wrote a story on beagles, which led to the story on Frankie Fury.

John Dehner Movie Find!:
Denver Pyle and John co-starred in *Cast a Long Shadow* [1959].

With Peter Lawford.

## "Doris at Sea"

Production Dates: November 15-18, 1971
Original Airdate: January 3, 1972
Directed by: Marc Daniels

While visiting Doris at her office, Dr. Peter Lawrence gets an emergency call to fly to the yacht of billionaire Nicholas Kavros, who is in dire need of medical attention. Because of a tie-in with an economic story *today's world* is working on, Cy forces Doris to join Peter and interview Kavros. As Peter gets ready to take off on a helicopter, Doris—dressing as a nurse—begs him to take her, assuring him she has all the medical training necessary to assist him. Mr. Kavros has a severe appendicitis attack and Doris helps Peter in the surgery with sutures and swabs. After the surgery, Peter needs to leave suddenly and perform other medical duties. Mr. Kavros is very happy to have Doris stay with him for a few days, giving Doris the opportunity to conduct her interview. Doris and Mr. Kavros rapidly become good friends, but then the unthinkable happens: Mr. Kavros asks Doris for her hand in marriage. Peter, at first finds this whole thing very humorous, but suddenly starts getting jealous. But does he really have a reason to?

Written by: Laurence Marks; Peter Lawford as Dr. Peter Lawrence, Karl Bruck as Captain, Anthony Caruso as Nicholas Kavros, Ben Wrigley as 1st Reporter, Larry McCormick as Jim, David Frank as Harry, Gavin James as Pilot, Vern Rowe as Messenger, Tom Stewart as 2nd Reporter

Groovy Day Facts:
   Because of late night dates with Dr. Peter Lawrence, Doris was late for work every day this week and fell asleep during editorial meetings.
   Doris and Peter make out in her office—twice.
   Doris weighs 122 pounds.
   *today's world* is a $15 million magazine.

*today's world* the now magazine:
   A story on inflation.
   An interview with Nicholas Kavros.

Denver Pyle Movie Find!:
   Anthony Caruso was in Denver's *Fort Massacre* [1958].

**"The Sorrow of Sangapur"**
Production Dates: November 1-4, 1971
Original Airdate: January 10, 1972
Directed by: William Wiard

On the Mistral Express Train from Paris to Nice and Marseilles, Cy and Doris are traveling on a secret mission. On the train they first encounter the Maharajah of Sangapur, the richest man in the world, and his wife, the Maharani. Cy already dreams of the possible interview for "the mag" and follows him. Doris suddenly hears a gunshot and a man falls at her feet. Doris Martin is now involved with an intrigue of international proportions. The jewel, the Sorrow of Sangapur, owned by the richest man in the world, needs to be returned to the people of his country and is about to be stolen. Several people on the train could be responsible for its disappearance for different reasons: from a fake Scotland Yard Agent, to an Indian student, to a true Interpol officer all get involved. he jewel itself eventually ends up in Doris's new camera, putting her life in danger.

Written by: Richard Powell; Lloyd Bochner as Stephen, Henry Corden as Maharajah, Larry Hovis as Hassan, Arlene Martel as Maharani, Ben Wright as Medoc

Groovy Day Facts:
Hassan says the jewel, which happens to be one of the world's most valuable gems, belongs to the six-million people of the British-owned province of Sangapur.
The custom in Sangapur to kiss an unmarried lady's hand.
Cy drinks Bourbon and Coke.

*today's world* the now magazine:
A story on the Maharajah of Sangapur.

John Dehner Movie Find!:
Series alumni Denver Pyle and John appeared in *The Left Handed Gun* [1958].

**"The Blessed Event"**
Production Dates: November 8-11, 1971
Original Airdate: January 17, 1972
Directed by: Bruce Bilson

In a crazy misunderstanding in Pallucci's Restaurant, Doris overhears Angie on the phone talking about a "blessed event," thinking Angie is pregnant when it's really Sophie, her dog. Doris throws a baby shower and celebrates in grand style with many of Angie's friends. During the surprise shower hosted by Doris and Jackie, Cy Bennett arrives. He's received an exciting job offer in New York, and he needs Doris to help him with his portfolio as soon as possible. Angie's completely embarrassed that she has been thrown a shower for a baby rather than a dog. Convinced by Louie, she tells Doris the truth. Doris is just as happy and offers to keep Sophie, in her delicate state, while Angie and Louie enjoy a trip to Las Vegas. Doris, taking good care of Sophie, brings her to the office in her last hours of pregnancy. Of course, during Cy Bennett's very important meeting, the litter of puppies start arriving.

Written by: Arthur Julian; Kaye Ballard as Angie Pallucci, Bernie Kopell as Louie Pallucci, Henry Hunter as Randolph Chandler, Paula Victor as Nina, Joan Lemmo as Stella Nordimi

Groovy Day Facts:
Cy wants Doris to go to New York if he gets the job, but she refuses.
Doris wears an "I Love Dogs" charity pin.
Doris and Cy eat lunch at Pallucci's.
The Palluccis' dog, Sophie, eats Italian food.
Sophie delivers three female and three male puppies; the Palluccis give one to Cy.
The last appearance of both Louie and Angie Pallucci.

Doris Day Album Find!:
"What Every Girl Should Know" from *What Every Girl Should Know* [1960]

**"Who's Got the Trench Coat"**
Production Dates: December 7-10, 1971
Original Airdate: January 24, 1972
Directed by: William Wiard

Jackie gives away to the Mercy Missions, Cy Bennett's most treasured possession, his trenchcoat. For his birthday she gathers from everyone in the office and buys a new one. On the day of his birthday, they gather around his desk and give him the present. He is thrilled. The coat is nice and comfortable, and he is very happy to hang it next to his old one, which has disappeared. When he finds out what happened, he is devastated. Doris takes a long journey to find the missing coat, which starts with a cold front coming in from Canada, and ends with an old trenchcoat that has given a "useless old man" a new life.

Written by: Don Genson; Regis Toomey as Charley Smith, Charles Wagenheim as Milt Schnitzer, Paula Victor as Sister Clara, Ben Wrigley as Harry, Larry McCormick as Jim, Louise Lane as 1st Secretary, Geraldine Ewing as 2nd Secretary

Groovy Day Facts:

$83 was raised by the magazine team for Cy's birthday gift.

Cy's trenchcoat was filed under the condition "disgraceful" by the Mercy Missions.

Cy called the old trenchcoat "Old Blood and Guts," as it was a reminder of many memorable occasions: A bullet hole from D-Day; a rip in the back from a spear during an uprising in the Congo; and a beer stain from a Shriner's Convention at the Fairmont.

Charley was known as Charles Milburn Smith, publisher/editor of the *Denver Dispatch*, two-time-winner of the Harland Award for journalistic achievement.

After being given Cy's trenchcoat, Charley Smith considers it his good luck piece. He finds employment at Benny's Beanery burger joint—his first steady job in 15 years—and he hasn't had a drink in eight days.

Doris eats burgers and drinks beer.

This was a wonderful episode with a cause written by producer Don Genson. It was very important to Genson at the time to showcase the plight of so many great men in San Francisco that have been forgotten by hands of time and needed a boost.

*today's world* the now magazine:

Sponsors and serves a meal at the homeless shelter.

Jackie Joseph Movie Find!:

Larry McCormick appeared with Jackie in *A Guide for the Married Man* [1967].

**"Doris' House Guest"**
Production Dates: November 19-24, 1971
Original Airdate: January 31, 1972
Directed by: Bruce Bilson

Col. Fairburn and family impose once again on Doris. Cy brings Col. Fairburn's sister-in-law, Thelma King—who had recently been left at the altar—to stay with Doris until she stops crying. Thelma suddenly develops a crush on Mr. Jarvis. And it's a mutual one. Willard and Thelma grow closer and closer when suddenly Henry Thruston, the man who abandoned Thelma, comes to visit her at Doris's. When he sees Thelma with another man, he leaves, thanking Doris for ruining his life. Doris talks to Henry and convinces him the only way to get Thelma back is to make her jealous, something she obviously learned from the magazine's psychiatrist. But will it work for Thelma and Henry? And what will become of Mr. Jarvis?

Written by: Arthur Julian; Billy De Wolfe as Mr. Jarvis, Barbara Hale as Thelma King, Jack Dodson as Henry Thurston

Groovy Day Facts:
  Mr. Jarvis's list of complaints:
  Her hi-fi is too loud.
  Doris is a "door nicker" and parks too close to his car and nicks the car door.
  Doris's plants are growing over the terrace wall, strangling his rhododendrons.
  Every time he is halfway through his shower Doris starts hers, which takes the hot water and leaves him freezing: "Just bathe a little later. I take my shower precisely at 7:31. My shower takes exactly four minutes except on Tuesdays and Thursdays…[when] I take a pine tar shampoo for my dandruff. My dandruff is caused by tension. With you as my neighbor, I should look like Snow White." "I thought you did!" Doris retorts.
  Noise coming from her apartment: the clink of glasses.

Tod Starke Movie Find!:
  Jack Dodson was in *Angel in My Pocket* [1969] with Tod.

## "The Crap Shooter Who Would Be King"
Production Dates: June 14-17, 1971
Original Airdate: February 7, 1972
Directed by: Edward H. Feldman

Cy Bennett, using the reporter's most valuable asset—his nose, senses a revolution happening in the European country of San Réatta, where Prince Rupert is a virtual prisoner in his own castle. Doris and Cy, using his faithful trenchcoat, fly immediately to the "powder keg" of Europe to cover the event. There, Doris meets Bruno, the palace butler who is impersonating his distant cousin Prince Rupert. She follows him on a two-day adventure that takes them to a casino where Doris breaks the bank with a throw of the die and wins the kingdom for Bruno.

Written by: Richard M. Powell; John Banner as Bruno, Lee Bergere as Rupert, Henry Corden as Emile, Richard Angarola as Antoine, Lou Massad as Ricardo, Sid Conrad as Man

Groovy Day Facts:
Cy Bennett's credo to good reporting:
"A reporter only knows one law: get the story. When one ruse doesn't work, he'll try another immediately. Moderation at the expense of news is no virtue. Extremism on behalf of the mag is no crime. Like a bloodhound setting up on the trail, a reporter will not rest, eat or drink until he gets his story."
Doris dines at Maxim's while in San Réatta.

*today's world* the now magazine:
Story on the revolution in San Réatta, and the "official" story of King Rupert's abdication.

Doris Day Movie Find!:
The theme song to *Julie* [1956]

**"Cover Girl"**
Production Dates: November 30-December 3, 1971
Original Airdate: February 21, 1972
Directed by: Bill Wiard

In order to increase sales and compete with *Time* magazine, *today's world* decides to hire Carlo Benedetti to paint an exclusive new cover. Carlo arrives in San Francisco and sees Doris every morning, every afternoon, and every night, completely neglecting his art piece. Cy starts to worry that his expense account is growing while his work isn't showing up. Cy and Matt (another reporter at *today's world*) discuss Doris's situation with Carlo, and the fact that Carlo has not drawn a single "doodle" since his arrival. They decide to visit *today's world* psychiatrist, Dr. Backschneider, who suggests that the only way to get Carlo working again is to make him jealous. Doris invites Carlo to dinner and introduces Matt as her fiancé. Carlo leaves disappointed, bitter and angry. Will he go back to Italy? Will he complete the cover? Will he ever speak to Doris again?

Written by: Laurence Marks; Cesare Danova as Carlo Benedetti, Rory Calhoun as Matt, Norman Stuart as Dr. Backschneider, Larry McCormick as Reporter

John Dehner and Jackie Joseph.

Groovy Day Facts:
Doris doesn't like cherry & custard Danish. She prefers prune.
Cy says it costs $12/minute for a telephone call from San Francisco to Rome.
Carlo was paid $5,000 plus expenses to design an issue cover for *today's world*.
Carlo's painting was hung in Doris's office.
The split-screen editing of the telephone conversation is reminiscent of Doris's films *Pillow Talk* and *Lover Come Back*.
Matt has worked at the magazine for years, but this episode is his only appearance.

*today's world* the now magazine:
Matt writes a biographical piece on Carlo Benedetti.

Doris Day Album Find!:
"Summer Has Gone" from *Latin for Lovers* [1965]

Guest Star Mini-Bio:

Rory Calhoun starred in more than 80 films and 1,000 television appearances. Among his films include *River of No Return*, *How to Marry a Millionaire* (both with Marilyn Monroe) and *I'd Climb the Highest Mountain* and *With a Song in My Heart* (both with Susan Hayward). He starred in the CBS series *The Texan* and in the 1980s played Judge Judson Tyler in CBS's daytime drama *Capitol*. His final screen appearance was in the film *Pure Country* in 1992.

**"Gowns by Louie"**
Original Airdate: February 28, 1972

[see "Doris—a la mode" section]

**"There's a Horse Thief in Every Family Tree"**
Production Dates: July 6-9, 1971
Original Airdate: March 6, 1972
Directed by: Norman Tokar

Doris Martin fights for her job as major advertiser Lady Domonic beauty products threatens to pull out of the magazine following a story Doris wrote on its principal stockholder. Doris's story exposed Nesbitt Townsend's ancestor as a horse thief in the pre-mechanical age when horses were vital in providing transportation and labor. Doris infiltrates the Townsends' household as a new maid to plead with the Townsends into keeping their advertising and to secure her job with *today's world*.

Written by: Phil Sharp; Harriet E. MacGibbon as Mrs. Townsend, Robert Emhardt as Mr. Townsend, Sandy Kenyon as Randolph, Ceil Cabot as Cook

Groovy Day Facts:

When Doris is fired, Jackie offers to quit in protest.

The cook describes the Nesbitts as "batty."

Mr. Townsend collect stamps and lost a rare Blue Malays that Doris found.

Mrs. Townsend was in burlesque and known as "Tanya the Dove Goddess."

Cy is referred to as "The Tiger."

*today's world* the now magazine:

Memo to: Doris Martin
From: Cyril Bennett
Re: Nesbitt Townsend story

Brilliant idea Doris. Super construction. Devastating humor.
Gratefully, Cy

Jackie's Far-Out Look:
The Polka-Dot look.

Jackie Joseph Movie Find!:
John Dehner was in *The Cheyenne Social Club* [1970] with Jackie.

### *today's world*—THE NOW MAGAZINE

San Francisco-based *today's world* is one of the leading magazines in the country with the largest circulation on the west coast. Although aimed at a family audience, its articles ran the gamut from current affairs to gossipy bits—not unlike most leading magazines at the time. It won an award for its series on Far Eastern Cults.

When Doris Martin joined the staff in 1969, *today's world* was a monthly periodical, and the magazine borrowed $100,000 from a bank for improvements. Although a published writer, Doris was not hired for her writing skills, but as the executive secretary to managing editor Michael Nicholson. Ron Harvey was the assistant editor, with Myrna Gibbons as his secretary. When Doris arrived, there was no woman in a executive capacity at the magazine. This resulted in Doris being asked to do certain assignments, including trying, to secure serialization rights.

Mr. Nicholson gave the stockholder's report in 1970: "Though taxes and expenses increased, circulation increased by 12% and advertising by 14%, profits of margin is 15% higher." Under Cy Bennett's tenure, *today's world* is a $15 million weekly magazine. In 1972, its sales, however, are declining, while *Time* magazine's is increasing. *Today's world* is located in

John Dehner and Jackie Joseph.

"The Today's World Building," a 23-story skyscraper.

By 1971, Doris was promoted to associate editor and worked under city editor Cy Bennett. She then researched and wrote several stories, most of which were published.

The magazine has many employees, including receptionist Helen [who appeared in several episodes], office boy Dave, reporter Ed Ferguson, Harry, who offered an article entitled "Are Monkeys People?" and with Jim discussed a story on inflation. Charlie and Jim are editors, and Campbell is a writer at the magazine. Dr. Backscheider is a psychiatrist at the magazine.

Matt Lawrence has been at *today's world* "for years" and stands in as Doris's boyfriend to get Carlo Benedetti to finish his painting for a cover of the magazine. Jack is first given a story to do on Sir Robert Kingsley, while Doris is assigned one on the women tax reform movement. Leon works in accounting and had a set of twins in 1971. Bob Singer is also in accounting and is known as "Broom Closet Bob."

Sam Johnson is retiring at age 65, the mandatory age. He's been with the magazine for 40 years and is married to Bertie. He works in the printing area and Harry is a co-worker in the department. Marvin, who works in shipping, has a wife who's a singer. Sam does retire, but was rehired as a consultant.

Jack Reilly is another writer who is to do a story on a Tokyo trade show. Writer Barnes suggests running a nude centerfold, which Cy nixes. Wally is the mail delivery person in 1972.

*Today's world*, like most any work place, has its problems. In season two, Col. Fairburn brings in an efficiency expert to correct "the casual slipknot attitude of the employees... the work produced [compared] to man hours [is] very bad."

Personal calls are allowed, and that leniency is taken advantage by all, including Doris. There is, however, a no-moonlighting policy [which Doris broke]. Drag races in the elevators occur during the annual office Christmas party, as does a lot of drinking, dancing and romance.

In 1972, Col. Fairburn is once again concerned with the lowered productivity in every department—art, research and editorial. For example, Morgan and Damell wrote a story on the Montana senatorial election which had several inaccuracies.

Rival *Prestige* magazine editor John Scott offers Doris twice the salary she's getting at *today's world*. She leaves the magazine for *Prestige* after Cy tears up an article she's written on a woman's view of football because *today's world* is not a sports magazine. With Doris's leaving, several other workers at the magazine follow suit, including writers Harry and Jim, Schneider in accounting, illustrator Frank Kramer, and Cy Bennett's secretary, Jackie Parker.

Some of *today's world's* more important stories include the serialization rights to Supreme Court Justice William Forester's memoirs as well as the novels *After Normandy* and *Africa Reborn* by Sir Robert Kingsley; the memoirs of Mill Valley's Doc Wagner as a country doctor; and a special issue on the pioneers, whose cover was designed by Amanda Merriwether. Two other covers were designed by Italian artist Carlo Benedetti. All three special issues boosted the magazine's circulation.

By the end of the series' run, plans were for a new *today's world* building to be built housing not only the magazine but a television studio as well.

## *THE DORIS DAY SHOW* LOOK: THE SETS

Money apparently was no object when it came to the sets for *The Doris Day Show.* The details of every set were evident, from the massive farm setting in the first season through the apartment in San Francisco to the last.

The *today's world* set was a large one as well, and unlike other news programs on the air at the time, this set looked like an actual business. While the printing and other departments were shown in episodes but not widely seen, the path from reception area to the main office was seen, and it consisted of practically four sets in one. From the reception area, with its paneled walls and sitting area, one entered into a working area that consisted of a group of secretaries sitting at desks with typewriters preparing the final copy for the upcoming edition. The door straight ahead leads to the secretary office of Doris (and later, Jackie Parker), with desk, typewriter, telephone, file cabinets, and cushioned chairs for visitors. This leads to Mr. Nicholson's (and later Cy Bennett's) office, which has the regular items an executive needs, as well as a couch, cushioned chairs and coffee tables used for private meetings. A long glass-topped table, with multiple matching chairs, was brought into the office for editorial meetings. The office also has a kitchenette behind louvered doors, complete with a hot plate, mini-refrigerator and sink to prepare food and drink for visiting clients, businessmen and women, and interview subjects. The office furnishings were provided by Steelcase, a leading office supply company.

Perry Ferguson II and his talents deserve much of the credit for the success of the series' sets. Each set, whether used once or a hundred times, was believable and detailed. From the expensive Steven's jewelry store to the small, family-owned Pallucci's Restaurant, each set was not simply thrown together, but time was taken to make them right. Although this was television, they had the look of a feature film.

Two of the series' major and most memorable sets were the homes of Doris Martin, the first in the country, the second in the city.

## The Home In Mill Valley

With the ranch setting, the sets were built on a soundstage. The house itself was complete in that the actors could walk from the frontyard, inside through the main floor living room and into the kitchen and dining area, and out into the backyard. This was highly unusual. Most of the time there is the exterior, which is a facade built outside with only a shell: once a person walks inside, there are no living quarters on the other side. The interior scenes are filmed in another location inside a soundstage. Then the shots are edited together to make both locations appear as one.

## The Apartment in San Francisco

When Doris Martin decided to move from the farm to San Francisco, she found this two-story apartment above Pallucci's Italian restaurant in a turn-of-the-last-century brick building. Although two stewardesses had lived there prior, the apartment looked as if it had been uninhabited for many years. The walls were shades of gray and black, and the carpet badly worn. But it was converted into one of the coolest apartments ever on television. Unlike the farm set, interiors of the home were shot on a separate stage from the exterior shots of the apartment building.

From the apartment's front door, which was later painted a bold red, one enters into the living room into the cheery living room, with yellow walls and painted white trim and woodwork similar to the color scheme used on the farm. The room extends to a sitting area and a dining area, which house many antiques from the farm set.

Jim Hassinger, who worked with Perry Ferguson on the sets for *The Doris Day Show*, described the setting and Doris's style at the time: "At home, the San Francisco apartment and her three-room dressing room suite, Doris uses color and a mix of wood, wicker and plants. The colors are basically the same: Yellows and lettuce green with pinks or off-reds for dramatic contrasts. Gold carpeting, butter yellow walls and an oversized sofa with corn yellow textured silk in a corner. A caramel-colored corduroy couch, backed with a long table in the living room. A fireplace and two chairs that were hand rubbed with an antique finish and accessorized with subdued green cushions.

"A white wicker chair complements a lift-top lacquered school-type desk. Matching white wicker chairs form a conversation area before ceiling-high windows that faces the terrace. Ferns and other plants surround the base of the metal spiral staircase and hang from the ceiling. Doris favored printed valences over long curtains for the apartment."

Past the living room is a small, but practical kitchen, which has a sitting bar and stools which are usually used for the breakfast meal. The kitchen has a dumbwaiter that connects to Pallucci's Restaurant below. There is also a bronze turtle whose shell lifts when you step on a secret pedal, which reveals itself as an Early American spittoon.

A French door in the dining area opens into a brick terrace with a terrific view of the city. It features many of Doris's plants from the farm, a white wicker ensemble with flower print cushions, and a round glass patio table with white metal chairs.

The second floor has a bathroom and three bedrooms, although the audience is shown only Doris's bedroom. It looks similar to her room on the ranch with the furnishings and color scheme. Many of the pieces of furniture used in the farmhouse were utilized in the apartment set.

Doris Day paid particular attention to the sets, especially the home dwellings. She liked items to be placed just so and even went around with a dust rag at times to tidy the place. Don Genson recalls one day when Doris looked as though she planned to dust the walls. "Do you know if you take time to do that, it will cost us about $1,000?" he quietly remarked to her. She stopped, surprised with the comment, then grinned. She did not attempt to dust the walls again.

One of the most distinctive aspects of the apartment is the metal spiral staircase leading to the upstairs. The staircase was a working one and was used in many episodes. Today, it resides in Doris Day's actual home.

Props were just as detailed with each set. The offices had ashtrays, potted plants and dried arrangements, staplers, pencils in pencil holders, notepads on the desks, filing cabinets with files containing papers—everything one would expect in an office at that day and age.

Restaurant, party, hotel suites and other scenes were also detailed in set design and props. So were other character's apartments. Even if they were used only once, each was made to look real and lived-in: shelves were lined with books and knickknacks, and a character never opened a cupboard that did not have something sitting inside of it.

## A CHAT WITH KAYE BALLARD

*You first appeared on* The Doris Day Show *in season two's "Kid-napped"…*

Yes. I played the wife of a mobster. Then they hired me for the third season playing the Italian with Bernie Kopell.

*How much of the character of Angie Pallucci was you or came from the script?*

Of course. A lot of that came from me because I gave them the name of the restaurant, thinking of a restaurant in New York—Pallucci's in the village. I'm sure it's still there—it's been there forever. And it was lovely working with Bernie Kopell. The Jews and the Italians seem to be one alike. There's a great empathy with them.

*And Bernie said he learned a lot of Italian from you.*

All dirty words! Ha—"emotional" words. The chemistry between Bernie, myself and John Dehner—what a man. He was a thrill to be on-stage with.

*One of Pallucci's most famous customers was Tony Bennett.*

Yes, and I got Tony to do that. I asked him, 'Would you like to do *The Doris Day Show?*' And he said, 'Oh I'd love it!'

*There was the episode "The Blessed Event," in which you worked with a lot of dogs.*

Nothing thrills me more than working with dogs. So Doris and I— we love animals the same way.

*There was a lot of food being prepared and being eaten on the series. Do you recall where that came from?*

The commissary would cook the food, or it'd be brought in from an Italian store. But we did eat a lot of it.

*You looked very comfortable in Pallucci's Restaurant—and in the kitchen. Are you in real life?*

Oh, I am. I cook, but I didn't cook on the show. And I love eating. Can't you tell?!

Doris Day and Kaye Ballard.

*I've seen you through the years and in recent interviews and must tell you how terrific you look.*

Well, that's good! You know what it is? When you're not trying to be thin and not trying to be beautiful. You know, it's interesting. For example, I saw a movie the other day and [the actresses] looked wonderful, natural and they haven't done anything to themselves. But [another actress] looks like she has anorexia. It's tragic. She has collagen lips. And you think, 'My God, she's a good actress, she doesn't need all of that.' I honestly believe you should grow old gracefully because it's going to happen no matter what you do.

*Angie Pallucci had a habit of trying to match Doris Martin up with any man.*

Oh, I did that in real life too, trying to find someone for her! She is very special, and I tried to introduce her to people that I thought she might have fun with. She was very much alone. Preferred to be alone. And with all of the disappointments at that point in her life, she preferred to be with her animals. And I understand that completely.

*You were in the television show* The Mothers-in-Law *before* The Doris Day Show. *Was the transition from one to the other difficult?*

That show was the easiest show in the world to do because she made it that way. When the top is professional and wonderful, everything else is. And Doris is, and she was at the helm. She made it totally pleasant. Totally.

*Was there ever a time when you and the cast read a script and decided to make changes, or wasn't that allowed?*

Things came up naturally. Nobody ever tried to do anything—tried to make an impromptu. And it just came out naturally and it worked.

We made changes as we went along to make it better, but we were doing a one-camera show. With an audience and a three-camera show, then it's difficult to make changes and the tension is always there. But one-camera is a joy, and you can make changes as you go along.

*You also appeared on* Doris Day's Best Friends *series. How do you recall doing that show?*

That experience was wonderful because she was in her own environment with a lot of puppies. She made it very easy—like you weren't doing an interview or a show at all. It looked like an afternoon tea with animals running around, and it was lovely. They shot it very, very quickly. It was a lovely day and they shot [part of] it outside.

*What was Doris Day like and what was it like to work on her CBS series?*

Doris Day was a giant star but never acted like it. We had a lot of fun. There was a lot of breaking up, too. She'd make me laugh or I'd make her laugh or John Dehner would make us laugh. It was a joy to do. Effortless joy.

# Season Five: 1972-1973
## "Doris Martin: Investigative Reporter Gets the Story"

The previous season's format remained consistent in the fifth season of *The Doris Day Show*. Another opening credit was made—the series' fourth such change—for a few of the later episodes. This one had Doris Martin walking down her spiral stairway in a black dress to open her front door, with scenes from the fashion show episode included.

After the Palluccis sold their apartment building to concentrate on their restaurant business, Mr. Jarvis eventually bought it this season. In doing so, he became Doris's landlord. Doris continued working at *today's world*, but there seemed to be more of an emphasis on Doris's romantic involvements, which steered toward a more adult audience. While this season seemed light years from a majority of season one's episodes, it nonetheless exemplified the progression of character and situation.

This was the last season of the series. While CBS was willing for *The Doris Day Show* to continue, Doris said no. She was tired and felt five seasons was enough. "There are so many other things to be done and said, and doing a situation comedy week after week is no longer fulfilling for me," she said at the time. "[Television] has provided me with a good living for many years. But it is not the alpha and omega of the world.

"There is really no reason why prime-time TV must devote so much time to pure entertainment. TV is the most powerful medium in the world, and Hollywood, its prime source of material, has used it almost entirely for entertainment."

A dozen years later, Doris would use the medium to provide the audience with more than "entertainment." She used *Doris Day's Best*

*Friends* to educate the public to a cause close to her heart, that being the well-being of animals.

## CBS PRESS RELEASES TO PROMOTE *THE DORIS DAY SHOW*:

August 31, 1972

### Doris Day "Discovers" a New Director—Peter Lawford

Peter Lawford, who has been an actor for a good many years, made his debut as a director during the recent filming of an episode to be seen during the fifth season of *The Doris Day Show*, which begins on the CBS Television Network Monday, September 11 (9:30-10:00 PM, EDT).

Asked why he chose that particular episode to direct, Lawford explains that "nobody ever asked me to direct anything before."

It was Doris Day, the star of the series, who did the asking. Lawford has been a frequent guest in the recurring role of Dr. Peter Lawrence, swain of Doris Martin (Miss Day). He was performing as Dr. Lawrence one day when Miss Day popped the question.

"I've always noticed that Pete gets along well with people," Miss Day says. "It seems that no matter how temperamental a person is, Pete has the knack of doing it. I decided that for that reason he'd make a good director for our series. I'm sure I was oversimplifying the requisites for the job, but anyway I suggested he give it a try.

"He was thrilled to death at the idea, and I was kind of surprised to find out that he hadn't done any directing before. I just thought that he probably had done it somewhere along the line."

As a director, Lawford made a hit with the series' producer, Ed Feldman. He completed filming of the episode in a record three days and, considering the money saved, that makes any producer enthusiastic.

### CBS Television Network Nighttime Program Notes

Doris Day, pert and vivacious as ever, opens her fifth season on the CBS Television Network when *The Doris Day Show* has its 1972 Fall premiere on Monday, September 11, in the same 9:30-10:00 PM, CNYT, time slot.

In the popular comedy series Doris portrays Doris Martin, energetic staff writer on "Today's World," whose job is always hectic and exciting as she confronts a constantly changing assortment of people and events to get her stories for the magazine. Romance is often lurking around unexpected corners, too, with Doris meeting some of the handsomest, most talented and eligible (if not always legally) men around. While her home base continues to be San Francisco, her exploits sometimes take her to many different—and fascinating—parts of the United States and the world.

John Dehner continues in the role of editor Cyril Bennett, still looking back upon the days when he was a dashing foreign correspondent and still envisioning himself as a man in a trenchcoat who could pound

out a graphic, award-winning story under the most trying of circum-stances. In fact, though he'd never admit it, he tends to get rattled a little easily. Bennett's secretary (Jackie Joseph) is the medium through which most of the serious contact between Doris and her boss takes place.

In one of the new season's episodes Doris will write an article called "Forgive and Forget," but she finds the title easier to write than to put it into practice when she believes her occasional boyfriend, a doctor played by Peter Lawford, has stayed overnight at the home of a beautiful and none-too-seriously ill patient. In another story, Doris thinks she's being watched by a Peeping Tom. She asks her boss, who is about to be nomi-nated San Francisco's "Man of the Year," to find out who he is, and when the police find Bennett prowling around the grounds in search of evi-dence they arrest him in a very embarrassing case of mistaken identity.

*The Doris Day Show*, an Arwin Production, is filmed at CBS Studio Center in Hollywood, with Edward H. Feldman as producer.

**THE EPISODES:**

[Authors' Note: The chronological listing of episodes is changed from the actual airdates to help better explain the progression of Doris Martin including her relationships, career and home life.]

**"No More Advice...Please"**
Production Dates: July 25-27, 1972
Original Airdate: September 11, 1972
Directed by: Marc Daniels

Guess who's coming to dinner? Everybody's mother, Cy Bennett. Doris and Peter Lawrence are hosting Cy at her apartment. In Cy's eyes, the two of them look so comfortable that it's time for them to "pay the parson." Doris thinks he's just completely old fashioned and out of step with the times. Cy doesn't agree and is determined to give them advice (good or bad) to make this happen. Unfortunately, Doris is very busy interviewing Professor of Anthropology and popular writer Eric Stewart about his new book *Every Day is Mother's Day* for *today's world*. When Eric suffers from back problems, Doris advises him to see Peter. While in Peter's office, Eric admits to him that he has fallen in love with Doris and is thinking of marrying her. Peter makes the mistake of taking Cy's advice.

Written by: Laurence Marks; Peter Lawford as Dr. Peter Lawrence, Don Chastain as Eric Stewart, Luis de Cordova as Jules, Melissa Whittaker as Melissa

*today's world* the now magazine:
An interview with Eric Stewart on his book *Every Day is Mother's Day*.

Doris Day Movie Find!:
"What Does a Woman Do" from *Midnight Lace* [1960]

**"The Great Talent Raid"**
Production Dates: July 17-20, 1972
Original Airdate: September 18, 1972
Directed by: William Wiard

Doris gets a job offer at *Prestige* magazine, at double the salary she's making at *today's world*, but Doris is happy where she is and declines the offer. When Cy rejects her story on a woman's view of football, Doris gets very upset, and he threatens her job so she literally walks across the street to *Prestige* and starts working there. Even though happy and comfortable, she quickly realizes that she misses her old home and wants to go back. But she has a firm contract that she cannot break. Doris decides to put her football story into action, and starts trading staff members from one magazine to the other until almost everyone has been replaced, leaving both sides unhappy. Doris needs to find a way to put everyone - including herself—back in their original jobs.

Written by: William Raynor, Myles Wilder; Billy De Wolfe as himself, Ralph Story as John Scott, Glynn Turman as Al Davis, Luis de Cordova as Jules, De De Young as Ellen, John Kroger as Jim, Tom Stewart as Harry

Groovy Day Facts:
The combination to Cy's office wall safe is 18 left, 25 right, two times around, stop at seven. He keeps an extra set of car keys there.
Doris had lunches that lasted one-and-a-half hours at *today's world*, but those were reduced to one hour at *Prestige*.
Billy De Wolfe makes a surprise cameo in the restaurant scene.

*today's world* the now magazine:
"A Woman's View of Football" by Doris
"Why I Take the Pill" by Jim
"The Decline and Fall of the American Bra" by Harry
A ballet review by Cy

Jackie Joseph Movie Find!:
Glynn Turman was in *Gremlins* with Jackie.

Guest Star Mini-Bio:
Ralph Story is a well-known TV personality in the Los Angeles area. His "Ralph Story's Los Angeles" on the CBS station KNXT-TV ran from 1963 well into the next decade. Also, he preceded Regis Philbin as the host of "A.M. Los Angeles" on KABC-TV in the 1970s and 1980s.

## "Just a Miss Understanding"
Production Dates: June 26-29, 1972
Original Airdate: September 25, 1972
Directed by: Lee Phillips

Doris, who is expecting a huge bonus from *today's world*, buys Peter Lawrence a very expensive attaché case with a wireless phone. When she receives her bonus, it is disappointingly not nearly enough to cover the cost of Peter's birthday present. Doris has no choice but to get another job at night. Doris goes to KBEX radio, where she had been offered a job before and asks for a temporary job. Luckily, Miss Understanding is on vacation and she can replace her. Her schedule is from midnight to 5:00 A.M., and Doris luckily happens to be free. She gives Peter the birthday present and for weeks she struggles with her job at *today's world*, dating Peter in the evening and working all night, finding herself completely exhausted. Peter, worried about her, thinks that she is seeing another man at the same time. But one night while listening to the radio, he hears...

Written by: Charlotte Brown; Peter Lawford as Dr. Peter Lawrence, Joe Hoover as Jim, Jack DeMave as Dave Genson

Groovy Day Facts:

Doris's profit-sharing twelve months previous was $600, but only $84 for the current year due to several things, including the increase of expenses and upgrading equipment for the magazine.

Doris says she gave Cy an "executive yo-yo" for his birthday.

Although Doris takes a second job, *today's world* has a "no moonlighting" policy for its employees.

Doris falls asleep not only while dancing with Peter and riding the elevator in the office building, but also during an editorial meeting.

Peter makes scrambled eggs for a breakfast with Doris.

Doris and Peter plan to take a trip to Big Sur. [She later goes there with Jonathon Rusk.]

*today's world* the now magazine:

A story on consumer protection by Doris

Doris Day Movie Find!:

The title song to *Caprice* [1967].

## "The Press Secretary"

Production Dates: August 7-10, 1972
Original Airdate: September 25, 1972
Directed by: Richard Kinon

Journalist Jonathon Rusk, a very dear, old friend of Doris's, is running for Congress and asks Doris to be his press secretary. Cy gives her a leave of absence in exchange for an exclusive interview with the candidate. Doris works hard for the campaign and Jonathon enjoys her participation very much. Their relationship builds to what it was years ago, but Jonathon is married and Doris feels that she has gotten herself into something she doesn't think she can handle, so she resigns from the campaign. Jonathon promises Cy an interview with the President if he can convince Doris to return as his press secretary. She does accept to go back but sets clear boundaries between the two of them. Their work relationship flourishes and the campaign works well. When Jonathon's wife arrives, she becomes suspicious of Doris's closeness with her husband. But with the help of Jackie and Cy, she is assured that nothing has happened. Now they patiently await the election results.

With Patrick O'Neal.

Written by: Laurence Marks; Patrick O'Neal as Jonathon Rusk, Julie Adams as Louise Rusk

Groovy Day Facts:

It was rare for women to be press secretaries for high political offices and campaigns at this time.

First appearance of Jonathon Rusk.

Jonathon Rusk was Doris's hometown friend and the pair had dated. He once siphoned gas out of his car so that it would run out, and he insinuates that they were intimate at a boathouse.

Jonathon mistakes Cy as a caterer.

*today's world* the now magazine:

An exclusive interview with Congressional candidate Jonathon Rusk.

Doris Day Movie Find!:

Patrick O'Neal was Doris's leading man in *Where Were You When the Lights Went Out?* [1968].

**"Peeping Tom"**
Production Dates: June 19-22, 1972
Original Airdate: October 9, 1972
Directed by: Marc Daniels

Cy drops by Doris's apartment and he is bursting with happiness. He's been nominated for Citizen of the Year Award for a series of brilliant articles on community involvement—which Doris Martin wrote. Although Doris is very happy for him, she is very busy getting ready for a date. While Doris is changing upstairs, Cy yells out his practice acceptance speech to her. Doris notices out the window that someone is watching her through binoculars. She is completely petrified and asks Cy to go across the street and check it out. Cy goes across the street, finds the binoculars, and the police soon arrive to arrest him. The next day, Doris and Cy explain the situation to the police, who start an investigation. Doris asks Jackie to stay with her until they find the peeping tom. Cy stops by Doris's to make sure all is well. After receiving a prank phone call, Cy decides to spend the night on the couch. When the cleaner arrives in the morning, he makes an interesting comment about a dress to Doris that he never could have seen her in. She believes he's the peeping tom so she informs the police. But what is it he is really looking for?

Written by: Arthur Julian; Larry Hovis as Larry Madison, John Stephenson as Sgt. Murdock, Joseph Perry as Sam

Groovy Day Facts:
Cy loves peanut clusters.
Cy's competition for the Citizen of the Year Award is J. Robert Stafford, who gave San Francisco a $12 million medical facility.
Doris hears the doorbell, asks who it is, Cy replies, "Jack the Ripper."
Doris, Jackie and Cy watch the movie *Dr. Jekyll and Mr. Hyde* at her place and cooks breakfast for them the next morning.
Cy is given two citations: the Courageous Citizens Award from the San Francisco Police Department, as well as a parking ticket for an expired meter.

Denver Pyle Movie Find!:
Joseph Perry appeared with Denver in *The Left Handed Gun* [1958].

**"Forgive and Forget"**
Production Dates: June 12-15, 1972
Original Airdate: October 16, 1972
Directed by: William Wiard

Doris feels that a lot of her friends are breaking up and not always for the best reasons. She feels that sometimes understanding another person's flaws would be the best way to build on a relationship, so she decides to write an essay—an opinion piece on separation and divorce with the main thrust being, in Cy's words, "to err is human, to forgive divine." When the article comes out a few weeks later, it causes quite a sensation. At a party with Peter, Doris is confronted by a group of married women who feel that she may not quite understand what their married life is all about. Doris is suddenly faced with the same situation and spends a sleepless night while Peter takes care of a beautiful patient in the middle of the night.

Written by: Laurence Marks; Peter Lawford as Dr. Peter Lawrence, Ginny Golden as Toni Rolfe, Noah Keen as Dr. Jerry Kruger, Murray Pollack as Walter Mercer, Jo De Winter as Marcia Kruger, Alene Towne as Louise Mercer, John Kroger as Herb Franklin

Groovy Day Facts:
Jackie says she's been dating Harry for two years, but they breakup after he has a fling on a business trip to Los Angeles.
Col. Fairburn owns 67% of the magazine's stock.
Doris's story was liked by Col. Fairburn, but not Mrs. Fairburn.
Doris sleeps on the job—again.

*today's world* the now magazine:
"Forgive and Forget"

Doris Day Movie Find!:
Raquel Welch is mentioned in this episode and made a small appearance in *Do Not Disturb* [1965].

**"Debt of Honor"**
Production Dates: July 10-13, 1972
Original Airdate: October 23, 1972
Directed by: Peter Lawford

Doris returns early with a book full of notes from her interview with the governor and his wife, and is ready to start working on the next article. Doris starts writing the story and receives a letter from a financial company. She is in debt of $1,100, a loan she had made to friends years ago that they had never paid. All of a sudden, she is completely broke. Jackie immediately offers her $8 from her savings account, and Doris starts calling friends to whom she'd lent money: Lenny, Barb, Joe, Connie, Harry and Wally, but nobody can help. She eventually asks Cy as well, but he refuses. Doris, who has been a good friend to everyone, being caring and generous, is now faced with a very difficult problem. She contemplates selling pieces of jewelry and then remembers selling an old car to Greg Mitchell, who never actually paid for it. She arranges a meeting with him with the hope that he will come through, but suspects that he may be deadbeat.

With Ed Begley, Jr.

Written by: Phil Sharp; Richard Schaal as Greg Mitchell, Sid Melton as Al, Ed Begley, Jr. as Wally, Luis de Cordova as Maitre D'

Groovy Day Facts:

Wally, the young man who delivers the mail in the office, is growing a beard. Unfortunately, he's the only one who sees it.

To raise money, Doris decides to pawn a ring given to her by an oil millionaire. She discovers its worth is only $20.

When Doris dines with Greg Mitchell in order to get the $800 he owes her from the sale of her car six years earlier, the cost of the meal is $84—and Doris almost thinks she'll have to pay the bill.

This was Luis de Cordova's fifth and last appearance in the series.

*today's world* the now magazine:

An interview with the Governor.

Doris Day Movie Find!:

The title song to *Lover Come Back* [1961].

Guest Star Mini-Bio:

Although he had a diverse acting career in films including *Shadow of the Thin Man* (1941), *White Heat* (1949) and *Lady Sings the Blues* (1972), Sid Melton's work in television made him a recognizable face, if not a name. Perhaps best known as Charlie Halper in Danny Thomas's show *Make Room for Daddy*, *The Danny Thomas Show*, *The Danny Thomas Hour* and *Make Room for Granddaddy* (from the late 1950s through early 1970s), Melton's recurring role as carpenter Alf Monroe on *Green Acres* cemented his fame. He made many more television guest appearances throughout the years, including three on *The Doris Day Show* and as Salvadore Petrillo on *The Golden Girls*.

"Peter Lawford directed that episode," Sid Melton says, "and he was a wonderful man, a wonderful guy. No problems and a very capable director. Doris was a wonderful performer and the cast and crew were very easy to work with. I enjoyed it and working with them very, very much."

## "Jimmy, the Gent"

Production Dates: August 28-31, 1972
Original Airdate: November 6, 1972
Directed by: Marc Daniels

A man commits twelve robberies in three weeks, and *today's world* has been covering every single one of them. It looks like the work of famous thief Jimmy the Gent, who nobody's ever been able to pin down. He is currently a patient at General Hospital where Dr. Peter Lawrence works. Doris asks Peter if she could pretend to be a patient at the hospital and try to do an interview with the gangster. Peter completely refuses. The hospital is too busy to have pretend-patients occupying beds. When Jackie is in a small elevator accident, Doris sees the opportunity to go to the hospital and pretend that she was injured. Once inside the hospital, Doris finds Jimmy the Gent's room and starts communicating with him, but he is very suspicious of her injuries. She continues anyway she can to talk to Jimmy, but it is the real Jimmy the Gent?

Written by: Laurie Samara, Courtney Andrews; Peter Lawford as Dr. Peter Lawrence, Elvia Allman as Nurse Howard, Walter Burke as Jimmy, Charles Wagenheim as Jenkins, Florida Friebus as Miss Peabody

Groovy Day Facts:

Cost for Doris to stay in the hospital is $75 a day. The price includes TV rental, which was a common practice at the time.

Doris goes undercover at General Hospital in order to meet with Jimmy. She is first admitted as a patient, then changes into a nurse to move about the hospital. After her nurse's uniform is discovered and removed, she becomes a candy striper after swapping her street clothes with a hospital volunteer who is going on a date.

Doris says she's a size 8.

Cy has a date with Nurse Howard and the two invite themselves to Doris's apartment—so Doris and Peter escape to his.

*today's world* the now magazine:

Stories on the crime wave in San Francisco and the true culprit.

Jackie Joseph Movie Find!:
Charles Wagenheim was with Jackie in *A Guide for the Married Man* [1967].

Guest Star Mini-Bio:
While she appeared in several films as varied as *The Nutty Professor* (1963) to *Breakfast at Tiffany's*, Elvia Allman was a constant personality on many television shows, including *The Bob Cummings Show*, *The Abbott & Costello Show* and *The Jack Benny Show* and three different roles on *The Doris Day Show*. She also played recurring—and different—characters on sister shows *The Beverly Hillbillies*, *Green Acres* and *Petticoat Junction*, where her most memorable role was as wealthy snob Selma Plout.

**"The Music Man"**
Production Dates: September 5-7, 1972
Original Airdate: November 13, 1972
Directed by: William Wiard

Doris is asked to do an in-depth story with the hottest rock star of the moment, Johnny Reb. Her mission is to follow him around for a few days, going everywhere he goes. Her first stop is a midnight recording session. Doris stays with him while he creates, writes, mixes, sings and produces all the songs for his new album. Johnny, who has a huge entourage, breaks up with his girlfriend because he has fallen madly in love with Doris. The rumor of their relationship is the talk of the town. During a party at Doris's apartment, without first telling her, Johnny announces to all of his and Doris's friends that they will be married.

Written by: Laurence Marks; Paul Hampton as Johnny Reb, Eldon Wuick as Mr. Barton, Melissa Whittaker as Mrs. Barton, Anne Randall as Nancy, Ed Garner as Charlie

Groovy Day Facts:
Johnny Reb records for Equinox Records, which was an actual record label and production company owned by Doris Day and Terry Melcher.
Melissa Whittaker also appeared in "No More Advice, Please." She later became Doris Day's real life daughter-in-law. In life imitating art, Melissa's

picture is on the back cover of Terry Melcher's solo album which was released through Equinox—the same company that appears in this episode.

Both Cy and Jackie temporarily lose some standing in their friendships with Doris when they question her relationship with Johnny.

This is one of only two times that the end credits deviated from the series' standard images and theme song. For *The Music Man*, the credits are run over footage of Doris and Johnny walking, with a Johnny Reb song instead of the instrumental "Que Sera, Sera" played on the soundtrack.

*today's world* the now magazine:
A profile on rock star Johnny Reb

Jackie Joseph Movie Find!:
Anne Randall was in *The Split* [1968] with Jackie.

Guest Star Mini-Bio:
In the British rock music journal "Footsoldiers and Kings," Paul Hampton is listed as one of the 100 major architects of American rock 'n' roll. While attending Dartmouth college, Hampton was signed by both Columbia Records and Columbia Pictures to write music with Hal David and Burt Bacharach. Hampton's songs have been recorded by many artists, including Johnny Cash, Elvis Presley, Merle Haggard, Bette Midler, Tom Jones, Sammy Davis, Jr., Eddy Arnold and Rick Nelson. He is also an ASCAP award-winning songwriter for "Sea of Heartbreak."

**"Defective Story"**
Production Dates: August 14-17, 1972
Original Airdate: November 20, 1972
Directed by: Richard Kinon

Doris and Cy are at a party for General Smaltzoff, who is arranging diplomacy talks with the U.S. Marvin Patterson is trying to convince Cy to buy his story for $10,000 on the general's planned defection from his eastern European country. Doris is convinced that Marvin is making up the story just to get the money. So she decides to become friends with the general and get information on him herself. Her only way in is with Cy's big foot—"The Cyril." The general, however, tells Doris that he has no intention of defecting. But is he telling the truth?

Written by Charlotte Brown; Roger C. Carmel as General Nikoli Smaltzoff, Alan Oppenheimer as Marvin, Joseph Perry as Guard #2, Dave Morick as Guard #1, Lidia Kristen as Zelinka, Ford Lile as Reporter

Groovy Day Facts:
When Marvin Patterson gives Doris a thank-you gift, he may have an underlying contempt toward her. It is a plant whose common name is Mother-In-Law Tongue.

*today's world* the now magazine:
Exposing General Smaltzoff's defection?

Doris Day Album Find!:
"Christmas Present" from *The Doris Day Christmas Album* [1964]

**"The Co-op"**
Production Dates: August 1-3, 1972
Original Airdate: November 27, 1972
Directed by: Roger Duchowny

Mr. Jarvis informs Doris that their building is about to be sold. Upset with the news, Doris invites a very reluctant Mr. Jarvis and the other tenants to form a co-op. After a few meetings, where no one agrees with anyone, the partnership dissolves and Mr. Jarvis decides to buy the building himself. The first thing on his agenda is to raise everybody's rent. Doris encourages the tenants to take action and put Mr. Jarvis on 24-hour call with a huge list of repairs and hopefully change his mind about the rent increase.

Written by: Arthur Julian; Billy De Wolfe as Mr. Jarvis, Alan DeWitt as Lester Hansen, Henry Corden as Mr. Lohman, Lester Fletcher as Lance Baker, Paula Victor as Mrs. Lohman, Dan Keough as Mr. Sinclair, Misty Rowe as Mrs. Sinclair

Groovy Day Facts:
The landlord of the building, Mr. Carter, died at the age of 92 and the estate has put the building up for sale. Apparently, the Palluccis sold it to him—but kept their restaurant—as they had owned it when Doris moved in.

Trans Industrial Corporation, who has business interests in brassieres, tractors, electric typewriters and guided missiles, is interested in purchasing the building.

We see all of Doris's neighbors: Mr. Jarvis, years-married Mr. and Mrs. Lohman, newlyweds Mr. and Mrs. Sinclair, and Lance Baker and Lester Hansen, interior designers.

Arguably, the first series to show an openly gay couple.

Golda Meir, prime minister of Israel, is mentioned.

Cy refuses to co-sign a bank loan for Doris since her only collateral is "freckles and a great wardrobe."

"Ne-vah touch a landlord!" Mr. Jarvis now says.

Doris remembers a very cooperative Mr. Jarvis after getting him very drunk at the office and does the same here to get the rent lowered.

Doris Day Movie Find!:
Billy De Wolfe was featured with Doris in *Tea for Two* [1950].

**"Anniversary Gift"**
Production Dates: September 25-28, 1972
Original Airdate: December 11, 1972
Directed by: Richard Duchowny

It is Doris and Peter's first anniversary of the first day they met. As a present, Peter recalled Doris had admired a beautiful, old car on that day. He buys it and she baptizes it Clara. Doris is completely in love with Clara, except that Clara is making Doris's life a wreck. Clara only functions once in a while, which causes Doris to be late for work, appointments, dates, and sometimes even has to be towed from place to place. But she refuses to give up on Clara, almost losing her job and almost even losing Peter.

Written by: Arthur Julian; Peter Lawford as Dr. Peter Lawrence, Richard Hurst as Herbie, Kay Stewart as Mrs. Winston, William Tregoe as Mr. Winston, Dick Van Patten as Sam

Groovy Day Facts:
Peter and Doris first date was dining at Lobster House.
Because of Clara's unreliability, Doris is late for work five times.

The statue in Hancock Park is that of Lin Ching Phong, first mayor of Chinatown, who owned the first Chinese restaurant there.

Cy takes away Doris's parking space privilege because Clara doesn't fit in with the image of the magazine.

Peter cooks pot roast for a dinner with Doris.

Peter has made spaghetti, but has an office call so Doris invites Jackie over to eat with her.

There is a cabdriver convention in San Francisco, which results in a 45-minute wait for a ride when Peter needs to get to the hospital.

*today's world* the now magazine:
The unveiling of a statue in Hancock Park of the first mayor of Chinatown.

Doris Day Album Find!:
"Time to Say Goodnight" from *I Have Dreamed* [1961]

**"The New Boss"**
Production Dates: July 3, 5, 6, 1972
Original Airdate: December 18, 1972
Directed by: Marc Daniels

Col. Fairburn feels the magazine is slipping and decides to make some drastic changes for one issue. He asks that every senior executive step down and have someone under him take over his job, including Cy. Cy, always thinking about himself, picks Doris to take over his job, knowing that she may not be quite up to par. Although a little uneasy at the beginning, Doris moves well with the different departments and learns quickly how to make the right decisions regarding art, ideas and editorial. At the end of the week she has created quite a favorable sensation with Col. Fairburn, who couldn't be happier with her performance. Cy feels that he has been stabbed in the back by a "black widow fink." Doris, however, gives the credit for her success to Cy, saying that he was behind her 100%.

Written by: Laurence Marks; Edward Andrews as Col. Fairburn, Jack Wells as Fred, Joe Hoover as Jim, John Myhers as Mr. Grainger, Ben Wrigley as Charlie

Groovy Day Facts:
Col. Fairburn says efficiency has fallen in every department of the magazine, from art and research to editorial, which has run stories with inaccuracies.
Doris suggests *today's world* consolidate offices to reduce overhead in U.S. and overseas.
Cy says he does 100 pushups a day.
Doris plays hardball with advertiser Tom Grainger of Associated Aluminum, who pays almost $500,000 annually in advertising to *today's world*.
Col. Fairburn says he believes Doris will be the magazine's next editor.
Last appearance of Col. Fairburn is in this episode.

*today's world* the now magazine:
"Cuba Today" that ties in with economic conditions in Florida.

Jackie Joseph Movie Find!:
Edward Andrews was in *Gremlins* [1984] with Jackie.

**"Follow That Dog!"**
Production Dates: October 23-26, 1972
Original Airdate: January 1, 1973
Directed by: William Wiard

Following a *today's world* story on a canine adoption center in desperate need of financial support, George Cantrell, a rich investor, brings Doris a huge donation of $10,000 for the center on one condition: as he's traveling to London, England he needs someone to take care of his very precious dog, Tiger. Doris wholeheartedly accepts, not knowing just how very precious this dog really is. Could tiny, little Tiger actually hold the key to a world of crime and corruption?

Written by: William Raynor, Myles Wilder; Bruce Gordon as Benedict, Joe Ruskin as Harry, Paul Stewart as Cantrell, Jack Griffin as Adams, with James B. Sikking, Dave Morick and John Stephenson

Groovy Day Facts:
It is believed that Barney Moore, who had kidnapped Doris a few years ago, has changed his name to Benedict and is working for another crime syndicate in the Bay area.

Cy accidentally eats Tiger's Doggie Num-Num snacks.

Doris has a door in her kitchen which opens into a stairwell that leads to the basement.

Doris and Cy are held at gunpoint by Benedict and the Family mafia.

*today's world* the now magazine:

A story on the Canine Adoption Center.

Doris Day Album Find!:

"Time to Say Goodnight" from *I Have Dreamed* [1961].

**"The Hoax"**
Production Dates: November 6-9, 1972
Original Airdate: January 8, 1973
Directed by: Lee Philips

While Doris and Jackie are lunching in a restaurant, a talent agent, Mitch Folger, comes to their table and asks Doris if she would like to come to Hollywood and try to be an actress. He feels that she has great potential. Doris politely turns him down. When Cy finds out about the offer, he tells Doris to jump at the chance as they are doing a great series of stories on "charlatans" who have fake talent agency and acting school who are making a lot of money off of innocent victims. Cy makes Doris go to Hollywood and enroll as soon as possible. Doris goes through the process of paying for everything and anything, from photos to classes to film tests and flies back and forth between Hollywood and San Francisco to report. Mr. Folger discovers that she is doing a story on him, so he casts her in a real commercial. Now that her cover is blown, will she do it?

With Andy Griffith

Written by: Laurence Marks; Andy Griffith as Mitch Folger, David Frank as Ozzie, Ryan MacDonald as James Waterhouse, Ceil Cabot as Woman, Alan DeWitt as Man, Read Morgan as George

Groovy Day Facts:
Mitch Folger's business is the Associated Talent Agency and Drama School in Hollywood.
There is a $50 registration fee against future commissions, $50 for photos, and another $50 for four acting sessions. Also, $2,000 for a screen test, but Folger brought the price down to $400.
The TV commercial is for Smoothie Liquid Shampoo.

*today's world* the now magazine:
Illegitimate talent agencies.

Doris Day Movie Find!:
The title song to *Lover Come Back* [1961].

Guest Star Mini-Bio:
A Tony nominee for *Destry Rides Again* and *No Time for Sergeants*, Andy Griffith reprised the latter for a film version. This was followed by the provocative—and prophetic—film, *A Face in the Crowd*. While a regular guest on television's *The Ed Sullivan Show* and *The Steve Allen Show*, Griffith starred in *The Andy Griffith Show,* which had a long run in the 1960s. He returned to series work in the 1980s with a second successful show, *Matlock*. Griffith is also a Grammy Award winner for the gospel album *I Love to Tell the Story*.

**"The Last Huzzah"**
Production Dates: October 30, 31, November 1, 2, 1972
Original Airdate: January 15, 1973
Directed by: Richard Kinon

Cy informs Sam Johnson, to Doris's distress, that the time has come for him to retire. Sam, who has been a vital part of *today's world* printing department, is at first happy with that decision, but after spending a week home with his wife, he asks Doris to find a way to bring him back. Doris discovers that Cy's absentee and sick days could also make him eligible for retirement himself, which leaves negotiating room for Sam to come back.

Written by: Arthur Julian, Rick Mittleman; Henry Jones as Sam Johnson, Dan Keough as Mike

Groovy Day Facts:
Cy needs glasses as he cannot read, and later gets contact lenses.
Cy suggests giving a $7.50 plaque for a retirement gift. Doris and Jackie want the magazine to give Sam a $300 watch, and thrifty Cy gives $25 toward its cost.
This is the first appearance of the *today's world* printing area, where there is a picture of Peter Lawford's former brother-in-law President John F. Kennedy.
Betsy is the name of #3 printing machine
Sam has worked at *today's world* for 40 years and reached the age of 65, which is the mandatory retirement age at the magazine.

Tod Starke Movie Find!:
Henry Jones co-starred with Tod in *Angel in My Pocket* [1969].

## "A Small Cure for Big Alimony"
Production Dates: November 13-16, 1972
Original Airdate: February 12, 1973
Directed by: Lee Phillips

Cy Bennett's ex-wife, Donna, is in town to ask perhaps for more alimony, but she's actually there to inform him that she's getting married to Jeff O'Neal, and that they are opening a restaurant together. She only needs Cy to finance it. Cy refuses at first, then accepts, considering he may be rid of his ex-wife. Doris, who is a restaurant expert from living above one for many years and eating in them all over the world, gets very involved in the design and concept of Cy's newly-owned restaurant, to great results. Jeff, however, makes a pass at Doris, who is very blunt in saying she is not interested. It is also discovered later by the captain of the restaurant that Jeff is a thief.

Written by: Arthur Julain; Norma Crane as Donna Bennett, Lee Bergere as Jeff O'Neal, Marcel Hillaire as George Moreau, Buddy Lewis as Artie

Groovy Day Facts:
Cy pays monthly alimony checks to ex-wife Donna.
Doris and Cy meet for lunch at his usual place—a hot dog stand.
Cy lends $10,000 to Donna to get her restaurant business started.
The restaurant is called The Press Box since its location is close to news organizations.
Doris suggests booths over tables for the restaurant.

Doris Day Movie Find!:
"There's a Rising Moon" from *Young at Heart* [1954]
"You Make Me Want You" from *With Six You Get Eggroll* [1968]

Doris Day Music Find!:
"Sorry" single [1967]

**"Hospital Benefit"**
Original Airdate: January 22, 1973

[See "Doris—a la mode" section]

**"Byline——Alias Doris"**
Production Dates: October 16-19, 1972
Original Airdate: March 12, 1973
Directed by: William Wiard

A reporter from *today's world* magazine named Scotty tells Doris he is going to be fired if his next story isn't good. He asks Doris to edit, thinking this is his last chance. Doris happily agrees and makes some key changes in his initial storyline. Cy adores it and is very impressed with the changes in Scotty, so much so that he puts him in his top team of reporters and transfers Doris to the women's section. Doris is furious, but agrees as long as it is only temporary. Doris is assigned to interview a famed television chef. Cy then gets Doris to cover the Miss Cable Car beauty contest. Scotty is assigned a story on Senator Bergson—which Doris was supposed to do. When Scotty learns about the change, he and Doris swap assignments, then turn in their stories with the other's byline. Is Cy able to recognize each story's true author?

Written by: Laurence Marks; Joey Forman as Scotty, Paul Fix as Senator Bergson, Ceil Cabot as Melissa Murphy, Louise Fitch as Louise Bergson

Groovy Day Facts:

Doris has been doing hard news for three years to this point.

The famous chef Melissa Murphy makes $300,000 a year and has a television audience of 20 million. Her two words of advice to housewives: Eat out.

This was the third role by Joey Forman and the fourth by Ceil Cabot in the series.

The last aired episode.

*today's world* the now magazine:

The Ferguson Trail

Interview with Mrs. Murphy, the lady with the golden hands

Interview with Senator Bergson

The Miss Cable Car Beauty Contest

Story on jewelry store holdup, two murders and a bank robbery

Doris Day Movie Find!:

Paul Fix played Doris's father-in-law in *The Ballad of Josie* [1967].

**"Family Magazine"**
Production Dates: November 20-22, 1972
Original Airdate: February 5, 1973
Directed by: Lee Philips

Sir Robert Kingsley is on a lecture tour and Cy assigns Jack to do an interview with him, even though Doris is a close, personal friend of his. Doris is very upset and convinces Cy that she is the only one who can give this interview justice. Doris and Sir Robert are thrilled to see each other again, and they spend a lot of time together. Cy starts following them around, imagining all sorts of things. He confronts Doris at the office and accuses her of "hanky panky" with Sir Robert, and maybe she isn't quite right to be working for a "family magazine." Doris decides to teach Cy a lesson. When he learns that Sir Robert has written a new book called *Africa Reborn*, Cy is extremely anxious to get the rights to the book. Doris and Sir Robert announce to him that she will soon be Lady Kingsley—and his negotiator for the serialization rights to Sir Robert's new book.

Written by: Don Genson, Laurence Marks; Jon Cypher as Sir Robert Kingsley, Martin Ashe as Willoughby, Dick Wilson as Motel Manager, John Kroger as Jack

Groovy Day Facts:
Doris calls Cy "the San Francisco Strangler."
Sir Robert Kingsley's previous book, *After Normandy*, was serialized in *today's world* and helped circulation increase by 9%.
*Africa Reborn*, Sir Robert's new book, is dedicated to Doris and whose serialization rights *today's world* purchases for $200,000.
Sir Robert dines at Doris's and compliments her on the meal. She remarks that she's mastered the art of defrosting and then the final preparation is "all downhill."
There is an interesting continuous shot of Cy and Sir Robert in his hotel room where the two talk in the living room, then continue their conversation in the dining area while being filmed from behind a bookcase. The camera moves from the bookcase to the two characters as they complete their talk in the living room.

*today's world* the now magazine:
   A story on tax reform movement.
   The serialization of *Africa Reborn*.

Doris Day Movie Find!:
   "Au Revoir Is Goodbye With a Smile" from *Do Not Disturb* [1965].
   "You Make Me Want You" from *With Six You Get Eggroll* [1968].

## "The Magnificent Fraud"
Production Dates: August 21-24, 1972
Original Airdate: February 19, 1972
Directed by: Marc Daniels

Doris's favorite uncle, August von Kappelhoff, has just been released from jail and surprises Doris with a terrific German meal at her apartment. Uncle August is also there to ask Doris for a small favor. He tells Doris that four years ago he left a real Vittorelli painting hidden in her house. Now that there is going to be a Vittorelli exhibit in San Francisco, the actual painting in the show is a fake and it has to be replaced by the real one. Doris manages to get Cy involved, and during a photo-op with Vincent Bissel, the sponsor of the exhibit, they are able to switch the paintings. On the way home, Cy and Doris see Uncle August in front of her building talking to a friend. Doris tells Cy that the man is Professor Gluten, an art expert she's just met with; however, Cy knows Professor Gluten as his weekly bridge-playing friend. Putting two and two together, they realize they have just stolen the real Vittorelli.

Written by: William Raynor, Myles Wilder; Bernie Kopell as Uncle August, Dan Tobin as Vincent Bissel, Kay Kuter as Professor Druten, Betty McGuire as Woman, Towyna Thomas as Maid, Martin Ashe as Butler

Groovy Day Facts:
   Doris says she almost called the Salvation Army to pick up the suitcase that held the painting.
   Uncle August's last name is von Kappelhoff—Doris Day's real last name.
   Doris gives up her two weeks vacation to work on Cy's World War II memoirs when he helps him switch the paintings.

*today's world* the now magazine:
An interview with Vincent Bissel.

Doris Day Movie Find!:
Bernie Kopell was in Doris's movie *The Thrill of It All* [1963]

**"Meant for Each Other"**
Production Dates: December 4-7, 1972
Original Airdate: February 26, 1973
Directed by: Roger Duchowny

Jackie announces to Cy that Doris is in LOVE—and it all of a sudden just happened—with an attractive man in the same business as Doris. It is television news foreign correspondent Jonathon Rusk. He is back in town and in Doris's life, and this time he is free. Cy is under the impression that Doris has fall in love with him. That misunderstanding is cleared up quickly, and Jonathon, after a very long, developing friendship through years of separation for reasons of life and work, finally proposes marriage to Doris, and she sincerely accepts. Unfortunately, time, work and events could separate the couple again.

Written by: Courtney Andrews, Laurie Samara; Patrick O'Neal as Jonathon Rusk, Peter Hobbs as Roberts, Joe Ross as Mr. Wilson, Jack Wells as Announcer, Louise Lane as Nurse, Sharyn Wynters as Madame Singh

Groovy Day Facts:
Jonathon did a series of stories on New African nations.
Jonathon interviews a visiting prime minister, Madame Singh.
Doris calls herself an "absolute nut" after thinking Jonathon was cheating on her.
There is an unusually long, uncut shot of Doris and Jonathon in her living room. The scene runs without interruption of the pair sitting on her couch, following her to the kitchen for a cup of coffee, and returning to the living room. The ability to do such a shot is not only difficult, but is an example of the talented cast and crew on the series under director of photography Richard Rawlings.

*today's world* the now magazine:
   An interview with the Governor's wife
   A story on septuplets (which turns out to be quadruplets)
   "Fire at Docks May Be Arson"

Doris Day Movie Find!:
   "We'll Love Again" from *The Man Who Knew Too Much* [1956]
   "You Make Me Want You" from *With Six You Get Eggroll* [1968]

**"Welcome to Big Sur, Sir"**
Production Dates: November 27-30, 1972
Original Airdate: March 5, 1973
Directed by: William Wiard

Jonathon and Doris finally have some time to themselves, so Doris pleads with Cy to get another day off so they have a long weekend alone in Big Sur. Jonathon has made all of the arrangements, and they are ready to go. As they are about to leave—surprise, surprise—Jackie and her friend, Sid, who is on his way to a jewelers' convention, have missed the bus to Los Angeles. They made a change of plans and decided to join Doris and Jonathon in Big Sur, taking their chances on having no reservations. When they arrive there is no room for them at the hotel, and after looking for miles around, they discover there is no room for them in town. Feeling guilty, Jackie moves in with Doris while Sid moves in with Jonathon, not at all the weekend that they had planned. Oh yes, just one more thing—Cy decides to join them, too, and puts Doris to work.

Written by: William Raynor, Myles Wilder; Patrick O'Neal as Jonathon Rush, Sid Melton as Sid, Paul Vaughn as Clerk

Groovy Day Facts:
   Instead of bartering with Cy to get a day off, Jackie simply called into work sick.
   Jackie eats half a ham sandwich since her mother is Jewish but her father isn't.
   Cy contacted Jackie's mother to find out where Doris was staying for the weekend. He told her Jackie would get a raise in exchange for the information.

Rooming with Sid, Jonathon discovers that he not only snores, but his suitcase is filled with ticking, waterproof wristwatches.

While on her long weekend, Cy and Doris stay up until 4:30 A.M. to complete a story for the magazine.

Last appearance of Jonathon Rusk in the series.

*today's world* the now magazine:
A story on cryogenics.

Doris Day Movie Find!:
"You Make Me Want You" from *With Six You Get Eggroll* [1968]

Sid Melton appears in this episode as Jackie Parker's friend. He later became Jackie Joseph's brother-in-law, and shares his memories of working on the series: "Jackie was great. She was perfect as the secretary, and we went with Doris and her boyfriend on their vacation and intruded on them. It was a lot of fun, too. I was pretty fortunate working with these people, and the scripts were great.

"I haven't seen Doris in a few years, but she called a while back. It was easy to work with her. And to work with Doris, the biggest box office actress of all time, was just wonderful."

**"It's A Dog's Life"**
[In the chronology of the series, "It's A Dog's Life" is the last episode]
Production Dates: October 2-5, 1972
Original Airdate: January 29, 1973
Directed by: Roger Duchowny

Doris finally finds the love of her life. After losing a husband, moving a few times, changing jobs, traveling all over the world and countless marriage proposals, Doris Martin meets Biggest and falls in love instantly. After finding him abandoned, lost and alone, she brings Biggest home and the chemistry is perfect. The battle now begins with her new landlord and old nemesis Willard Jarvis, who doesn't allow pets in his apartment building and doesn't like dogs. Mr. Jarvis firmly believes at the moment that a man's friend is not a dog, but his mother. Of all the battles Doris fought through the years—some won and some lost—she *must* win this one...

It is her biggest win: Not only can Biggest stay, but Doris and Mr. Jarvis have finally found a common ground: the well-being of animals. Mr. Jarvis actually adopts two dogs himself, agrees to let renters have pets, and they all lived happily ever after.

Note: The future building of *today's world* is seen in this episode. Cy Bennett reveals that it will have everything you need to publish a modern magazine: electronic printing presses, a TV scanning screen (computer) connected to its correspondents all over the world (satellite), a whole network of "laser beams" and a television studio for news broadcasts. He also tells Doris that "by the time this building is completed you may not be with this magazine anymore." (Maybe in Carmel with Biggest? See *Doris Day's Best Friends* series.)

Written by: Arthur Julian; Billy De Wolfe as Mr. Jarvis, Henry Corden as Mr. Lohman, Ford Lile as the Policeman, Cliff Norton as the Animal Control Man (Mr. Genson), Biggest and Myra Muffin as the canines (actually two of Doris Day's dogs).

Groovy Day Facts:

Neighbors Lance and Lester throw a party until 3:00 A.M. and the sound of music, dancing, stomping and high heels keeps everyone in the building awake—then the girls arrive.

Doris visits with Mr. Lohman in the laundry room about pets in the building. He then says he'd better get back to his wife because she is jealous of her.

As for the newlyweds, the Sinclairs, the honeymoon is over. Her mother's loudness keeps the neighbors awake and he's now sleeping on the couch.

Biggest retrieves Mr. Jarvis's wallet—like Nelson had earlier with Jarvis's personal items.

Doris threatens to write a story and expose Jarvis—not unlike when he worked for the electric company and Mr. Nicholson made a similar threat.

Mr. Jarvis says man's best friend is not a dog but "is his mother." Mr. Jarvis calls his dog Myra, which was his mother's name.

Name droppings in the episode include Cy saying he dined with the Rawlings. The name of the man with the animal shelter is Genson.

The last appearance of Mr. Jarvis.

*today's world* the now magazine:

An article about no pets allowed in apartments

The "future of news" through *today's world* magazine

### *THE DORIS DAY SHOW* SPECIAL EPISODES

While each episode of the series can be considered special in its own way, there was a handful in which a standard theme (i.e., Christmas) or a unique storyline (Doris befriending a millionaire) was incorporated into the show. The following are these special episodes:

### DORIS AND THE MILLIONAIRE

In the course of *The Doris Day Show*, there was a pair of special two-part episodes. Together, the episodes ran for an hour but were aired separately in the half-hour time allotted for the series. Both of these featured multimillionaire William Tyler, a recluse who not only valued his privacy but Doris Martin as well.

Lew Ayres played William Tyler in the episodes. Doris Day remarked that he was one of her favorite stars when she was growing up and she used to watch his movies as a child. She also said he was a beautiful person who shared her passion for peanut butter.

## "Doris Hires A Millionaire"
Production Dates: November 3-6, 1969 (part I); December 19-23, 1969 (part II)
Original Airdates: February 23 and March 2, 1970

Written by Budd Grossman [part I]; Norman Paul, Jack Elinson [part II]; Lew Ayres as William Tyler, Paul Smith as Ron Harvey, Ross Elliott as Mr. Clark, John Stuart as Mr. Bradford, Issa Arnal as Helen, John Lawrence as Policeman

Part 1: *today's world* could get the scoop of the year: they have received a tip that reclusive millionaire William Tyler is in San Francisco. The last picture of him was taken 30 years ago, so Mr. Nicholson sends ace reporter Ron Harvey on the chase. Mr. Harvey, using his expense account, will stop at nothing covering every bar and strip club in the city where he thinks a millionaire would be. During her lunch hour in the park, Doris meets a nice, older, down-on-his-luck gentleman, who is being harassed by a policeman. Doris defends him and then shares her lunch with him. She finds this man (who introduces himself as Bill Th-

With Lew Ayres.

ompson) is very intelligent and different. She decides to help him find a job. Doris first asks *today's world* and then discovers he's worked on a farm. So she brings him home to meet Buck and the kids, and he is hired to replace Leroy B. Simpson (who now operates a local gas station). Bill Thompson ends up doing a great job, but seems to have a secret identity. Is Doris Martin about to discover who he really is??

Part 2: *today's world*, unable to find millionaire William Tyler for their next cover story, decides to finally abandon the idea, but are left with no cover story for the next issue. Doris suggests her new friend Bill Thompson, a down-on-his-luck man who is now working on her farm, who's had a very interesting life. Mr. Nicholson loves the idea and sends Ron Harvey to cover it. On the farm later that day, Billy and Toby discover Mr. Thompson's true identity: he is millionaire William Tyler. Doris and Buck, who have grown fond of him, are surprised, but decide to keep his identity a secret. But Mr. Harvey is on his way with camera in hand. Will he expose the real William Tyler?

Groovy Day Facts:
We learn that the evening meal at the farm is at 7:00 P.M., since Doris started working.
Buck likes to play gin rummy.
Under the alias Bill Thompson, William Tyler is hired as Buck's farm-hand for $50 a month, room and board included.

Doris Day Movie Find!:
Lew Ayres was once married to Ginger Rogers, who starred with Doris in *Storm Warning* [1951].

**"Doris Leaves *today's world*"**
Production Dates: August 3-6, 1970 (part I); August 10-13, 1970 (part II)
Original Airdates: October 12 and 19, 1970

Written by: Jack Elinson, Norman Paul; Lew Ayres as William Tyler, Teru Shimada as Mr. Orokumu, Richard Angarola as Mr. Constantine, John Stuart as Jameson, J. Pat Cranshaw as Fred, Rob Hathaway as Tom Roberts, Tamara Mosahid as Dancer

Part 1: After she has worked at *today's world* for more than a year, Mr. Nicholson gets Doris a $10 raise for all of her good work. Later, while eating her lunch in the park, Doris meets her old friend, multimillionaire William Tyler. He is in San Francisco to hire—with a huge salary—a new secretary: Doris Martin. After much thought, Doris accepts. She is given a wonderful going-away party at the magazine and a standing offer to return if she wishes. Doris's new job includes a brand-new office with a private

entrance for William Tyler and her very own male secretary. Her very first task comes in the middle of the night when she is assigned to go to Tokyo, Japan, where she begins a worldwide, nonstop adventure.

Part 2: Starting in Tokyo, Doris is adjusting well to her new job as William Tyler's secretary. She travels constantly from Japan to San Francisco, to Switzerland, to a small country in Africa, and to the deep sea. One thing isn't quite right with her new job: Billy and Toby miss her very much and she misses them as well. She is heartbroken after canceling a baseball game she had promised to take them to. While on a long business trip in Greece with Mr. Tyler, Doris is anxious to go home to her family. She discusses her problem with Mr. Tyler who promises to give it all of his attention. The next day, however, while still in Greece, Doris receives an emergency phone call from San Francisco. Billy tells her that when Grandpa went to pick up Toby from school he wasn't there. Doris is in a panic and in another continent, far, far away from her missing son...

Groovy Day Facts:

To prevent the publication of a recent photograph they acquired, William Tyler purchased the *Washington Herald* newspaper.

Tyler offers Doris a starting salary of $25,000 a year as his secretary, which is more than what Mr. Nicholson earns.

The gift Doris receives from *today's world* at her going-away party is a framed cover of the first magazine she worked on while there.

Mr. Tyler's private cook is Chef Pierre.

Doris Day Movie Find!:

This episode is reminiscent of Doris's *The Man Who Knew Too Much* [1956], and the mother separated from her missing child.

Doris also went to Switzerland in *Caprice* [1967].

Guest Star Mini-Bio:

He starred with Garbo in *The Kiss*, but it was his role of Paul Baumer in the original *All Quiet on the Western Front* that brought Lew Ayres critical and commercial success. He furthered his standing with audiences with *Holiday* and starring in a series of Dr. Kildare movies. When he declared himself a pacificist during WWII, Ayres suffered a severe backlash from the press and theater owners. He did, however, serve the U.S. heroically as a medic in the South Pacific and as a Chaplain's aide during the war. After the war, Ayres made a successful return to film in *The Dark Mirror*, *The Unfaithful*, and *Johnny Belinda*, for which he was Oscar-nominated. Later work included parts in *Advise & Consent*, *The Carpetbaggers* and *Battle for the Planet of the Apes*.

## DORIS'S CHRISTMAS PRESENT

Like many other television series, *The Doris Day Show* had the obligatory Christmas shows, of which there were three. The first two involved much of the holiday spirit and customs, from exchanging gifts to having parties, as well as allowing Doris to sing holiday tunes. The third Christmas show, however, was unlike traditional fare in that it featured a murder!

**"A Two Family Christmas"**
Production Dates: October 20-23, 1969
Original Airdate: December 22, 1969
Directed by: Lawrence Dobkin

The staff at *today's world* and Buck at the ranch are all getting ready for Christmas. Buck has a 22-pound turkey and asks Doris to invite her friends at the magazine to celebrate with them and the kids. Unfortunately, they have other plans. Meanwhile, Mr. Nicholson is worried about another bad and embarrassing office Christmas party. As he explained to Doris before she started working there, he now asks her help to prevent another fiasco. Doris reluctantly accepts and works her Christmas magic to create harmony and love in the office. Doris finally comes home, where Billy and Toby are finding it hard to get to sleep. Toby is worried about Santa Claus's journey when, in a big surprise, carolers are heard outside the house. It is Mr. Nicholson, Myrna and Mr. Harvey, who changed their plans to celebrate the holiday with their favorite family.

Written by: Jack Elinson, Norman Paul; Paul Smith as Ron Harvey, David Manzy as Dave, Carleen Frans as Eileen, J.B. Douglas as Mr. Singer

Groovy Day Facts:

Myrna plans to go to Squaw Valley while Mr. Nicholson has reservations at Palm Springs and Ron Harvey is flying to Acapulco for the holidays.

To keep the party crowd from getting out of hand, Doris waters down Ron's holiday concoction, introduces Myrna to Mr. Singer, who works in accounting, and hooks up Ron with the magazine's new research assistant.

Doris and Buck almost give the secret away as Toby walks down the stairs.

With Philip Brown, Denver Pyle and Tod Starke.

Buck has a picture of Doris on a bearskin rug—as a baby.

There is an antique player-piano in the living room.

Doris Day Movie Find!:

Myrna does Jimmy Durante impersonations. Durante co-starred with Doris in *Billy Rose's Jumbo* [1962].

**"It's Christmas Time in the City"**
Production Dates: October 26-29, 1970
Original Airdate: December 21, 1970
Directed by Denver Pyle

Mr. Jarvis, a big fan of Dickens' *Scrooge*, is desperately trying to forget all about Christmas, his worst time of the year. The Palluccis decorate the building in grand festive style, and Louie prepares a feast fit for a king. Doris has decorated her apartment beautifully and many guests will be gathered for her Christmas party: Buck, Angie and Louie Pallucci, Mr. Nicholson, Myrna, Ron Harvey and Ethel. Mr. Jarvis is also invited. Not only does he decline, but threatens to do all he can to stop it. Will he succeed? Can Doris use her Christmas magic on Mr. Jarvis?

The cast of season three.

Written by: Jack Elinson, Norman Paul; Kaye Ballard as Angie Pallucci, Billy De Wolfe as Mr. Jarvis, Denver Pyle as Buck, Bernie Kopell as Louie Pallucci, Carol Worthington as Ethel, John Lawrence as Santa Claus

Groovy Day Facts:

Although they agreed not to exchange gifts, Doris gives Myrna a $29.95 evening bag and Myrna gives her a $32.50 jewelry box.

Toby wants a rocketship toy for Christmas—even though he broke Billy's in season one.

Ron dances with Ethel and also plays a miniature trumpet.

In addition to the Mr. Jarvis's aforementioned grievances, he finds the clanging of bells irritating. Also, Christmas lights are much too bright and could overload the circuits. They are also a nuisance in that should they should fall and break, shattered glass would cover the walk.

Doris succeeds in winning over Mr. Jarvis after he hears her singing "Silver Bells."

Carol Worthington was seen in four episodes as different characters before playing Doris's sitter Ethel. This was her last appearance.

The last appearance of Buck Webb in the series.

## "Whodunnit, Doris?"

Production Dates: October 25-28, 1971
Original Airdate: December 13, 1971
Directed by: Marc Daniels

As Christmas approaches, Doris gets involved in a holiday murder mystery. Doris is returning to her car from an appointment and sees a Santa Claus going down a chimney. As a good reporter and always prepared, with camera in hand, she takes a picture of him. As she returns to her car, she hears a gunshot. She runs into the house and finds a victim on the floor, and a Santa Claus holding a gun. With the help of Jackie, a few of Santa's helpers, and a skeptic Cy, Doris has to prove, with a little of her Christmas magic, Santa's innocence before Christmas.

With Charles Nelson Reilly.

Written by: Gary Belkin; Charles Nelson Reilly as Ralph Mantley, Cliff Norton as Harry Miller, Ken Lynch as Detective Broder, Kennedy W. Gordy as Boy, Walter Sande as Head Santa Claus

Groovy Day Facts:

Detective Broder recognized Doris from an earlier jewel robbery ["Mr. & Mrs. Raffles"], recalling she gave him "a lot of trouble."

97-year-old Nelson Mantley not only stole his nephew's girl, but owed Harry Miller $200 for a TV repair bill.

Doris is held up at gunpoint once again.

Harry charges Cy $100 to fix his TV set. Had it been Doris's set, he would have done it for free.

Santa's Helpers is an actual group of businessmen and women who help out the less fortunate during the holiday season.

Walter Sande appeared three previous times as a Mill Valley doctor.

Doris Day Music Find!:

Songs heard in the Christmas episodes include:

"Deck the Halls"

"God Rest Ye Merry Gentlemen"

"Jingle Bells"

"Silent Night"

"Silver Bells"

"There's a Rising Moon (for Every Falling Star)" from Doris's film *Young at Heart* [1954]

## DORIS—A LA MODE

There were four "fashion shows" throughout the series in which Doris Martin was called upon -either willingly or by accident—to present the latest designs. And the episodes were exceptional. Doris wore trendy, stylish and sometimes outrageous clothes [i.e., a gown made from a garment bag in season three]. Doris Day may have been over 40 when she started the show, but she was extremely fit and beautiful. These episodes were favorites with viewers and Doris herself. In all likelihood, she can be credited with starting with what is known as "Fashion Television."

"We did the fashion shows," Doris remarked to an audience of fans in Carmel in the 1980s. "And what a time we had with Barbara [Lampson] working out hairdos and to have all these different things going. And Barbara and Connie [Edney] and I did that. The three of us did those fashion shows and worked everything out. They were really, really well done, I have to admit it. We did an awful lot in a half an hour. That was great fun."

**"Doris, the Model"**

Production Dates: September 29, 30, October 1, 2, 1969

Original Airdate: November 17, 1969

Directed by Hal Cooper

Written by Norman Paul, Jack Elinson; Johnny Haymer as Montagne, Paul Smith as Ron Harvey, Gail Stevens as Yvette, Arlyn Genson as Simone, Paul Marin as Hal, Larry Gelman as Nat, Sam Javis as the Waiter, Jerry Fitzpatrick as the Valet

When Doris Martin started her workweek, she had no idea that she would end up on the runway. *today's world* is doing a story on fashion designer Mr. Montagne's new fashion collection. Mr. Nicholson asks Doris and Myrna to pick up Mr. Montagne and his models at the airport. Coming in from Paris on a long flight, the models are hungry. Mr. Montagne informs Doris that his beautiful models are on a strict diet but have a secret passion for food, especially for American delicatessen food. So security guard Doris Martin offers her services with Myrna's help to keep an eye on the models. They both do a good job intercepting food, but eventually they fall asleep while the models run away and disappear…At the event, hosted by Ron Harvey, Doris, by default, trepidation and ultimately success, becomes the only model for the show.

Groovy Day Facts:

Nat & Hal owned a delicatessen in the show. This is a homage to Doris's favorite deli in Beverly Hills.

Doris Martin acknowledges that she wears wigs in this episode and tries to convince Myrna to do the same.

**"The Fashion Show"**
Production Dates: August 17-20, 1970
Original Airdate: October 26, 1970
Directed by Reza Badiyi

Written by: Jack Elinson, Norman Paul. Johnny Haymer as Montagne, Miguel Landa as Jacques Giroux, Harriet Medin as Marie

A year later, Mr. Montagne is back with a new, top secret, exciting collection. This time his designs are specifically tailored for his new favorite model, Doris Martin. Mr. Nicholson reluctantly agrees to lend Doris for the fashion show as long as she keeps working for the magazine. He needs to deliver a very important stockholder's report without the aid of Colonel Fairburn and needs Doris's help to prepare. So designer, fitters and publishers all work with Doris at the same time. Meanwhile, the House of Robert is out to sabotage the Montagne collection and will stop at nothing—even using Myrna—to steal Mr. Montagne's masterpiece…Ron Harvey hosts the fashion again and the show is a stunning one as promised, until the end when the *piece de resistance* is missing.

Groovy Day Facts:

Added to the end credits: All Furs Used in The Fashion Show Sequence Are of Synthetic Material.

Reza Badiyi was born in Tehran and became an accomplished and respected television director. Reza gave series their signature look including *Baywatch* and *Buffy the Vampire Slayer*. He won the Directors Guild Award for directing the most hours of television. He created the memorable opening sequences for *Hawaii Five-O* and *The Mary Tyler Moore Show* as well as directing episodes of *Mission: Impossible*, *The Six Million Dollar Man* and *The Rockford Files* among many others. Although he disliked directing sitcoms, but directed more episodes of *The Doris Day Show* than any other comedy in his long career. He said the series was not like a standard sitcom; everything was above par from the talents to the production. His masterful rhythm and editing of his fashion show episode is one of his greatest achievements.

## "Gowns by Louie"
Production Dates: December 14-17, 1971
Original Airdate: February 28, 1972
Directed by: William Wiard

Written by: Arthur Julian; Werner Klemperer as Jacques Moreau, Joseph Mell as Louie Salkawitz, Lester Fletcher as Claude, Charles Cirillo as Vito

Jacques Moreau is organizing an event of international proportions: a fashion show involving every top fashion designer from Europe—but no American ones. This is a very important cover story for Cy Bennett and the magazine. At the last minute, Marcel from Marseilles, who is one of France's very best, cannot make the show with his designs. Jacques is in a panic and needs another designer to take his place. After being impressed with Doris's wardrobe, she convinces him to use her designer, Louie. Jacques believes that Louie is French and Doris persuades Louie to share his fashion designs with the world, although he must do so with an acute case of laryngitis. Jackie is the host for the festivities and the fashion show is perfect until the discovery of Louie's Dry Cleaning and Alterations.

Groovy Day Facts:

In the end title credits there is the statement: Fur coat worn in fashion show sequence is of synthetic materials.

Mr. Jarvis makes a cameo appearance at the dry cleaners.

Mrs. Feldman is referred to as one of Louie's customers.

*Frankenstein* is mentioned in this episode as well as Doris's film *Please Don't Eat the Daisies*.

Doris Day Movie Find!:

Joseph Mell appeared in Doris's film *Pillow Talk* [1959].

## "Hospital Benefit"

Production Dates: September 18-20, 22, 1972
Original Airdate: January 22, 1973
Directed by Roger Duchowny

Written by: Laurence Marks; Peter Lawford as Dr. Peter Lawrence, Lee Meriwether as Lois Frazer, Noah Keen as Dr. Robertson, Peggy Rae as Mrs. Dawson, Betty McGuire as Nurse, Jeffrey Mannix as Mannequin

Peter Lawrence wants to generate funds for a new hospital wing. He has tried different ideas but nothing has worked. Doris suggests one of her fashion shows as a fund-raiser and Peter agrees. Doris first meets at the hospital with Lois Frazer. Lois not only listens to her pitch, but shows great concern for Peter, which surprises Doris. Peter then talks to the committee about Doris's idea, but they refuse. Doris, having already done the work of organizing the show, is very upset and furious that they have turned her down. But Cy, with the power of the press, sees that the event is back on. During the extraordinary show, Doris finds out from Jackie, who is hosting the evening, that Lois Frazer is Peter's ex-wife. She also sees that the two are attending the show together.

Groovy Day Facts:

The film *Night in Berlin* was originally to be shown for the hospital benefit, but the movie company backed out.

End credits for *Hospital Benefit* include scenes from the episode's fashion show rather than the usual San Francisco scenes. Fourth and last appearance of Peggy Rae in the series.

Last appearance of Dr. Peter Lawrence.

Guest Star mini-bio:

Lee Meriwether was Miss America 1955 and then was the "Today Girl" on NBC's *Today* show. She then turned to acting and played lead characters in several episodes of *Dr. Kildare*, *The F.B.I.*, *The Time Tunnel* and *Mission: Impossible*. She played Catwoman in the 1966 theatrical release *Batman* and was in *Angel in My Pocket* with Tod Starke. In the 1970s, Meriwether was on the long-running detective series *Barnaby Jones*. Interestingly, Jackie Joseph wrote an episode of *Barnaby Jones*.

Doris Day Movie/Music Finds!:

Songs featured in the fashion show episodes include:

"Au Revoir Is Goodbye with a Smile" from *Do Not Disturb*

"Caprice" from *Caprice*

"Christmas Present" from *The Doris Day Christmas Album*

"Daydreaming" from the album *Duet*

"I'm in Love" single [1948]

"Periwinkle Blue" from the album *I Have Dreamed*

"Pillow Talk" from *Pillow Talk*

"Send Me No Flowers" from *Send Me No Flowers*

"Sorry" single [1967]

"There They Are" single [1966]

"Twinkle and Shine" from the album *Bright & Shiny*

"What Does a Woman Do" from *Midnight Lace*

"What Every Girl Should Know" from the album *What Every Girl Should Know*

"You Oughta Be in Pictures" from *Starlift*

## *THE DORIS DAY SHOW* LOOK: THE CLOTHES

In the first season, Doris Martin's clothing consisted primarily of light, short dresses and occasional slacks, but mainly denim jeans since they were the most practical for day-to-day living in the country. The style, although practical for the setting, was light years away from the sophisticated fashions audiences came to acknowledge with Doris Day in her films.

"I was so connected with clothes in my films," Doris remarked. "I love wearing beautiful things on the screen and paying a lot of attention to what I'm wearing because I think the audience loves it. They like to see you look pretty and smart."

"Doris was uneasy about [the series'] concept from the beginning. In time, we knew it wouldn't work," Don Genson said during the series' run. "When the storyline changed Doris into a well-dressed careerist who has to go into the world and cope with life outside the family home, she felt her role acquired better viewer identification and was closer to her own established image as well. The ratings proved right, for the results were electric. The show moved into the top ten rating and stayed there ever since.

"Recently, for a talk show, Doris decided, mostly for personal reasons, to have a simple hairdo done at home, none of her usual elaborate film makeup and to wear a midi dress with boots. It wasn't a preseason test or anything like that, but it might as well have been because the results were so impressive. Doris simplified her usual TV make-up, which automatically eliminated the early call, and also decided to endorse the midi look for her clothes for the 1970-71 season. She hopes to show it can be individual, exciting and practical. And it must be all of those things for a working woman to move about in it with ease and style.

"[T]here are misconceptions. Many assume that whatever Doris wears, it has to be expensive. This is not necessarily true for her TV series. To stay within the budget and life pattern of the character she plays, Doris's TV fashions come from the stock of a major store in our area. They are geared to the Doris Day image through occasional, minor design changes and with the addition of major and totally personal accessories.

"For one gaucho outfit, Doris substituted a $3 blouse for the original designer's top. For another, she added a $4 hat. And another time, aware of the fashion changeover problems of other women, she used an orange-colored mini under a midi jumper!

"In the past Doris has favored quiet colors and lots of white. Now she used bright yellow and other bold colors. It gives her wardrobe new dimension."

Connie Edney: "Doris has the finest color sense of anyone that I have ever worked with, plus a sure instinct for line. She could easily have been a designer in her own right. This can be seen in the way she has adapted the midi to her needs. Someone else could have made a similar fashion changeover and failed to confidently and successfully walk the thin line between dowdy and the far out. Doris, in my mind, manages the transition so well that I think most people who see the midi on her will look at it and say: 'Gee! That's great. I could wear that!'

"For the show, although we don't do any original designing as such, we do change the clothes enough to make them fit Doris's figure and preferences. One of the things she does, that many women should do and don't, is to simplify everything. Those of us in the fashion field know that inexpensive clothes have more trim than the expensive. The more costly the costume, the closer you come to pure line. So where others may put it on, Doris takes it off. The clothes she wears on this season's shows should fit into the average woman's wardrobe because they are not really expensive, and those that are in, say, a higher price range, can often be found in a modified version, in a less expensive copy.

"Typical of the clothes Doris wears, even in this show, is the long sweater coat this is less than $35 retail. The shirt worn under the coat costs less than $25. We made characteristic Doris Day changes for this. Doris took off the wide belt and substituted a narrow, string one to lower the waistline, added fake snakeskin boots and a bold Western hat! It came out pure Day!

"We also have an evening gown with matching velvet coat that required some changes. The collar is too wide for someone with broad shoulders. So we made the collar seem skinnier by making it a simple, standup collar. We also added fake fur to the hemline and made a matching Cossack hat that can even be used as a muff. Any woman can do the same—even to lengthen a coat—because the fake fur is available by the yard now. I assume that everyone knows Doris used fake fur because she is against the use of animal pelts for fashion and endorses the preservation of wild life movement."

Connie felt that the most important single fashion designer tip Doris would give anyone is to "Think young; welcome change." As for the model herself, Doris Martin weighed 122 pounds in 1972, and was a size eight.

**That little something extra ...**

In many episodes, the cast improvised a bit from the written script, which added to the series' charm. One of the longest improvs occurred in the episode "The Woman Hater," with Doris Day acting without a script throughout the restaurant scene. Most of the time it was Doris herself who diverted just a bit, either on the spur of the moment or by accident. Among the episodes with an unscripted moment that became something extra include:

"Singles Only": Doris tells Billy while he is swimming not to forget to get out of the pool if he has to go to the bathroom.

"The Co-Op": When Mr. Jarvis begins to fix Doris's bath, he accidentally knocks over what Doris says is her "good bath oil." His reply: "It's annoying me!"

"Doris' House Guest": In the office, Cy talks on the telephone while Doris sits on his desk. During the conversation, she accidentally knocks over the pencil holder, emptying the container, but he continues the scene—and she doesn't put them back in place.

"Debt of Honor": When Doris receives cash payments in dollar bills, Jackie touches the money. Doris then jokingly slaps her hand.

"Peeping Tom": Doris, Jackie and Cy sit on her couch and remark they are going to watch the movie *Dr. Jekyll and Mr. Hyde*. Doris then lets out a quick scream, which causes Jackie to jump.

"The Father-Son Weekend": While fishing with Toby, Doris helps pull in his catches. But at one point she leans a little too forward and almost loses her balance.

"Peeping Tom" with John Dehner and Jackie Joseph.

"Sheik of Araby": While giving a speech, Doris loudly bangs her finger on a table, says, "Oww!," then continues with the scene.

"The Songwriter": When Doris sits at the piano, with Billy and Toby on either side, she accidentally bumps Toby. She improvises by apologizing before continuing the scene.

And there are countless episodes in which Doris appears to misstep while walking in a room. Those were quite real as there were electrical cords on the bare floors, hidden under carpeting, which were used for various reasons to film scenes. Rather than do another take, they were kept in. Sometimes she'd say, "What's that on the floor?" and "I tripped on your carpet" while delivering her lines, and other times she continued speaking as if nothing had happened.

## A DISCUSSION WITH JACKIE JOSEPH

*How did you learn you were going to be part of* The Doris Day Show *and what was your reaction?*

My first inkling was from my agent. She said, I know that you don't want to do a series and that you want to stay at home and be Mommy, but they want you for *The Doris Day Show*. All you have to do is say yes, and they promise that if you do the show, they'll only call you in the hours that they need you. That no day would start before twelve. That was their rule. But if you have a late shot, you don't need to show up until later, and only work a few days a week. I've never felt so wanted. And it happened to come, I think, just a few minutes after my husband said you really need to go back to work, because he thought he would never work again.

*Your character, Jackie Parker, had her own "style"—mainly kooky. Where did the idea come from to make her look so unique?*

I think Doris, first of all, got to know me better, just like anyone working on the show. I think after she had gotten to spend time in Hemet [California], where Terry was recuperating after his [motorcycle] accident, she came back laughing at some of the styles and that's where the big hair came from. She called it the Hemet Hairdo. And she thought it was just fun for me to be outrageous, but still behave like nothing was different. It wasn't, "How do you like my hair?" It was the same person while being a little bit more bizarre. But she thought it was funny, and I think there was a "nothing really matters that much" attitude since this was a comedy.

*Your wigs and clothes must have been stored in a special place.*

That was all in the wardrobe department and the hair department. And I think Barbara Lampson, who had been working with Doris for years, and Connie Edney were just having fun. There were times when I might have something from home that could be used, like one time I came back from Hawaii with a muumuu and I'd wear that.

That reminds me. I would have been in two more shows but I had the opportunity to take my mother-in-law and her mother and my children to Hawaii for two weeks. I asked Doris and the producers and they said it was no problem. So they actually wrote me out of two so that I could go and do a family thing. But then I came back with my muumuu, so that explains that.

*Doris obviously loved her clothes, and there were episodes of fashion shows that got bigger with each year.*

Playing dress-up was fun for her and she also thought the audience enjoyed seeing it, like looking through a magazine, seeing styles, and there was so much cuteness it was adorable. You had to sustain belief that one person could model everything in a fashion show and within the blink of the next model a whole set could change. She did two I believe.

Jackie Joseph

*She did two with you and two previously.*

Oh, she did fashion shows in the other life? Interesting. [But] I think for her they had to be fun and continue being glamorous. And the variety of the people she could be when she modeled.

*There were several guest stars on the series and some who became famous after the series. One was Ed Begley Jr.*

Oh yes. I think that was his first job and he was very quiet, very serious. And it's funny. From then on you're always friendly. I see him at events or he'd come help with Actors and Others for Animals. It's like for the rest of your life, because of that one day or one week, you're always friends with the person. He turned out to be an impressive man.

*Peter Lawford?*

I never chitchatted with him. First of all, I don't like to intrude on anybody because I always feel they are thinking what they're going to do next, planning what their work is. Unless someone wants to come to me and make small talk, I believe in people being private on the set. Peter was kind of serious around then. He wasn't silly at all, not like one of the Rat Pack. And Doris was giving him an opportunity to learn how to be a director. I don't think he had done much directing prior to that. I think he was in Peter

Lawford trouble, whatever that was. He lived hard and was extremely nice and there were never any problems on the set as I recall. He was a pretty big star, but to be in a sitcom was something he probably hadn't planned on.

When he directed the show in which I had my fever blister, I think that was his first show ["Debt of Honor"]. I had gotten something on my upper lip and I didn't know what to do about it. It looked like a burned marshmallow. It was huge. I came in and said, "I don't know what to do." The make-up [people] tried to cover it, but Doris came in and said, "Well, that happens to people. Why don't we just act like you've got a thing on your lip?" She referred to it in the show very briefly with "Oh, you've got that thing." So for the rest of the show I had this thing that looked like something should be knocked off of my mouth—but it was my mouth. Several weeks later, because there was a close-up of a conversation, sitting at a little ice-cream table or something in-between Doris and I, I got a sheet asking for a reshoot of it, they wanted to do it over again. That had never happened before. So I looked at the sheet and it said, "Reshoot due to ugliness." It was the funniest call sheet I ever got.

*One of Doris's oldest friends was Billy De Wolfe; however, one wouldn't know that watching the pair in character on the series.*

They were great buddies. They were a lot of fun. He amused everyone by being quietly wry and hysterical. He wasn't a big, loud comic, just an English, civil man.

Billy was such a nice man. My daughter was on a field trip for summer camp and she was standing backwards when a photograph was taken and printed in the newspaper. When she came to see me on the set, Billy came over and said, "Excuse me. Didn't I see you in the newspaper the other day?" And she said, "Yes." He said, "I thought I recognized you." Now that was the kind of sweetness he had, and I think that the interesting thing about people like Billy and Doris, and what certainly spilled over to just about everybody who was ever on the set, was that there were no harsh words. They didn't exist. The word harsh didn't exist. No confrontations. No temper tantrums. That just didn't live there.

*Patrick O'Neal was another leading figure on the series. What were your feelings about him?*

He was kind of mysterious. He played a romantic figure, and of course he would come in from New York and he was married. He was very classy and yet he owned a bar. He was that kind of class.

*And there was Kaye Ballard, too.*

She was always fun. And as fun as she was, that's how kind she was. A very thoughtful woman. Once I went to New York and she took me to what she thought was the best ice cream parlor in New York. Just making people feel important and special. Extremely warm and kind, and of course a brilliant talent.

*John Dehner played your boss and in fact had experience in news reporting before becoming an actor.*

I didn't know that. He certainly had something to reach for. His demeanor was always as a gentleman. Almost a country gentleman. He was a refined, comfortable member of the cast. Easy to be with. It seemed like he was a visiting from the Royal Shakespeare Company, sitting in on a sitcom for a while. It was a job and he enjoyed [it] and there was never any contention on the set, so what wasn't there to enjoy? And he was very nice to my children and me. He had a nice boat and took us all out one day.

*Many times as Cy Bennett he would look like a volcano ready to explode, or his hypochondria would creep in and he'd be sick. How much of his performance, do you feel, was ad-libbed and how much was directed?*

I don't know how much direction there was with his way-out behavior. Say, like during rehearsal, he would try, "Doh-RUS!" or something like that, and Doris would laugh she'd say, "Oh, you got to do that. That's so funny." Or he'd stick his head out the door and go, "JJJahkee!" She just thought that was hysterical because it was so imperious and so lighthearted. And it became part of his character.

*Were you or others able to ad-lib or did you stay strictly to the scripts?*

I think it happened a little, but it usually came out at rehearsal. I mean, it was never while we were shooting. Basically, Doris's show was her script and the costumes. I think a lot of the sets were either from her home or made like a place where she'd live. She worked closely with the set designer, and wanted to be comfortable wherever she was. It's not always too easy.

*Another of Doris's guest stars happened to be Biggest, one of her dogs.*

Oh, she loved him! I think he was so conspicuously special because he was so big!

*How did you become involved with Actors and Others for Animals?*

It was a double whammy for me because it was within the same couple of days of starting the series, Doris leaned over to me and asked, "Do you like animals?" and I said, "Yes." And then I was at a parents' meeting at my children's school and I was [asked the same thing]. I thought what's going on here with the animals? Then there was a meeting and talking about animals and pulling in a few people to form a nucleus, and so that was the beginning. The premise and the intelligence of it all is that anything about animal welfare was on the back page of a throwaway newspaper. They felt if actors did something conspicuous about helping animals and being kind, and spaying and neutering, that people who like actors would do the same. So they decided to become front-page people.

The biggest thing that first happened was, literally at night, when we went to a place where the animal shelter wouldn't deal with this severe problem, where someone had too many animals and it had gotten out of hand. The animals had become basically carnage. So, with Doris, Richard Basehart and a few volunteers, we raided this place and we told the police we were going to do something illegal, so they had to come because something illegal was happening. They didn't arrest us, but Mr. Basehart, that wonderful man, actually got away with a dog under his coat. Then we got to go to the Burbank City Council and tell them why we did that. And at that meeting, there were all these reporters and cameras, and it became front-page news material. We realized how strong the power of the press was when actors were doing this.

*Was the set visited by Doris's film co-stars or famous friends?*

The set wasn't a place where people hung out because it was one constant workday. It was a very busy time considering how relaxed it was, they still pumped out a show every week. It was a place of work. The main time was when there were celebrities in the show itself, like Van Johnson.

*What did a typical day on the set entail?*

We'd get there about twelve, and midday she would have sandwiches brought in from Art's Deli—giant sandwiches, all sorts of wonderful deli sandwiches because there was no lunch break. You'd work from noon til six or seven—and the crew loved that. You'd have your mornings; you could always sit and have a sandwich while shots were being set up; and she loved to eat half a cantaloupe with Rocky Road ice cream. Loved it.

*Did you rehearse much? Did you get your scripts in advance?*

On the first day of work was always a rehearsal. We really came in and, somehow, we walked the show a bit. We rehearsed a bit, but not a lot. Maybe not the day players. I think the show was moving so fast that they didn't have the luxury of sending a script.

*Which one was your favorite episode?*

A lot of them were fun. The going to Big Sur episode with Sid [Melton] was fun because I was such an irritating person. I liked the political one ["The People's Choice"] because we got to be outrageous and wear funny little hats. I loved "Peeping Tom," and I loved Larry Hovis in it. We were good friends.

*Other than Doris Day, what were the constants on the series? For example, were the main sets frozen [kept untouched and off-limits] after each week?*

The sets stayed basically the same. There might have been a few minor changes, sprucing up, but otherwise things like that was a constant—and so were the sandwiches. It mainly was the people and the stories that changed. There was always a happy ending, even if she lost her Italian lover, it was "well, it appears that wasn't supposed to happen." One would hope one's life was as good-natured as that series was.

*Do you recall Doris disliking a scene or a script and requesting a rewrite?*

If there was ever a time where she wanted something changed, it was never in front of the cast and crew. Any of that kind of business was done privately with the producers or Eddie Feldman or whoever she worked with. She was never a conspicuous boss.

*In the fifth season, Doris became executive producer of the series. Was there a change in the way business was conducted?*

If there was, it was not part of her demeanor. She never displayed her "in-chargeness"—only when it came to parties or things like that. Obviously, she was giving them and the fun of having them. We knew she had some kind of clout.

Now, at the end of the day, if she wanted to bring her dogs onto the shooting, she had to get the OK. I guess what I'm trying to say is she never flaunted her position. She really was kind of one of the cast as far as her behavior.

And I was also very impressed that she started her day by swimming every day. She swam and swam and swam then went to work.

*When did you learn that the series was going to end, and what was your reaction?*

I think at some point in the middle of the last year it was a given that that was going to be the last year, and because it was less than a job. It was like an errand. I never put great emphasis on it being a career move. It was just a lucky thing to do, an unexpected.

I just reported to duty. I was disinterested and have been in the business long enough to know work is there and work is gone. You just show up, do the job, and then wait to see if you get another job.

*A few years ago you and Doris privately met in Carmel. What was that like?*

When I went up to Carmel, it was very sweet. She had a suite for me at the Cypress Inn and I remember, I never had a bath with a whirlpool in it,

Jackie Joseph, Pierre Patrick and Doris Day

so I emptied this little thing with bath foam in it, not realizing that when you turn on the whirlpool, one would literally get lost in the suds. I thought I would have to call for help. I was under this mountain of bubbles.

It was fun meeting with her at the country club and having lunch. She was so kind to her fans, and the busboy—she knew everybody by name. I think it was after people had taken pictures of her hiding behind a bush, picking up debris or something and thinking she was this reclusive weird person. But she was sociable and darling, friendly to everybody and loved her new environment.

Going to the house was interesting. I think when we met it was a combination of Easter and her birthday. You had to literally walk over boxes of fan mail and little gifts throughout her house. She said it was more mail than she ever got while working. People are discovering her all the time, and I think she was very serious about wanting to answer all of her mail. For a while we went through it. It was a full time job—and a half—to tend to her thank yous.

*What do you feel was the uniqueness of* The Doris Day Show?

It was glamorous, even though it was light-hearted and fun. It wasn't the glitzy-glamorous. It was a kind of escape that was attractive—like "Oh, I'd like to live in that apartment" or "I'd like to have that kind of job." It didn't have big messages except for a few episodes. It was easy on the eyes.

Our show was kind of easy-going, wasn't it [compared to the CBS comedies]? I don't think of it in those terms. My happy surprise about being on the show was what a nice group of family and friends I fell into. And how kind they were to understand that my main work right then was raising my children. I remember I had a call that was at five o'clock in the evening. They would call me when they knew they needed me in an hour and a half. I didn't live too far and I could get into hair and makeup and they had it all figured out. I was in the pool with my children and the phone would ring: "Can you come in now?" They trusted me that much that I would do that, and it was a very luxurious way to be a mommy. That was the way my main thinking was.

## THE AUDIENCE NUMBERS

While *The Doris Day Show* had an irregular yearly Nielsen rating, it consistently ranked #1 in its time slot. In the five-year season averages [from September 1968 through March 1973], *The Doris Day Show* achieved a 21.1 rating with a 33% share, compared to ABC, who had a 18.3 ratings/ 28% share with various shows, including *Monday Night Football*, and NBC's *Monday Night at the Movies'* 19.6 rating/31% share. Just under half of the series' audience were adult women from 18-49; however, 27% were adult men and the same percent for children and teenagers.

For Season One [1968-1969], the average Nielsen rating was less than 21.0 and placed #30 for the season among all shows on television. CBS's Tuesday night line-up for the season was *The Red Skeleton Show*, *The Doris Day Show*, *60 Minutes / Specials*. NBC aired a movie of the week to compete with *The Doris Day Show*, while *N.Y.P.D.* was shown on ABC.

In Season Two [1969-1970], when CBS moved the series from Tuesday to Monday nights for the remainder of the run, the average Nielsen rating jumped to 22.8 and the series placed #10 for the season. CBS's Monday night line-up consisted of *Gunsmoke*, *Here's Lucy*, *Mayberry, R.F.D.*, *The Doris Day Show*, *The Carol Burnett Show*. Competing against *The Doris Day Show* was a movie of the week on NBC, while ABC aired *The Survivors*.

As for Season Three [1970-1971], the average Nielsen rating slipped to 20.7; however, *The Doris Day Show* placed #20 for the season among all shows on television. CBS's Monday night shows were the same as the 1969-70 season. Competing against *The Doris Day Show* was a movie of the week on NBC, while ABC premiered *NFL Monday Night Football*.

With Season Four [1971-1972], the series' average Nielsen rating increased to 21.2 and placed #23 for the season. CBS's Monday night shows were *Gunsmoke*, *Here's Lucy*, *The Doris Day Show*, *My Three Sons*, and *Arnie*. NBC showed a movie of the week, while ABC aired *NFL Monday Night Football* opposite *The Doris Day Show*.

There was a slight decline in Season Five's [1972-1973] Nielsen rating, with an average of about 20.0. After a three-season battle, ABC's *Monday Night Football* overtook the series in the year-end ratings; however, *The Doris Day Show* continued to lure audiences from the games. Only after *The Doris Day Show* left the air did *Monday Night Football* become a big rating's winner. For the 1972-73 season, the CBS Monday night line-up included *Gunsmoke*, *Here's Lucy*, *The Doris Day Show* and *The New Bill*

*Cosby Show.* Airing opposite *The Doris Day Show* was a movie of the week on NBC.

*The Doris Day Show* began airing in foreign markets while it was originally airing on CBS. It was distributed by Pearson International for the world outside the U.S. The show was dubbed into French, Italian, German, Spanish and Japanese. Surprisingly, in the U.K., where Doris has had a huge fan base, *The Doris Day Show* was not shown in its entirety. In fact, only 26 episodes culled from the last two seasons were aired, from July 9, 1973 through February 12, 1974, on ITV. However, in France and Canada (where the series' title was changed to *Que Sera, Sera*), the first three seasons were televised in French and were met with large audiences. In 1976, Worldvision Enterprises licensed the rights for 25 years to distribute the series worldwide, covering both foreign and domestic (North America) markets. It was acquired by a few U.S. locals channels, including KONG-TV in Washington state, as well as on the CBN cable station in the 1980s.

# The Television Specials

The 1960s and '70s were a great time for television variety shows and music specials, from Dean Martin to Streisand, Elvis, Ann-Margret, Sinatra—even the famous mime, Marcel Marceau—had a few. Doris was already on her 70th charted single and had yet to present a vocal performance on television, although she had been seen singing on film. After a few years into her television series, CBS wanted a Doris Day "concert" for television where she would finally perform those magical songs that people had loved for the past 30 years. Rather than one, it was agreed to do two television specials, which fulfilled Doris's contract with the network.

## THE DORIS MARY ANNE KAPPLEHOFF SPECIAL
[also known as *The Doris Day Special*]
First televised March 14, 1971, CBS-TV

Doris Day's first variety special opens with a filmed montage (shot by *"The Doris Day Show"* cinematographer Richard Rawlings) of her singing "Secret Love" and then bicycling through parks and schools accompanied by a group of children on bicycles and policemen on motorcycles. Over the segment she sings "Who Will Buy?," "Feelin' Groovy" and "Ob-la-di, Ob-la-da."

The remainder of the program is set in a garden. Doris sings "It's Lovely Up Here," then introduces five of her dogs and sings "You Must Have Been a Beautiful Baby." Guest Perry Como arrives and after a short banter with Doris, he sings "Didn't We?"

281

In a fashion show segment, Doris models several new designs through still photographs and comments on the styles. Two production numbers are integrated: "Gypsy in My Soul," with two male dancers in Spanish-influenced costumes, and "Them Was the Good Old Days," with several male and female dancers, in which Doris wears a current fashion influenced by the flappers of the 1920s.

Back on the garden set, Doris joins Perry in a medley of "When You Were Sweet Sixteen," "Everybody Loves a Lover," "Meditation," "Quiet Nights of Quiet Stars" and "If I Had to Live My Life Over."

Doris reminisces about her early days in show business and then presents film clips from *Calamity Jane*, *That Touch of Mink*, *Pillow Talk*, *Young at Heart*, *Love Me or Leave Me*, *By the Light of the Silvery Moon* and *Midnight Lace*. In each, she is either whimpering or crying hysterically. Rock Hudson makes a cameo appearance, in which she introduces him as Roy Fitzgerald from Illinois, then calls him Tab Hunter. He storms off, so Doris stomps her foot and demands "Tab" to return and kiss her goodbye. Rock returns, dips her in his arms, and carries out her request.

Doris concludes with "Both Sides Now," "It's Magic" and "Sentimental Journey" in the garden set that slowly turns to black. By the time of "Sentimental Journey," the sole lighting is on Doris, which demands attention by the viewer to her still powerful voice.

CREDITS:

| | |
|---|---|
| Origination: | Hollywood (tape and film) |
| Star: | Doris Day |
| Special Guest Star: | Perry Como |
| Executive Producers: | Don Genson and Terry Melcher |
| Produced: | Saul Ilson and Ernest Chambers |
| Directed: | Bill Foster |
| Written: | Saul Ilson, Ernest Chambers, Garry Belkin and Alex Barris |
| Choreographer: | Kevin Carlisle |
| Music Arranger and Director: | Jimmie Haskell |
| Vocal Arrangements and Musical Material: | George Wyle |
| Art Director: | Michael Baugh |
| Costumes: | Sal Anthony |

| | |
|---|---|
| Dance Sketching: | Hal Hidey |
| Production Manager: | Abby Singer |
| Lighting Director: | George Schamp |
| Technical Director: | Dick Hall |
| Set Decorator: | Charles Kreiner |
| Theme Song: | "Sentimental Journey" |

Doris finally offered her millions of fans what they were waiting for with this special: a comfortable set, 22 wardrobe changes, and the song selection with music that was perfect. She combined standards along with current songs, which were suggested by Terry Melcher. Although the special was an hour long, additional segments and extended scenes were filmed but did not make it into the final cut, including Doris talking about her journey from Cincinnati to Hollywood and singing (with a humorously exaggerated New York accent) "You Ought to Be in Pictures."

Jimmie Haskell, who was already familiar with Doris by working on her television series, was hired as the musical director for the special. Haskell is a three-time Grammy winner in the Best Arrangement Accompanying Vocalist(s) category. He won in 1967 for "Ode to Billie Joe," recorded by Bobbie Gentry; 1970's "Bridge Over Troubled Water" by Simon and Garfunkel; and Chicago's "If You Leave Me Now" from 1976.

The special was actually produced in April 1970, but CBS held off airing it until the following year when it was televised with a group of specials by others, including Barbra Streisand and Burt Bacharach. The reason for this delay was simply the network's idea of a major event, which consisted of a night of variety/music specials to grab high ratings.

**Would you believe a night big enough to hold "Born Free" Burt Bacharach Rudolf Nureyev Tom Jones Barbra Streisand Doris Day and Perry Como?**

You better believe it:
7 pm. **Born Free** starring Bill Travers and Elsa, the Lion.
9 pm. **The Burt Bacharach Special** *(Not seen on Ch. 16)* starring Burt Bacharach, with Rudolf Nureyev, special guest star Tom Jones. And a special appearance by Barbra Streisand.
10 pm. **The Doris Mary Anne Kapplehoff Special** starring Doris Day and her special guest Perry Como. *(Not seen on Ch. 16)*

**TONIGHT ON CBS◉2,9,16,43**

The unconventional title stemmed from the fact that several specials by entertainers were simply titled with the star's name. Doris thought it would be cute to use her real name instead, and although CBS was hesitant at first, they agreed. This provided the network to promote the special with the tag "Who is Doris Mary Anne Kapplehoff?" and enticing the television audience to view it. In addition, Doris's name was misspelled in the title. Kappelhoff is the correct spelling.

## CBS PRESS RELEASES TO PROMOTE THE SPECIAL:

February 10, 1971

### Doris Day: A Hard Day On a Bicycle

"I thought riding a bicycle was easy until I rode with 20 children, the Los Angeles Police Department motor drill team and a camera crew—all at the same time," explains Doris Day, an avid bicyclist.

The bicycle riding that Miss Day is referring to is part of the opening segment of her first television special, "The Mary Anne Kapplehoff Special," to be broadcast Sunday, March 14 (10:00-11:00 PM, EST) in color on the CBS Television Network.

Miss Day begins her ride traveling through a plush golf course, then on to an elementary school where she is joined by some 20 boys and girls between the ages of 8 and 12.

"Those kids, none of them professional bicyclists, did some pretty fancy riding. While I pedaled a relatively straight line, the director had them weaving in and out of buildings and all around me.

"Up to that point, my job was pretty simple, then came the police on their motorcycles. While they went through some of their precision maneuvers, I was supposed to ride through their lines singing.

"I must admit I was a bit leery about the whole thing, but their expertise made the ride extremely safe. Timing was crucial; I had to speed up, slow down, turn, go straight and all the time the cameraman was trying to follow me and avoid being run over by the motorcycles."

To accomplish this feat, the cameraman did some pretty fancy maneuvering too. With a hand-held camera, he seated himself in the middle of the moving wheels, lay on his back at the edge of a motorized figure eight performance and at one point even mounted, backward, one of the motorcycles being driven by a highly skilled policeman.

"Needless to say, I was pretty tired after all that riding," concluded Miss Day. "I am, however, proud of myself for not falling off the bike once. But from now on, I think I'll restrict my bicycling to leisure riding."

"It's no secret, I should think, that I'm a dog lover," Doris remarked at the time of the special. "On my CBS Television Network special my only guests were six dogs and Perry Como. The six dogs happened to have been mine. An enterprising friend is betting on when the next dog will be born and has promised to donate half the proceeds to the Fund for Animals.

"Whenever I get depressed about how little I can really do about all the homeless strays in the U.S. alone, I think of those people who so often complain at election time that theirs is only one vote and what possible good can it do. It can—and does—do a lot of good. Forty million of those one votes will put a man in the White House—not a single voter has more than that one lone vote."

"I guess I'm a bike nut. I acquire and dispose of them the way some car nuts changes cars. Right now I have an English lightweight, an ordinary American balloon-tired job, a chain-drive tricycle with a big cargo basket mounted between the rear wheels, and what may be the only bicycle ever manufactured in India. At least, I've never known anyone

else who had one."

Doris purchased a bicycle at a police auction and raved that it "was a terrific buy. It cost me only $15. It looks like any other standard lightweight, and it was by accident, long after I bought it, that I happened to spot 'Product of India' stamped on the frame. I was thrilled. For me, acquiring bikes is a lot like acquiring antiques. The real fun of it is digging up unusual bargains, especially at unexpected sources. Just about anybody can go into a bicycle store and buy a shiny new one. But what's the fun in that? As a matter of fact, I think I've owned only one brandnew bike in my entire bicycling career."

"I'm not particularly mechanically inclined," Doris admitted when it came to fixing bicycles. "But I can take a bike apart and put it back together again pretty well—all except for coaster brakes. I tried that once, and once was enough."

February 23, 1971

### Doris Day Wanted Realism and She Got It

The order of the day was beauty through realism. Nothing artificial was allowed.

The scene: A lavish garden patterned after Doris Day's own backyard.

The place: A studio at CBS Television City in Hollywood.

The purpose: The taping of Miss Day's first television special.

The result: "The Doris Mary Anne Kappelhoff Special," to be broadcast Sunday, March 14 (10:00-11:00 PM, EST) in color on the CBS Television Network.

It was decided that taping the show in Miss Day's own garden would be too difficult and might destroy it. So the producers of the special did the next best thing—they brought the garden to the studio.

Hundreds of yards of Kentucky bluegrass, bedded in sod, were laid over approximately 11,000 square feet of the studio. Carefully placed in

Singing "Both Sides Now" in the garden set.

With Perry Como.

the garden setting were over 500 assorted potted plants, 30 varieties of trees, numerous azaleas. Highlighting the flora was the yellow disks and white rays of hundreds of daisies, which are Miss Day's favorite flower.

Constructed in the garden was a pond complete with lily pads and water. Then came a gazebo, lawn furniture, two live doves and six of Miss Day's dogs.

Everything was placed so it was maneuverable. The grass could be lifted and the trees and plants could easily be moved out of the camera's way without damaging a single leaf. Hothouse temperatures were maintained, at the discomfort of the humans present, to avoid freezing the flora.

The scene was set—a very beautiful one at that—and the hay fever sufferer who worked on the show can attest to the realism that was attained by Miss Day and her producers.

Perry Como had never worked with Doris Day before her special and he was pleasantly surprised to find out her philosophy of performing was similar to his.

"Doris puts her all into every number. Work doesn't scare her," he said prior to the special's airing. "If it takes all night to do a number right, she'll stay up all night. She studies and plans every move, and when the cameras roll, she looks and acts totally relaxed. I guess the whole point is to make it look easy, even though you break your back to get it that way."

Como admitted when he made his debut as the featured singer for Ted Weems' band, at the age of 24, he had less than three years' experience singing in public. "That night was a trauma, but served to teach me a lesson—always be well prepared. I forgot my line, forgot the song and I even forgot where I was. From that moment on, I began practicing to be cool, calm and collected. Since that day, whenever I appear in front of an audience, I completely memorize everything, leaving nothing to chance."

## DORIS DAY TODAY
First televised February 19, 1975, CBS-TV

This high-energy variety special never stops in intensity from beginning to end. It begins with a montage of photos from her films to a dance explosion with her guests and the song "Anything Goes," showing how not only society has changed in the last few years, but she herself.

The set is a large stage decorated simply with several large panels of embroidered floral patterns and vertical stripes. Doris then sings "Day by Day," accompanied by both formal and casual dressed musicians, combining two appearance styles of the past and present.

"Whatever happened to the old band uniform?" Doris asks. "When I was singing with big bands, all the guys dressed alike—exactly alike. They wore the same shirts, ties, suits, shoes, socks. They even had matching wah-wahs. However, today dressing is a matter of personal choice."

She talks with John Denver and they sing "Exactly Like You," then playfully kid around with their real names—Doris Kappelhoff and John Dutschendorf—using them in various song lyrics including "Tea for Two,"

"Did You Ever See a Dream Walking?," "Give Me a Little Kiss," "On the Atchison, Topeka and the Santa Fe" and "Put on a Happy Face." John then sings "Follow Me," accompanied by Doris.

An unusual rendition of "My Baby Makes Me Proud"/ "Behind Closed Doors" has Tim Conway singing to his bored housewife [Doris], who dusts an unkempt living room and their young children, whose number increases as the skit progresses. When they get behind closed doors in their 18th-century French-styled bedroom, a still-bored Doris sits on the bed as Tim does a variety of speeded up macho moves, such as riding a motorcycle around the room, dressing as Superman, a boxer, and knight in shining armor, as well as swinging from the chandelier dressed as Zorro.

Doris is joined in a medley of songs from her films and many hit records. Rich Little appears in the sketch, imitating several famous men from Doris's film career. These include Alfred Hitchcock and James Stewart [*The Man Who Knew Too Much*], Kirk Douglas [*Young Man with a Horn*], Jack Lemmon [*It Happened to Jane*], Cary Grant [*That Touch of Mink*], Clark Gable [*Teacher's Pet*], Jimmy Durante

[*Billy Rose's Jumbo*], Rex Harrison [*Midnight Lace*] and James Cagney [*Love Me or Leave Me*].

Against a black set decorated with posters of some of her films, Doris sings "The Way We Were" over a montage of many of her leading men. The Sunshine Medley features Doris and John singing such songs as "You Are the Sunshine of My Life," "Sunshine on My Shoulders," "You Are My Sunshine" and "Walkin' in the Sunshine."

"Midnight at the Oasis" features Doris and Tim as motor home owners on vacation in a littered park, and she sings the song in a role reversal of their earlier skit. The Lockers then perform an elaborate dance routine choreographed by Tony Basil, the sole female member. Inside the camper, Doris and Tim wake to find their living arrangement is quite cramped, with Tim constantly underfoot and continually injuring himself as Doris looks on.

Doris closes the show with "Day by Day" onstage with a sky-blue background and white sheer panels.

CREDITS:

| | |
|---|---|
| Origination: | Hollywood (tape) |
| Starring: | Doris Day |
| Guest Stars: | Tim Conway, Rich Little and The Lockers |
| Special Guest Star: | John Denver |
| Produced: | George Schlatter |
| Directed: | Tony Charmoli |
| Choreography: | Tony Charmoli |
| Written by: | Digby Wolfe and George Schlatter |
| Musical Director: | Tommy Oliver |
| Art Directors: | Brian Bartholomew and Keaton S. Walker |
| Costume Designer: | Michael Travis |
| Associate Producer: | Lee Miller |
| Theme Song: | "Que Sera, Sera" |

George Schlatter was a producer of many television specials and variety shows. He had produced the first five episodes of *The Judy Garland Show*, the hugely successful *T.C.B* special, followed by being executive producer of *Rowan and Martin's Laugh-In* from 1968-1972. In 1975 he was producing the TV hit *Cher*.

Toni Basil was the only female member of the dancing group The Lockers. She later recorded the U.S. #1 song "Mickey," and was nominated for a Grammy Award. She was also Emmy-nominated for her choreography work in *The New Smothers Brothers Comedy Hour*.

Tommy Oliver, hired as the musical director of the special, had worked with Doris in the past, including the *Love Him!* album, and he conducted and arranged the Terry Melcher-produced work. He recalled being in awe of working with Doris. "I was terrified because she was such a big, big star," Oliver said. With *Love Him!*, Oliver hired a big orchestra and sixteen voices to make up the choir, all to accompany Doris in the recordings. "[The album] was a little different sound for her," he said. "Very, very lush." With *Doris Day Today*, Oliver used a successful combination of orchestration and rock music to present the past and present Doris Day. "I absolutely loved her. She is just a really nice, very talented human being."

A point of interest: The special was not recorded at CBS, but at its rival NBC studios in Burbank. This was arguably due to two facts: it was

the studio where producer George Schlatter worked on several shows and that the CBS soundstages were largely booked with other productions.

This special, along with *The Doris Day Show* episodes "The Job," "Doris Leaves *today's world*" and "Doris and the Doctor," were selected as shows available for viewing at the Museum of Television and Radio.

## CBS PRESS RELEASES TO PROMOTE THE SPECIAL:

January 13, 1975

## "Doris Day Today," Music and Comedy Special Highlighting the "Now" World, To Be Broadcast February 19 On the CBS Television Network

"Doris Day Today," a rollicking celebration in music and comedy of what's happening in the "now" world, plus a few glances back over the past, will be presented as an hour-long variety special Wednesday, Feb. 19 (9:00-10:00 PM, EST) on the CBS Television Network.

Joining Miss Day in songs, dances and comedy sketches are guest stars Tim Conway, Rich Little, The Lockers and special guest star John Denver.

Kraft Foods, represented by J. Walter Thompson Co., will sponsor the special...

January 29, 1975

## Rich Little Is a One-Man Band of Actors

Rich Little is everybody's favorite actor. He is also all of Doris Day's favorite leading men.

A talented young impressionist, Little recreates the romantic leads from a dozen Doris Day movies when appears with her as a guest star—or is it guest stars?—on "Doris Day Today"...

From Sinatra to Gable to Stewart to Cagney, the famous voices emerge through the vocal versatility of Little, who got his start doing imitations of his college teachers in Ottawa, Canada.

James Stewart, one of the most frequently imitated of all stars, was so taken with Little's performance on a show in which the two appeared together that he told Rich, "I wish you'd been around 20 years ago. You could have dubbed all my movies."

## DORIS DAY'S BEST FRIENDS

CBN [US cable; the Christian Broadcast Network/the Family Channel]
1985-1986; Premiered July 16, 1985
7:00 P.M. Eastern Standard Time, Sundays

CREDITS:

| | |
|---|---|
| Executive Producers: | David Freyss, Terry Melcher |
| Producer: | Dan Evans |
| Director: | Joe Coleman |
| Writers: | Terry Melcher, Dan Evans |
| Music Director: | Terry Melcher, Bill House |
| Director of Photography/ Post Production Supervisor: | Randy Franken |
| Features Producer/ Production Coordinator: | George Atkinson |
| Features Producer/Reporter: | Steve Reid |
| Videotape Editors: | John Rossi, Steve Childress, Dennis Gross, Brad Rothberg, Lisa Byrne, Roger Vater, Mike Malpass |
| Unit Production Manager: | Jerry Cardwell |
| Make-Up: | Michelle Rede |
| Wardrobe: | Connie Edney |
| Hairstylist: | Barbara Lampson, Jon Thanos |
| Assistant Director: | Dick Broder, Greg Quant |
| Researchers: | John Jenney, Carol-Ann Touchberry |

| | |
|---|---|
| Executive in Charge of Production: | Tim Robertson |
| Theme Song "Best Friend" written: | Terry Melcher, Bill House |
| performed: | Doris Day |

Doris Day returned to a weekly television series in 1985 with *Doris Day's Best Friends*, a project she felt was worthwhile to focus on the welfare of animals while also including skits, music and conversations with guests.

For years, the networks and film studios tried to get Doris Day to agree to appear in one project or another. After her commitment to CBS, Doris spent much of the time with her pet and animal foundations, with public appearances and private rallying to cajole public awareness and to change the laws to ensure better rights for animals.

In early 1985, the Christian Broadcasting Network (CBN) network approached Terry Melcher with an original program idea for his mother. The cable network, which combined religious programs with Westerns and sitcoms of the past, believed they could lure Doris Day back to television with an entertaining, informational series about animals, which would be produced in the Carmel area.

With Mary Tyler Moore.

With Lucille Ball at the Actors and Others for Animals rally.

There was no reason to turn down the CBN offer since Doris had by then completed her move to and her years-long home construction project in Carmel. She had also concluded the more than a decade battle with former business manager Jerome Rosenthal that began in 1968. In fact, Doris had returned to the recording studio to begin work on a new album when the offer for the series arose.

Doris recalled: "We started out to make an album and then that suddenly happened [the *Best Friends* series], so all the songs that we did for the album, we just ended up using them in the show. So it worked out very well, but we didn't have enough for a complete album.

"When I recorded up here, we used a small studio in Monterey that wasn't the greatest—and I'm being kind. It was really funny. There was a theater right outside the door—an adult theater, and the parking lot was right there. There was no air in the studio so I was going outside every few minutes to get a breath of air, and I'd see all these guys driving around. It was sickening!

"I came to work one day to record and I saw Terry and the men from the studio [cornering] a big dog, and he was beautiful. Well, the dog ran away and went up to the ticket office [at] the theater, and he put his feet up like he wants to go to the movies! That was Blue. I named him Blue— and it had nothing to do with the flicks. [He was] a Blue-Tick Hound."

The network hired Terry as co-executive producer for the series. In addition, Doris allowed CBN to air her *Doris Day Show* on the channel since she controlled the rerun rights.

"First of all it's great fun to be working again," Doris told reporters at the press conference announcing the series. "I'm looking forward to that. The show is called *Doris Day's Best Friends*. My best friends are people and animals—not necessarily in that order. That's a terrible thing to say. It's a chance to really work with the animals, to do musical videos, which I am loving, and it's great fun.

"We have a man-in-the-field doing all kinds of film on animals at the zoo. We want to raise money for all the humane societies all over the country. We want to make people more aware of the animal kingdom, and what it means to have a pet, how wonderful it is for the elderly to have pets. We're just going to do all kinds of things and have some funny things we hope. It's going to give me a chance to see some of my old friends, which is really neat."

Twenty-six half-hour episodes were produced in a short time, then aired and rerun on CBN from 1985-86. Doris herself hosted *Doris Day's Best Friends* and while the matter at hand was stories about animals, most episodes featured celebrity guests. Some of them worked with Doris in films or music where they reminisced about their projects of years past, and others were new friends of Doris's. Each included a sit-down chat and the topic of conversation evolved around animals.

There were also skits with some of the guests, which proved entertaining to the television audience. In addition, several episodes included newly recorded songs by Doris:

## EPISODES:

Guest: Rock Hudson

Doris invites Rock Hudson, one of her best friends, to her first show. With it being a new show the budget is small, so he has to come to Carmel all the way from Los Angeles on a very old bus. Rock arrives nine hours later, tired but happy to be with his buddy Doris.

The pair reminisced about their films together. They also talk about wanting to do another film together. Doris remarks her favorite film of theirs was *Pillow Talk*, while Hudson jokingly said his was *Ice Station Zebra*—a non-Day film, but a personal favorite of his.

Guest: Les Brown and His Band of Renown

Traveling with his band of Renown, Les surprises Doris when he arrives with his tour bus for a visit with their favorite lead singer. Doris invites everyone to dinner and to spend the night. During dinner Doris and the musicians reminisce about their days on the road. Band members joke with her as if a day hasn't passed, from talking about playing six weeks at the Café Rouge, where Terry and Doris's mother would come, "and she'd cook meals," to teasing Doris, and her dating Jack Carson in her early Warner Bros. days. Les takes Doris aside to try to convince her to come back with the band. For one magic moment she does as sings "Sentimental Journey."

Guest: Robbie Benson

On his way to visit Doris, Robbie encounters a stray dog that is being watched by a clown. He arrives to Doris's and tells her of the strange occurrence. They decide to retrieve the dog from the clown. Unknown to the pair, however, is that the clown is really a wealthy man and the dog's true owner, who have grown tired of "Barney."

Doris and Robbie take the dog to the veterinarian to be checked for illnesses. The vet tells them that they are required by law to put the animals to sleep "after about three days" if they are not claimed or adopted. Robbie suggests a friend of his may want to adopt Barney, sparing the dog's life.

Guest: Denver Pyle*

Doris is walking a dog when she sees exiting a pickup truck, Denver Pyle, one her dearest old friends, with a new dog that he has just picked up from a clown. Doris and Denver talk about the dog and then move onto *The Doris Day Show*. Doris divulges that she thought of him as her father. It was a touching revelation, and Pyle was moved that Doris held him in such high regard. "Now don't puddle up on me," he says as they hug. "You know what that does to me."

A clip with Doris and Denver from "The Con Man" episode of *The Doris Day Show*, in which he is giving advice his daughter sound advice.

Guest: Earl Holliman

A siren is heard and Doris sees Earl Holliman coming out a police care with a dog. Doris's neighbor's dog has run away again. Doris and Earl talk about the very first event for Actors and Others for Animals with Jackie Joseph at her kid's school. Many stars were in attendance and close to 18,000 people attended.

Steve Reeves has a special report for Doris on the current Actors and Others for Animals event. Stars gathered to talk about their pets and say hello to Doris: David Hasselhoff, Shirley Jones, Greg Evigan, Bo Swenson, Lee Meriwether, Erik Estrada, Jo Anne Worley, Lorne Greene, Peter Falk, Cindy Williams, Dick Sargent, Cesar Romero, Ted Shackleford, Melissa Gilbert, Beatrice Arthur, Ken Berry and Jackie Joseph.

Guest: Biggest*

Biggest's true story started when Doris was filming *The Doris Day Show*. Doris explained: "I think it was about 1970, maybe, and I heard through a friend that a family had left a dog on the porch of a house and they had moved away and left the dog sitting there without any food or water. Well, the rescue man who worked for our organization at the time his name is Ben Wrigley. I called him and he said, 'I would be happy to pick the dog up for you.' Which he did. And when he saw him, he was in terrible condition and had to be taken to a veterinarian and be shaved from head to toe. When I saw him, I wasn't quite sure what kind of dog he was because he was very strange, very funny look-ing—but cute.

"Anyway, I had many dogs at the time and decided that I couldn't keep him, that I would try to find a home. The first home that he was taken to, the people, when they saw him, they were disappointed. I could see that. And they said, 'Well, he's a little bit too big. We were thinking of something smaller.' And I said 'fine.'

"The second place was my secretary at the time and she really liked him and wanted him, but when the manager of the apartment complex saw him, he said that he thought he was too large. So he came back to me.

"The third person was a cousin to my stand-in and she loved him, but he didn't want to be there. And so he spent one night and the follow-ing morning—and by the way, I was crying all the time, every time he left. Something told me that he should stay with me. "But that night he had a very bad time at her house and the next morning she called and she said, 'Doris, [he] wants to be with you.' She said, 'he just doesn't want to stay in my house.' And I said, 'I will be out to get him.' I picked him up, and he has been with me ever since. And he is one of my very special treasures in this world. This is Mr. Biggest."

Guest: Joan Fontaine

Doris meets actress and Carmel resident Joan Fontaine, who had just acquired a new Labrador retriever. Doris convinces her to have the dog professionally trained rather than doing it herself, and lets her use her new trainer. Although Joan and Doris never acted together, they both worked with Alfred Hitchcock. Doris in *The Man Who Knew Too Much* [1956], and Joan in *Rebecca* [1940] and *Suspicion* [1941], for which she won the Best Actress Academy Award.

Joan joked that she had a hand in Doris's career in that she played her records over and over on the sets, and everyone who came into her dressing room heard Doris singing. "Everybody knew Doris Day before most people did." When Joan asked, "What are your plans?" Doris replied, "I never make them." "Who makes them for you?" the confused Joan asked. Doris laughed and explained that she takes one day at a time.

Guest: Cleveland Amory

Animal activist Cleveland Amory visits with Doris about his work with animal rights. He tells Doris how important her ad Real People Wear Fake Furs was the beginning of a great movement.

Guest: Gretchen Wyler

Doris tells the story of and visits the Monterey Bay Aquarium. Actress and animal activist Gretchen Wyler talks to Doris about her plea for animal rescues. Gretchen started the Genesis Awards, which are now seen on the Animal Planet station which presents, every year, the Doris Day Music Award.

Guest: Mickey Gilley

Country singer Mickey Gilley, famous for recordings as well as his Gilley's dance and nightclub, visits Doris. Doris secretly plans for him to leave with a new dog. Mickey shows interest in Barney, one of Doris's dogs. But she declines to give him up because Barney has "two wives. He's a Mormon." Doris suggests he go to the local SPCA and adopt a couple of dogs or cats.

Plus a visit with Judy Ruby and the Doris Day Pet Foundation.

Guest: Danny Cooksey

Doris is at the First Interstate Bank to get a loan for a new veterinarian clinic to provide low-cost medical care for pets and providing spaying and neutering. Bank president Danny asks her about her animals.

Doris tells him about them, and Danny says he'd like to see them. Doris replies he is welcome to visit—once the loan is approved. He readily agrees and she gets the loan. The pair is off for a fun day at Doris's ranch to view her animals.

Main story: The California Rescue Dog Association (CARDA)

The story of CARDA and how dogs are used in rescue situations, from earthquake and avalanche victims to missing people. Also, an explanation on how the dogs are trained to locate people.

Guest: Alan Shepard

Doris is working in her garden with Biggest when the ground starts to shake. A spaceship lands and famous astronaut Alan Shepard comes out with a dog which was sent to space that he is bringing back to earth. They talk about the importance of animals in the space program.

Guest: Howard Keel

On a peaceful country road, a stagecoach travels to its destination. We hear in the distance a bad cowboy shooting away, and he holds up the stagecoach and demands money or the dog, who happens to be Biggest. Doris (as Calamity Jane) sticks her head out and says, "Get lost you four flashin', bushwackin', ride-donkin' coyote!" The robber recognizes Doris, but mistakes her for Dinah Shore. Suddenly a man shooting from a galloping horse comes to her rescue. The robber decides to leave. He then says Doris is Patti Page. "Get lost you mangy varment!" she growls.

The man on the horse coming to Calamity's rescue is Wild Bill Hickok (Howard Keel). Howard and Doris reunite. Howard talks about acting in the show *Dallas* and recording his first solo album. A clip from *Calamity Jane* is shown.

At the end of skit, Doris leaves and says jokingly says she'll watch Howard on *Dynasty*. He, in return, bids adieu to "Dinah." Then the robber reappears and asks Howard if he isn't Gordon MacRae, who was a singer and Doris Day's leading man in four films. Howard chases him off.

Guest: Kaye Ballard*

Kaye Ballard telephones Doris (whom she calls Clara), tired of the hustle and bustle of New York and asks to visit her in Carmel. Kaye arrives with 80 pieces of luggage and, in her best Angie Pallucci, argues with the cabdriver about the baggage handling charge. When he asks for a tip, she slugs him in the arm.

Doris tells Kaye to enjoy her time there and to relax, and that the kitchen is off-limits—to which Kaye replies, "Rats!" When Doris returns from a walk with Biggest, Kaye has defied her and cooked an Italian meal for all the dogs. Doris tells Kaye her dogs can't eat that food, which leads into a discussion about canine nutrition.

Main story: The Monterey County SPCA chapter

The very first free spay and neuter day in Monterey is introduced by Doris and her pet foundation and the local SPCA. Today Spay Day USA has become a national day to have your pet spayed and neutered for free and is presented by the Doris Day Animal League and Animal Foundation.

Guest: Angie Dickinson

Doris invites Angie Dickinson for lunch at Quail Lodge to discuss her pet foundation. They have a wonderful lunch, and when the check comes, Doris discovers she has forgotten her wallet—and Angie did not bring hers, so they can't pay. Doris calls for the manager, Ed Habor. "By the way," she says, "I'm Doris Day. And this is my friend Angie Dickinson." "Oh sure," Ed replies. "I'm Cary Grant. Elmer take those desserts away. Ladies, we don't go for that Hollywood stuff up here. It doesn't make any difference here in Carmel." He refuses to make arrangements with the ladies and calls the sheriff. After waiting all day, the sheriff finally arrives. When he sees Doris Day, he is shocked and surprised and breaks into a beautiful rendition of Doris's classic "Secret Love."

Guest: Tony Randall

Doris is very excited as she is driving to the airport to pick up Tony Randall, who is flying in from New York for a visit. She tells her dog Otto about all the movies she and Tony made together: *Pillow Talk*, *Lover Come Back* and *Send Me No Flowers*. When she arrives to the Monterey Peninsula Airport, Tony isn't there. She telephones him to see what happened. Tony's dog Rose just had four sons and three daughters and he had to stay with her. Of course, Doris understands and gives him advice on taking care of Rose and puppies. Tony says he will visit Doris, but will pedal his way to Carmel—which should take about six months. Doris then convinces Ryan Paul Melcher to take over guest duties for this episode.

Guest: Loni Anderson

Doris is going whale watching today and is expecting Loni Anderson to join her at any moment. When Loni arrives in a long, black stretch limousine, she is dressed in a beautiful evening gown, not quite ready for whale watching. After a quick change of clothes, they set off on a boat for an unbelievable experience at sea. Terry sings "Sea Cruise."

Guest: Jill St. John

On a fun hayride, Doris and Jill St. John talk about their interesting wrangler who Jill thinks is very cute and hopes to meet with him. Doris remarks it is getting cold, and they decide to go back to the house. Doris visits with Jill about her husband and about her life in Aspen.

Guest: Robert Wagner

Doris and Robert Wagner enjoy horseback riding together. Doris rides Freckles beautifully and Robert, who is excellent, has been riding since he was a kid as he explains to Doris during his interview. They talk about his series *Hart to Hart*, his horses, his life with Jill St. John and his career. We learn he was the mysterious wrangler from the previous episode.

Guest: Gary Collins

Doris, driving her van with some of her friends on their way home from the vet, gets a flat tire. She flags down the first car she sees and it is Gary Collins in a limousine. Gary immediately makes a phone call for her to repair the van. He then gives Doris and her friends a lift home—not knowing her friends are eleven dogs. They like Gary so much they tear apart his new tuxedo. Doris invites him inside to change, but he is apprehensive about being with the dogs. "Oh they love you. They wouldn't play with you if they didn't love you," Doris answers.

Gary then sits with Doris and talks about his pets and his animal experiences in Kenya while making *Born Free*.

Guest: Gwen May

A fun visit with Carmel's Gwen May, who rescues animals in trouble. Through Gwen, Doris met Jim, who helped her acquire her Carmel property. Doris then enjoys horseback riding with her roving reporter Steve Reid.

Guest: Tony Bennett*

On a beautiful shopping day in Carmel, Doris visits a few local stores, signs autographs and goes to see Tony Bennett's art exhibit, which is presented by the artist himself. She compliments his work, especially one with a yellow taxi cab. He remarks he has never been in the area before and how beautiful it is.

Main story: Doris's family of dogs and Connie Edney*

Doris is in the meadow having fun with her friends, including Big Buster Brown, Biggest, Autumn, JoJo Brown, Snowy, Barney, Auddie, Leroy Brown and Elsie Shoecart. Connie Edney, Doris's longtime friend

and dresser from *The Doris Day Show* and this show, pays tribute to her dog Lulu with a lovely poem written by her and read by Doris:

> We walk along the road, my friend and I, both well past middle age.
>
> The sun is leaving, and its yellow light has turned her coat to reddish gold the way it used to be when we were young.
>
> Ahead of us two quail are hurrying home. Nose to the ground, she doesn't see them. So I nudge her with my foot. She looks.
>
> My mostly beagle dog, who used to point at anything that moved and then chased it while I vainly tried to call her back. But now she seems to say that was long ago. That game is over now.
>
> She looks into my eyes and tempori the way that beagles do, and sees that I am sad.
>
> A moment's pause, then suddenly she charges down the path. Ears flopping, eyes dancing, just as suddenly she stops. One paw lifted, tail ramrod straight. I smile, then sternly call her back. But when she's on her way again flying like the quails.
>
> The game's not over yet.

Guest: Leslie Nielsen

Doris talks about one of her favorite pets, Honey Day, and her recovery from cancer. Canadian actor-comedian Leslie Nielsen sits down with Doris for a fun conversation, including his empty reel of his Invisible Man audition, and a chat about a certain movie called *Airplane!* Leslie speaks about the series *The Blue Frontier,* which he hosted.

\*—worked or appeared on *The Doris Day Show* series.

New songs performed by Doris on *Doris Day's Best Friends* series:
"Best Friend"
"Crocodile Rock"
"Daydream"
"Disney Girls"
"Everyone's Gone to the Moon"
"It's All Happening at the Zoo"
"My Heart"
"Octopus's Garden"

"Rescue Me"
"Ryan's on His Way to the Roundup"
"Stew Beau"
"This Is the Way I Dreamed It"
"Wildfire"
"You Are So Beautiful"
"You Can Make It Big"

## DORIS DAY: A SENTIMENTAL JOURNEY
US PBS 1991

| | |
|---|---|
| Narrator: | Roger Ebert |
| Producer & Writer: | James Arntz |
| Co-Producer & Writer: | Katherine MacMillin |
| Editor: | Don DeMartini |
| Director: | Dick Carter |
| Executive Producer: | Glenn DuBose |
| Field Producer: | Nicolette J. Ferri |
| Associate Producer: | Michael D. McAlpin |
| Camera: | Roy D. Alan |
| Lighting Director: | Jim Gedwellas |
| Post-Production Audio: | James Guthrie |
| Audio: | Robert Dove, Tom Siegel |
| Research: | Mary Cleere Haran |
| Primary Archival Material: | Donald Chang |
| Research Consultants: | Donald Chang, Howard Green |

| Additional Crew / Doris Day Interview I | |
|---|---|
| Director: | Steve Norman |
| Director of Photography: | Richard L. Rawlings, ASC |
| Hair: | Barbara Lampson |
| Make-up: | Mark Bussan |
| Wardrobe: | Connie Edney |

Additional Interviews / Doris Day Interview II
On The Scene Productions, Inc.
Director of Photography:     Rick Walker
Audio:     Keith Winner

For Arwin Productions:
Coordinating Producer:     Linda Dozoretz
Executive Producer:     Terry Melcher

Song: "My Heart," Performed by Doris Day; Written by Terry Melcher & Bruce Johnson; Courtesy of Daywin Music, Inc.

Doris Day had done several interviews in print and on television throughout the years, but *Doris Day: A Sentimental Journey* was the first time she spoke about her life and career in documentary film form. It was a production of WTTW/Chicago Productions in association with Doris's Arwin Productions, Inc.

In addition to Doris Day, the hour-long program chronicling her life includes interviews with John Updike, Tony Randall, Betty White, Les Brown, Molly Haskell, A.E. Hotchner, Ross Hunter, Kaye Ballard, Terry Melcher, Rosemary Clooney, Kirstie Alley, Jacqueline Melcher and Clint Eastwood. Each spoke about Doris and her life, music, film, television and animal welfare work.

Clips from many of Doris's films and some of her music recordings were included. Unfortunately, with the wealth of Doris's contributions in the entertainment field alone, an hour was simply not long enough to do justice to her career successes. For example, there is no mention of *Please Don't Eat the Daisies, Midnight Lace* or *The Glass Bottom Boat*, three of her top-grossing films. Nor is there any reference to her bigger music hits outside of "Sentimental Journey," "Secret Love" and "Que Sera, Sera." Doris's work on television is relegated to a few seconds with the opening credits of the third season of *The Doris Day Show*. Doris and Hotchner commented how the series helped her both financially and emotionally.

Regardless, the main draw of the documentary, of course, is the appearance of Doris Day, who shares her memories of making movies, recording songs, as well as talking about her family, friends, and life. It showed her still attractive and active as she reminisced about things as if they happened only yesterday rather than decades earlier. This documentary gave Doris the chance to speak publicly and have her thoughts and recollections on record. The special was first broadcast on PBS stations throughout the U.S. in 1991 and was greeted with positive notices from both critics and audiences.

## *THE DORIS DAY SHOW* BEFORE *THE DORIS DAY SHOW*

From 1952-1953, Doris Day had a self-titled weekly half-hour radio program on CBS in the U.S. It was later heard in England and transmitted to Canada and Australia at different times. *The Doris Day Show* was a CBS and Martin Melcher production.

The show served three purposes: to promote her Warner Bros. films, to promote her new records, and to record new songs specifically for the show. One of the greatest satisfactions Doris had was answering fan mail on the air, especially those from soldiers fighting in North Korea who listened to the show overseas. The soldiers in return voted Doris the girl they wanted to take "a slow boat back to the States with" in a poll conducted by Armed Forces Radio.

After more than a year, CBS desperately wanted to keep *The Doris Day Show* on its radio airwaves. Doris simply had no time to continue with it in that she was shooting two to four movies a year and recording regularly for Columbia Records. But CBS would have Doris again on the air 15 years later with her own program for television.

While many of the shows exist in the hands of private collectors, not all were completely documented in terms of guest stars and performances. The following is a list of episodes, airdates and guest stars:

| Show # | Airdate | Guests |
|--------|---------|--------|
| 1 | 3/28/52 | Danny Thomas, Grace Kahn |
| 2 | 4/4/52 | Jack Kirkwood, Jack Smith |
| 3 | 4/11/52 | Frank Loesser, Ray Bolger |
| 4 | 4/18/52 | Mary Wickes, Ray Bolger |
| 5 | 4/25/52 | Marris & Miranda, Gordon MacRae |
| 6 | 5/2/52 | Liberace, Donald O'Connor |
| 7 | 5/9/52 | Gordon MacRae, Mary Wickes |

| 8  | 5/16/52  | Harry James, Guy Mitchell              |
|----|----------|----------------------------------------|
| 9  | 5/23/52  | Ray Noble, Dennis Day                  |
| 10 | 6/1/52   | Ronald Reagan, Bob Crosby              |
| 11 | 6/8/52   | Hal Peary, Dave Butler                 |
| 12 | 6/15/52  | unknown                                |
| 13 | 6/22/52  | Howard Keel                            |
| 14 | 6/29/52  | George Jessel                          |
| 15 | 7/6/52   | Frankie Laine                          |
| 16 | 7/13/52  | Dick Haymes                            |
| 17 | 7/20/52  | Sammy Cahn, Gordon MacRae              |
| 18 | 7/27/52  | Hal Peary                              |
| 19 | 8/3/52   | Jack Smith, Jack Kirkwood              |
| 20 | 8/10/52  | Gordon MacRae                          |
| 21 | 8/17/52  | George Murphy                          |
| 22 | 8/24/52  | Dennis O'Keefe                         |
| 23 | 8/31/52  | David Wayne                            |
| 24 | 9/7/52   | Jack Kirkwood, Johnny Desmond          |
| 25 | 9/14/52  | Dan Dailey                             |
| 26 | 9/21/52  | Donald O'Connor                        |
| 27 | 9/28/52  | unknown                                |
| 28 | 10/2/52  | unknown                                |
| 29 | 10/9/52  | unknown                                |
| 30 | 10/16/52 | Joan Fontaine                          |
| 31 | 10/23/52 | unknown                                |
| 32 | 10/30/52 | unknown                                |
| 33 | 11/6/52  | John Agar, Jack Kirkwood               |
| 34 | 11/11/52 | Cornel Wilde (show airs on new day of week) |
| 35 | 11/18/52 | unknown                                |
| 36 | 11/25/52 | Kirk Douglas                           |
| 37 | 12/2/52  | Gordon MacRae                          |
| 38 | 12/9/52  | Tony Martin                            |
| 39 | 12/16/52 | Jimmy Boyd                             |
| 40 | 12/23/52 | Jack Kirkwood                          |
| 41 | 12/30/52 | Danny Thomas                           |
| 42 | 1/6/53   | Loretta Young                          |
| 43 | 1/13/53  | Broderick Crawford                     |
| 44 | 1/20/53  | David Wayne                            |
| 45 | 1/27/53  | Howard Keel                            |

| 46 | 2/3/53 | Howard Keel |
| 47 | 2/10/53 | Broderick Crawford |
| 48 | 2/17/53 | Dan Dailey |
| 49 | 2/24/53 | Howard Keel |
| 50 | 3/3/53 | Gordon MacRae |
| 51 | 3/10/53 | Frankie Laine |
| 52 | 3/17/53 | Charlotte Greenwood |
| 53 | 3/24/53 | Gordon MacRae |
| 54 | 3/31/53 | no guests—new 15-minute format |
| 55 | 4/7/53 | " |
| 56 | 4/14/53 | " |
| 57 | 4/21/53 | " |
| 58 | 4/28/53 | " |
| 59 | 5/5/53 | " |
| 60 | 5/12/53 | " |
| 61 | 5/19/53 | " [last known broadcast episode] |

## TELEVISION'S DORIS DAY ON DVD

"It's a Beautiful Day… At long last, Doris Day's TV series comes to DVD," declared Tim Williams' June 12, 2005 story for *TV Guide* on the DVD release of *The Doris Day Show*:

"[Day's sitcom] was wisely built on her bona fide girl-next-door appeal. Critics at the time dismissed the show as poorly written fluff, but audiences spooned it up like a butterscotch parfait, and it ran for five successful seasons.

"True, the [first season] shows' plots make even *Everybody Loves Raymond* look multilayered. But it doesn't much matter when that sunny personality goes into overdrive. The show becomes as bright and pleasurably distracting as Day's groovy canary-yellow outfits (her TV wardrobe is rivaled only by Marlo Thomas' on *That Girl* for eye-popping style)…But the forgotten *Doris Day Show* is a testament to the power of pluck and stands as a charming snapshot of an extraordinary talent."

"Long anticipated" is an understatement regarding the wait fans have endured for Doris Day's television works to be seen again. Jim Pierson of

MPI Home Video spearheaded the DVD release of *The Doris Day Show* and Doris's specials. He says he was familiar with the series and learned none of Doris's television works were ever released to the home market. "I got a hold of Terry [Melcher] in June of 2004 to see if he was interested in getting the Doris Day TV material on DVD," Pierson says. "Doris owns the show so she had all the masters and they were in storage in Hollywood for all these years. Terry said yes. And it was a pleasure dealing with him, because he died a few months later."

Pierson recalls seeing the show as a child, but did not know all of the ins and outs of the series. "She started the series with a rural flavor that was popular with other CBS shows at the time like *Petticoat Junction* and *The Andy Griffith Show* and *The Beverly Hillbillies*, and the fact that she went cosmopolitan, a working mom, and that was before *Mary Tyler Moore*.

One of many never before seen sketches in the DVD sets include the "Que Sera, Sera Waltz" in *The Doris Day Special* DVD. This was cut from Doris's first special due to time constraints.

"I think what is interesting about Doris's show was the evolution of the format. The basic formula was playing off her. It all hinged on Doris's personality. The fact that the supporting cast changed, she was the glue that held the series together. She was the perfect television star: she was beautiful and she was appealing.

"The series wasn't slapstick comedy like Lucy. It was more plot-driven than joke-driven, unlike sitcoms today where it's all about goofy jokes, sexual innuendoes, that sort of thing. A lot these episodes have a dramatic storyline with comedic interface narrative to them. It's not like they were doing Maude having an abortion or dealing with heavy drug use. The James Brooks script ["The Job"] did have a pedigree that reinforced that highbred sort of format for the show. Quoting Philip Brown, he never thought of it as an out-and-out sitcom."

The episodes themselves were in very good condition, having been stored properly over the decades. One of Pierson's main hopes was to acquire additional footage to include in the DVD sets. Since a majority of such items are discarded as they are of no use to the finished episode, Pierson researched and found not only did Doris had some materials in storage, but CBS actually had all of the material from her first TV special in their archives.

"It was a bit of a fluke that the network had kept the original camera reels including all the takes and the prerecorded songs," Pierson says. "That was a real lucky thing. I spent a few days at CBS with the some of the engineers transferring all of the elements and supervising the restoration and reediting for the DVD bonus.

"Fortunately, the materials were not terribly problematic as they were well archived and preserved so there weren't any major technical challenges. The shows were transferred from the original negatives and original audio sources, and were then put through a digital sonic solution process to get rid of ticks and hiss sounds on the audio. It takes a fair amount of time to get it prepared, and to color correct the film. Actually transferring can take a couple of hours, the audio playback can be another couple hours. You can easily spend four hours working on a half-hour episode that need little work."

Pierson says the DVD sets sold very well: "Better than expected, but MPI didn't really know what to expect. We got a fair amount of ink on it with *The New York Times*, *The LA Times*, *USA Today*, *TV Guide* and *Entertainment Tonight* and we ran a couple of ads. It got mentions in a lot of places. MPI was very pleased."

Each season is sold in individual box sets, as are Doris Day's television specials. Each box set includes not only all of the respective season's episodes, but a plethora of bonus features, including network promos for the series; special Doris Day presentations and messages; never-before-seen outtakes and bloopers; her guest appearances on *What's My Line?*

Several DVD releases and box sets of Doris Day's films including a couple with Turner Classic Movies and The Doris Day Fox Collection with a special documentary produced by Cloverland have already been released to the home market.

## ARWIN PRODUCTIONS

At the end of every episode of *The Doris Day Show*, there is a credit which reads the show is an Arwin Production. What is Arwin? It is a production company started by Doris's late husband Marty Melcher in the 1950s when she was still under a long-term film contract with Warner Bros. *Young at Heart* was her last film with the company to fulfill the terms of the agreement, and it was with this film that bore the first imprint of the company name.

The idea of Arwin was to serve Doris well in that a majority of her post-Warner films were co-produced by her company. Arwin thus then owned a percent of her films, which resulted in continued royalties throughout the years. Don Genson worked for Arwin, as did Doris's brother Paul.

Arwin was also used when Marty started Arwin Record in the late 1950s, in which Doris's son Terry Melcher was involved. The label's biggest success was an early Jan and Dean record which was issued as Jan and Arnie. Daywin Music, Artists Music and later, Equinox, were publishing names used by Marty and Terry. Joe Lubin was a songwriter who worked for them. The company also owned music publishing for many of the songs Doris sang in her films and her Columbia Records releases, such as "Whatever Will Be, Will Be (Que Sera, Sera)."

In addition to *The Doris Day Show*, Arwin produced *The Doris Mary Anne Kapplehoff Special*, while the *Doris Day Today* special was done under the Equinox banner. Terry also oversaw a record label of the same name in the 1970s.

In the following years, Arwin, as a company, has been used occasionally as a business entity as needed. For example, the PBS documentary *Doris Day: A Sentimental Journey* was co-produced by Arwin. But no one—not even Doris herself—seems to remember exactly what the word Arwin stood for.

# A Thrill of It All: Doris Day Filmography

In this new century Box Office Champion Doris Day is becoming a very popular DVD franchise. TCM/ Warner Brothers has released three Mega Doris Day Box Sets. NBC/ Universal also gave us a special Doris Day Rock Hudson Collection. 20th Century Fox released their three Day films with some exciting new bonuses: a documentary that includes interviews with *Move Over, Darling* co-star Polly Bergen, costume designer Ray Aghayan and Doris's musical arranger and songwriter Mort Garson. These special featurette were produced by film expert John Cork who provided audio commentary—the first for a Day film—on *Caprice* with Pierre Patrick.

As you go through your own home DVD collection this list will provide you with some interesting information about each film:

- Premiere dates are the New York ones unless indicated in a different city
- Doris Day's leading men—sometimes two or three pursuing Day ending with the winner
- Film Director
- Film location where the story took place
- Doris almost always portrayed a working woman breaking new ground. We give you her different jobs— from advertising executive to factory worker to spy
- And yes, in many film she was a mother so we give a kid and gender count

6/25/1948 "Romance on the High Seas" Oscar Levant, Jack Carson, D-Michael Curtiz, New York, Cuba, Casablanca, Honky-Tonk Singer

4/15/1949 "My Dream Is Yours" Lee Bowman, Jack Carson, D-Michael Curtiz, New York, Hollywood, Jukebox Singer, One Boy

8/1/1949 "It's a Great Feeling" Jack Carson, Dennis Morgan, Errol Flynn, D-David Butler, Hollywood, Bushkin Corners, Wisconsin, Waitress, Taxi Driver, Elevator Operator

2/9/1950 "Young Man with a Horn" Kirk Douglas, Hoagy Carmichael, D-Michael Curtiz, New York, Big Band Singer

9/1/1950 "Tea for Two" Gordon MacRae, Gene Nelson, D-David Butler, New York, Broadway Heiress, One Boy and Girl

12/22/1950 "The West Point Story" Gordon MacRae, Gene Nelson, D-Roy Del Ruth, New York City, West Point, Film and Singing Star

1/17/1951 "Storm Warning" Ronald Reagan, Steve Cochran, D-Stuart Heisler, Cerritos, California, Waitress in Bowling Alley

3/26/1951 "Lullaby of Broadway" Gene Nelson, S.Z. Sakall, D-David Butler, New York, Cruise Performer

7/26/1951 "On Moonlight Bay" Gordon MacRae, Jack Smith, D-Roy Del Ruth, Indiana, Amateur Baseball Player

12/6/1951 "I'll See You in My Dreams" D-Michael Curtiz, Danny Thomas, D-Michael Curtiz, New York, Hollywood, Song Plugger, One Boy and Girl

12/14/1951 "Starlift" D-Roy Del Ruth, Hollywood, She Plays Herself

6/20/1952 "The Winning Team" D-Louis Seiler, Ronald Reagan, D-Louis Seiler, Elba, Nebraska, Baseball Inspiration

12/24/1952 "April in Paris" Claude Dauphin, Ray Bolger, D-David Butler, New York, Paris, Chorus Girl on Broadway

3/26/1953 "By the Light of the Silvery Moon" Gordon MacRae, Russell Arms, D-David Butler, Indiana, Auto Mechanic

11/4/1953 "Calamity Jane" Howard Keel, Philip Carey, D-David Butler, Deadwood, South Dakota, Real Life Jane Canary, Frontierswoman Doctor

4/9/1954 "Lucky Me" Phil Silvers, Robert Cummings, D-Jack Donohue, Miami, Superstitious Vaudevillian

1/20/1955 "Young at Heart" Frank Sinatra, Gig Young, D-Gordon Douglas, Connecticut, Talented Singer, One Boy (played by Doris's real-life nephew)

5/26/1955 "Love Me or Leave Me" James Cagney, Cameron Mitchell, D-Charles Vidor, Chicago, New York, Hollywood, Singer Ruth Etting

4/30/1956 (Paris, France) "The Man Who Know Too Much" James Stewart, Daniel Gellin, D-Alfred Hitchcock, Marrakesh, London, Retired International Singer, One Boy

10/17/1956 "Julie" Louis Jourdan, Barry Sullivan, D-Andrew L. Stone, Monterey, Carmel, San Francisco, Flight Attendant/Pilot

8/29/1957 "The Pajama Game" John Raitt, D-George Abbot/Stanley Donen, Cedar Rapids, Iowa, Factory Worker

4/1/1958 "Teacher's Pet" Clark Gable, Gig Young, D-George Seaton, New York, Journalism Teacher/Writer

11/21/1958 "Tunnel of Love" Richard Widmark, D-Gene Kelly, West Port, Connecticut, Expectant Mother

7/14/1959 (Denmark) "It Happened to Jane" Jack Lemmon, Steve Forrest, D-Richard Quine, (Fictional City of Cape Town, Maine) Shot it Chester, Connecticut, Raises Lobsters, One Boy and Girl

10/6/1959 "Pillow Talk" Rock Hudson, Tony Randall, Nick Adams, D-Michael Gordon, Manhattan, Connecticut, Interior Decorator

3/31/1960 "Please Don't Eat the Daisies" David Niven, Richard Hayden, D-Charles Walters, New York, Super Mom, Four Boys

10/13/1960 "Midnight Lace" Rex Harrison, John Gavin, D-David Miller, London, Millionairess

12/20/1961 "Lover Come Back" Rock Hudson, D-Delbert Mann, Manhattan, Advertising Executive, One on the way

6/14/1962 "The Touch of Mink" Cary Grant, D-Delbert Mann, Manhattan, Philadelphia, Bermuda, Unemployed, Keypunch Operator, Newborn

12/6/1962 "Jumbo" Stephen Boyd, D-Charles Walters, Traveling Circus, Circus Performer (Equestrian/Trapeze Artist/Clown)

7/17/1963 "The Thrill of It All" James Garner, D-Norman Jewison, New York, Commercial Star, One Boy and Girl

12/19/1963 "Move Over, Darling" James Garner, Chuck Conners, Polly Bergen(2nd wife), D-Michael Gordon, Los Angeles, Monterey, Castaway, One Boy and Two Girls

10/14/1964 "Send Me No Flowers" Rock Hudson, Clint Walker, D-Norman Jewison, Connecticut, Housewife

12/22/1965 "Do Not Disturb" Rod Taylor, Sergio Fantoni, D-Ralph Levy, London, Paris, Housewife

6/9/1966 "Glass Bottom Boat" Rod Taylor, Edward Andrews, Dick Martin, D-Frank Tashlin, Catalina Island, NASA Space Center, California, NASA Tour Guide, Assistant and Biographer to Astronaut, Mermaid on the Weekends

4/18/1967 "Caprice" Richard Harris, Edward Mulhare, D-Frank Tashlin, Paris, L.A., Switzerland, Spy

2/1/1967 "Ballad of Josie" Peter Graves, George Kennedy, Andy Devine, D-Andrew V. McLaglen, Wyoming, Sheepherder, One Boy

6/19/1968 "Where Were You When the Lights Went Out" Robert Morse, Terry Thomas, Patrick O'Neal, D-Hy Averback, New York, Broadway Actress, One on the way

8/7/1968 "With Six You Get Egg Roll" Brian Keith, George Carlin, D-Howard Morris, San Francisco, Lumberyard Owner and Operator, Three Boys and One Stepdaughter

6/1994 "Don't Pave Main Street" (Documentary) Clint Eastwood, D-William T. Cartwright/Julien Ludwig, Carmel, California, Herself

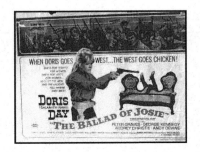

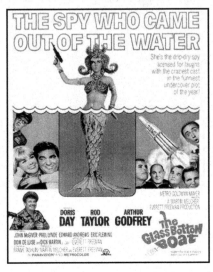

# The Doris Day Discography

At the 50th Grammy Awards on February 28th, 2008, Tony Bennett and Natalie Cole graced the great stage of the Staple Center, and presented Doris Day with the Lifetime Achievement Award. A montage of photos and Doris's music were seen and heard in the background as Tony and Natalie made the presentation. I was present as a long time Grammy member, and campaigned for many years to the Grammy committee for Doris to get this award. For the 50th Anniversary it could not have been more appropriate.

Doris sent this very special letter to Academy president Neil Portnow and the Academy Board of Trustees preceding the event:

"I was delighted and surprised to hear that the National Academy of Recording Arts and Sciences has voted for me to receive the Academy's Lifetime Achievement Award. My life has been devoted to music and I applaud the work of the Recording Academy, the creativity and talent of your members, the charity projects NARAS heads, and all you do to preserve and expose music to the world. I am sorry that I cannot attend the ceremony or the Grammys in person. My heart will be there with you and the music industry and I will be watching on television, of course. I am proud to be among this year's recipients and salute my fellow inductees. I have been blessed to work with some of the most wonderful and talented people in music and I want to share this wonderful honor with all of those with whom I worked. Again, thank you, with love, Doris Day."

Doris recorded exclusively for Columbia in the US and Philips in other parts of the world.

Her collection is completely available on CD through Bear Family and Collectors' Choice under Sony, and many are downloadable. The following are Doris's albums with US release dates:

"The Complete Doris Day with Les Brown", a compilation of her recordings from 1941 to 1946 which includes the #1 songs "Sentimental Journey" and "My Dreams Are Getting Better All The Time"

| 8/1949 | "You're my Thrill" Mitchell Ayers/Frank Comstock/Lou Bring, # 5 |
| 3/1950 | "Young Man with a Horn" Harry James, #1 |
| 9/1950 | "Tea for Two" Alex Stordahl |
| 3/1951 | "Lullaby of Broadway" Norman Luboff/Frank Comstock, #1 |
| 7/1951 | "On Moonlight Bay" Paul Weston/Norman Luboff, #2 |
| 12/1951 | "I'll See You in My Dreams" Paul Weston/Norman Luboff, #1 |

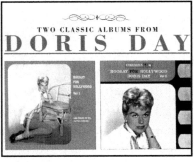

| 3/1953 | "By the Light of the Silvery Moon" Paul Weston/Norman Luboff, #3 |
| 11/1953 | "Calamity Jane" Ray Heindorf, #2 |
| 11/1954 | "Young at Heart" Percy Faith/Paul Weston, #15 |
| 5/1955 | "Love Me or Leave Me" Percy Faith, #1 (for 17 weeks) |

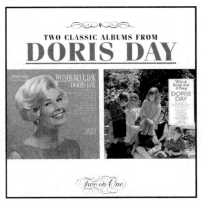

| | |
|---|---|
| 12/1956 | "Day by Day" Paul Weston, #11 |
| 8/1957 | "The Pajama Game" Ray Heindorf, #9 |
| 11/1957 | "Day By Night" Paul Weston |
| 10/1958 | "Hooray for Hollywood"- Vol. 1 Frank DeVol |
| 1/1959 | "Hooray for Hollywood"- Vol. 2 Frank DeVol |
| 3/1959 | "Cuttin" Capers" Frank DeVol |
| 1960 | "Listen to Day" Frank DeVol/Jack Marshall |
| 1960 | "What Every Girl Should Know" Harry Zimmerman |
| 3/1960 | "Show Time" Alex Stordahl |
| 3/1961 | "Bright and Shiny" Neal Hefti |
| 8/1961 | "I Have Dreamed" Jim Harbert, #97 |
| 2/1962 | "Duet" André Previn |
| 9/1962 | "You'll Never Walk Alone" Jim Harbert |
| 11/1962 | "Jumbo" George Stoll |
| 2/1963 | "Annie Get Your Gun" Frank Allers |
| 12/1963 | "Love Him" Tommy Oliver, #102 |
| 9/1964 | "The Doris Day Christmas Album" Dudley C. /Peter King, #92 |
| 10/1964 | "With a Smile and a Song" Allyn Ferguson |
| 3/1965 | "Latin for Lovers" Mort Garson |
| 7/1965 | "Doris Day's Sentimental Journey" Mort Garson |

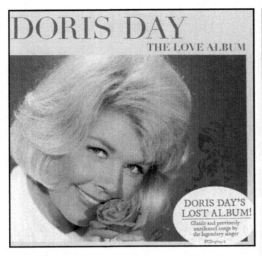

2/2006      "The Love Album" Jimmy Haskell

In addition to all these albums, Doris recorded hundreds of songs that were not included.

Doris Day's success as a recording artist speaks for itself:  77 charting singles. 21 hit the Top 10. Seven reached Number One.

In the mid 1980s and early 1990s Terry Melcher produced special recordings with Doris Day some were used on her *Best Friends* television series and could be released soon  under the direction of Jim Pierson who spearheaded *The Doris Day Show* DVD release.

The most recent Doris Day release was "Ludacrismas" with Ludacris which was part of the *Fred Clause* soundtrack in 2007.

# On Doris Day

## A NOTE FROM GARRY MCGEE

Doris Day once said: "I've done every kind of movie. I've done comedy and I've done drama. I've done the *Pillow Talk* thing and also the thrill-of-it-all of a married woman. And I've done musicals.

"It's wrong to give me that one image."

That is true.

In addition to her extraordinarily successful film and recording work, she was a television star, too. For six years and five seasons, *The Doris Day Show* not only won its time period, but introduced a growth and change in characters, which had been seldom seen in television comedies. Because of this evolution, the series was criticized for not staying with one formula throughout its run. But it is precisely that change which made the series uncommon and in retrospect, more entertaining. To me it's interesting how season one was considered simple and uncomplicated, but by the last season it had become more of an adult-type series. Once again, growth and an unfolding made the series both unique and entertaining.

I first became aware of Doris Day through her television show when I was a child. She was cool. And pretty. And funny. Her reactions were timeless. Her laughter, contagious. Her antics, outrageous. Her style, smooth. Doris Martin, however, was far from perfect. After all, she was in jail more times than the average person. But she did have that great looking Barracuda convertible that I was going to have when I grew up (never happened). Though I knew the reality of television, that there was not a Doris Martin living in San Francisco—or any of the other characters on TV— she and her TV friends and family were still part of my childhood. Monday nights were not the same in the fall of 1973 when *The Doris Day Show* was no longer on the air. I'd hoped it would be rerun, but that did not happen until a dozen years later when I was a young adult.

I proposed writing a biography of her life, but no publisher was interested in it (which shows how the publishing world doesn't know what it wants since other Doris Day works have since materialized). I decided instead to write a reference book to compile Doris's groundbreaking and extraordinary wealth of work in films, television, recordings, stage, radio and as an animal activist. The book, *Doris Day: Sentimental Journey*, was published in 2005 [McFarland], pleasing many fans who finally had a work that compiled most everything Doris had done, and amazing others who had not realized her many accomplishments.

Prior to the release of *Sentimental Journey*, Pierre Patrick contacted me and we discussed someday working on a project together. A few ideas were discussed. I remarked how terrific if there was a book on *The Doris Day Show* series since he had written a magazine article on the show for *Television Chronicles* a few years earlier. Through the years books have been published on several popular TV shows from the 1960s through the 1980s, but not one was done on this series. Pierre readily agreed to co-write one, but I was reluctant. We'd need many photographs and I felt that the voice of Doris Day had to be included to make the book satisfying to the reader. The former was taken care of, with much help from Jim Pierson, in addition to Pierre's and my collection.

I thought the latter would never happen since Doris Day seldom talks about her past. I knew she does not live in the past—nor does she dwell on it—because she lives for today and concentrates on things important to her. So I felt the chance of her talking about her television work was—well, winning the lottery seemed more probable.

It was quite a surprise when Pierre informed me Doris was very willing to answer our questions and discuss her career in television. She consented primarily because she knew Pierre and the work he had done in the past honoring her works. Through Pierre's and Jim Pierson's contacts, many of the people who worked on the series willingly spoke to us about their memories and experiences with Doris Day. Plus, Ben Ohmart with BearManor Media immediately accepted our proposal for this book before the interviews were set. Such was his faith in this work. We have been very fortunate, to say the least.

Except for a couple weeks, I spent every day from two to ten hours, for four months, writing and rewriting the work, transcribing interviews, taking notes for the short essays seen throughout, researching things from the series' co-stars and guest stars to its cars, and collaborating with Pierre throughout the process. My main thought was what you, the reader, would like to see and read: a work that is both informative and entertaining.

Today, with CDs, DVDs and cable television, Doris Day is constantly being discovered by new fans who now consider her en vogue, more appreciated by those who say she never went out of fashion, and more than a few envious critics who, while having dismissed her in the past, now beat their chests in praise of her talents. Personally, I consider her the best entertainer of all time.

Although I have never met the lady, I know she has done a lot and has given a lot in performing which has entertained millions of people. She also made the rights of animals a main topic in the 1970s and right through to the present. Doris Day used her name and her beliefs to help make the public become more aware of its treatment toward animals. But she went further and helped in seeing laws being passed to protect those who have no voice, yet serve mankind in countless ways. For that comes an additional, higher appreciation. And I know that there will never be another Doris Day.

## MY DREAM IS YOURS BY PIERRE PATRICK

As a child in Canada, I fell in love with Miss Doris Day. I was on vacation in Maniwaki, a small town in Quebec, when I received my very first single from my aunt Agathe Saumure, "Que Sera, Sera." It was her record when she was a little girl. Visiting my grandparents at the time with my Aunt Régine, I played this record for two weeks straight, except for watching *The Doris Day Show* twice a week in English and in French. My parents quickly got me the *Doris Day's Greatest Hits* album so I would play songs other than "Que Sera, Sera." Her voice was amazing and I couldn't stop listening to it from that moment on.

Years later in LA, on January 27, 1989, I was in Westwood Village, when I read Doris Day was to be in LA tomorrow to accept the Golden Globe's Cecil B. DeMille Award. This was to be her first visit in almost 10 years, and it was going to be an event. I had to be there.

I was determined to go to the awards and nothing would stop me. I had been to many awards before and met everyone from Elizabeth Taylor to Madonna, but this was *Doris Day* and the Golden Globes. I dressed in my Hugo Boss tuxedo, which I had gotten from my parents for Christmas, and went to Merv Griffin's Beverly Hills Hotel, where the ceremony was being held. I simply went to the back of the hotel, where the main entrance for the awards was, and, like magic, walked right through the lobby into the awards room.

And at the center of the room, where everybody was dressed in black, looking like an angel all in white, Doris Day was being escorted by nominee Clint Eastwood to her table. She was standing with Eastwood, who looked at me—I was holding a photo of Doris from her series and a pen in my hand. He seemed to be saying, "Oh no. Not one of my fans." I said to Doris, "Oh, Miss Day. I'm your biggest fan. I love you so much." I shook her hand and asked her to sign my picture. She asked me for my name. In a burst of excitement I think I said my brother's name, Jacques. But I finally said Pierre. Doris autographed it and said, "Thank you. It was so nice to meet you." I thanked her and walked away. I couldn't believe what just happened. It was an amazing moment, but now my challenge was to stay and watch her accept her award.

So I started walking around when someone asked me what I was doing there. It was Jimmy Smits, who was there with the nominated series *L.A. Law*. I decided to be honest with him, and told him the truth.

Doris Day at the 1989 Golden Globe Awards.

He arranged for me to sit at his table, which was actually overlooking Doris's table. At her table was Eastwood and Doris's son Terry Melcher (who was nominated for Best Song that year for "Kokomo") and Allen Carr, who was producing the Oscars that year and desperately trying to convince Doris to participate.

The masters of ceremony were Joan Collins and George Hamilton. The show was produced by Dick Clark, who was a very hands-on director. He also produced the American Music Awards, which I have attended many times.

The night was interesting for Doris as well. Not only was her son nominated, but her film co-star Jack Lemmon was, as was Barbara Hershey, her stepdaughter in *With Six You Get Eggroll*. And Clint Eastwood, her friend from Carmel, was nominated for Best Director for the first time, which he would later win. Also included in the audience were animal lovers and friends Betty White and Bea Arthur.

The evening was mostly wonderful except for River Phoenix, who spent most of the evening on his cell phone, which were new at the time. Winners that night were Jodie Foster, who guest-starred on *The Doris Day Show*, Candice Bergan, who was once one of Terry's longtime girl-friends, won for *Murphy Brown*.

The moment arrived: Clips were shown from several of Doris's films as was a special message from James Garner, which made Doris very happy. When Doris arose, the standing ovation was started by me. She gave a wonderful speech, thanking everyone from actors to crew members. She remarked that she had worked with the cream of the crop, and said to Clint she wanted to work with him, which made everyone laugh. She ended with: "The best is yet to come. And I want to do some more." Her words were touching and it led to a rebirth in Doris Day. New releases and tributes started appearing everywhere. The world's favorite star was to be celebrated in many ways.

Among the tributes that followed included not only television and re-cordings, including the entire Columbia discography released as mega-boxsets on CD for the first time by Bear Family. In the theater world, Jerry Goehring and Patty Carver worked very hard at putting Doris's music career on stage. The first was in New York in 1992 with "Day Dreams," a show actually seen by Terry Melcher who invited the couple to Carmel to meet Doris.

A transformation in the show was then done to emphasize the fan's point of view. *Definitely Doris* premiered in London at the King's Head Theatre in 1996 then in Boston, where it received glowing reviews. In 1998 it opened at TV and film director Garry Marshall's new theater called The Falcon.

Jerry had read an article I had written for *Television Chronicles* on *The Doris Day Show* and asked that I join the company as an associate producer. We assembled a won-derful cast, including appearances by two of *The Doris Day Show*'s alumni: Bernie Kopell and Jackie Joseph. The show was written by Leo P. Crusone and Patty Carver, who also starred in the production.

Patty Carver and Jerry Goehring with Doris Day.

During that time, Van Hise Films asked me to help with their A&E *Biography* on Doris Day. Their two-hour documentary on Doris Day was one of the highest rated *Biography*s ever.

I continued working with Jerry and moved to the east coast, where we produced another show entitled *My Doris Day*, and was joined by actor/producer William Suretté. The show was performed at Don't Tell Mama in New York City.

The next time I saw Doris was in 1993, for a Doris Day Best Friends fund-raising event that took place on October 9. It was heavily promoted and was presented on Vicki Lawrence's talk show *Vicki!* as well as *Entertainment Tonight* and covered by the international press.

Garry Marshall.

I met Les Brown when he was rehearsing with his band of Renown for a performance to be held that night. He was absolutely terrific and a very nice man. It was amazing to see Doris and Les Brown on-stage together again. The dinner and dance reception was private and great fun. The party went on until after midnight and Doris was one of the last to leave.

The next day I was at the Cypress Inn, Doris's hotel in Carmel. There was a man looking at pictures from the night before. He had one of Doris and me. I introduced myself and learned he was a good friend of Doris's called Bill Glynn. We became very good friends throughout the years.

A bit later, Doris arrived to do two interviews, one with Vicki Lawrence and one for an American Movie Classics documentary.

In 1996, after receiving one of the last dogs from the Doris Day Pet Foundation, Doris invited me to lunch in Carmel at the Quail Lodge Restaurant. I was joined with my then-girlfriend Jennifer Andrews and my dog Breezy. Doris made arrangements with the restaurant manager for Breezy to sit with us. She was a wonderful dog and well behaved, and Doris made sure she had some food while we ate.

I went back to Carmel a few times after that. One of those times was with Howard Green and Jackie Joseph. Jackie and Doris hadn't seen each other in almost 25 years even though they talked on the phone quite often. It was fun for them to have a mini-*Doris Day Show* reunion.

In 2006, a revival of *The Pajama Game* won two Tony Awards including Best Musical Revival. The film version was one of Doris's best musicals. This version was directed by Kathleen Kennedy, starring Harry Connick, Jr. with Kelli O'Hara in Doris's part. *Calamity Jane* could be heading for Broadway soon. A pilot version starring Louise Mandrell was presented in the fall of 2005 with the same team who brought *Definitely Doris* to stage.

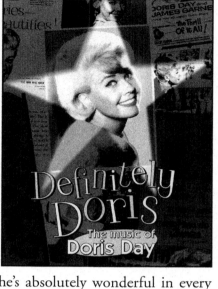

In all my visits with Doris, she is always gracious, funny, entertaining, and above all, extremely beautiful. She's absolutely wonderful in every way. John Updike said you almost want to be like Doris Day—not exactly like her, but almost as good as she is. She reflects that with most everything she has done, whether it's her career or her life.

Doris has risen to the top of every field—box office, music charts, Nielsen ratings, et cetera. With countless performances that live on, she has made many people feel good for a very long time. And for millions of people all over the world, she is at the very top of their hearts. On June 18, 2004, the Associated Press had this headline: "Pope, Doris Day Pick for President's Medal." Doris was bestowed with the highest honor that can ever be given to an American civilian, the Presidential Medal of Freedom for her distinguished service in the field of arts.

Eddie Miller and his mother Emiko outside the Cypress Inn.

Doris Day has become a solid franchise like Harry Potter, Batman and Jason Bourne. New books and special documentaries are constantly being released to the

1993 Carmel Benefit with Vicki Lawrence (Gramma Stewart in *Hannah Montana*).

Pierre, Doris and Breezy.

market. The magic of Doris Day is simple: she instantly makes people feel good.

I have been invited to contribute to some wonderful documentaries celebrating Doris Day's legendary career. In 2009 Florian Films produced a cutting edge film that included interviews with Peter Graves, Jackie Joseph and even Doris who was interviewed during her Magic 63 Birthday Radio Broadcast. This European feature was seen on ARTE TV and was a wonderful experience.

John Cork produced some great featurettes for the Doris Day Fox Film Collec-

William Suretté and Louise Mandrell flex their muscles for *Calamity Jane*.

tion DVDs.   Included is one called "Doris Day vs. Marilyn Monroe" with Monroe expert Sarah Churchwell.   It is interesting to watch Doris and Monroe doing the same scene (*Move Over, Darling/Something's Got To Give*) but even more revealing is the difference in acting style between the pair.   Monroe seems more unsure and insecure in her portrayal, considering she had attended Lee Strasberg's Actor's Studio in New York. Monroe was a stunning actress but never achieved Doris's famously organic performances.   Garry McGee wrote in his book *Sentimental Journey* that Doris was an acting school unto herself.   This is evident in her every performance.

Doris has always been supportive of all of my endeavors and projects, and her encouragement with this book has been terrific.   Doris also took the time to send a Happy 50th Anniversary greeting to my parents.

Ronald Reagan in *The Winning Team* said it for all of us:   "God must think a lot of me for giving me you."

## A VISIT WITH DORIS DAY

On the day of the telephone visit with Doris Day, it was apparently a typically busy day for her- overseeing her staff, pets to feed, obligations with her hotel, tending to business with new releases and her beloved animal foundation and league, as well as the continuation of major rescue efforts of pets who survived Hurricane Katrina's devastation, about which she spoke publicly to Liz Smith in *The New York Post*. But she was gracious to take the time to discuss her work in television for this book.

The lady's humor remains as strong today just as it did in the past. She still has that rare gift of giving a smile and a laugh as effortlessly as making a remark or telling a story on the telephone. But Doris Day also has the gift of memory. Although she seldom discusses her careers, she shared her memories and opinions of working in television—and a few other things as well:

(The interview is a continuation of an earlier discussion Pierre Patrick conducted with Ms. Day for his article on the series that appeared in *Television Chronicles*. Some quotes from that are included in the following transcription.)

*Have you watched* The Doris Day Show *on DVD?*

Oh yes, and I'm having a great time. I really am. One or two of the stories I think could have been a little funnier, but I really am delighted with it. Everything has changed in television, so risqué, and everything is right out there today.

But I'm just loving it. I shouldn't say that because it sounds like I'm conceited—I don't mean it that way. But I am enjoying it. And the relationships between me and the other characters on the show are just terrific.

I'm really in tears all the time. I know that sounds silly, but I see my pals and I go back and remember all the fun we had. And I cry because of the memories and I see Jackie Joseph and Jim Hampton, and then Philip, how adorable he was—I just love him. I felt like he was one of my own. And little Tod, I miss him. It was sad what happened. And Bernie—I just love him. We laughed all the time.

*Jim Pierson with MPI deserves much of the credit for spearheading the DVD release of the show.*

I think he has been spectacular. I'm so fond of him and don't really know him, and yet I'm very grateful that he was in charge.

*Originally, you did not want to do the series, but you made it work and made it great. How did you do that?*

I was a wreck the first year. I was in bad shape, but I didn't take that on the set. I believe in giving 100%. And if you don't, get out of it and don't do it. You have to give your all and do it wholeheartedly, really, with your heart.

*You worked with [director of photography] Richard Rawlings and his son, who did TV's* Desperate Housewives.

Really? His son is doing that?

*Yes, and when you look at* Desperate Housewives, *the style of photography is similar to* The Doris Day Show, *especially with lighting and the use of colors.*

Oh, for goodness sake. Isn't that interesting? It seems to me that he started coming on the set and worked as an apprentice on the show. And there he learned from the best—his father.

I loved his father. Dick Rawlings was one of the nicest men I've ever met in my life. He was the most perfect gentleman. He had a great sense of humor, and was a great, great cameraman—just perfect. And if his son takes after him, he'll be the best.

It saddened me when I heard that Dick Rawlings passed away. I had moved and hadn't seen him in awhile, but we had talked on the phone as I do with all of them. But I was saddened because he was a great, great person.

*The clothes you wore on the series were actually from stores and not specially designed for you. Isn't that correct?*

Connie Edney, the lady who always worked for me, always did the shopping for me at Joseph Magnin. And she would bring tons of things. My driver and the limo would take her all around Beverly Hills on a Friday. That's because Thursday would be the last day of filming an episode. On Friday morning, we would get a new script, read it, and rehearse. So while we rehearsed, she'd have time to leave. Connie would come back later in the afternoon. When she was ready for me, she'd come out on the set and say, "The dressing room's ready for you to take a look."

I would go in, and she would have all of these outfits put together, all around the whole place on hangers. She included a hat, the bag, shoes, the gloves, the belt, the blouse, the skirt, the coat, whatever. Then I would select what I wanted. That's the way we did it. And whatever accessories I needed, she would be sure that I had them because she was just perfect. She really was sharp and knew what I needed in clothes.

Joy Turney would do all the alterations. Joy was great and she took care of all the other women on the show, like Rose Marie and Jackie Joseph. Joy was an angel. She would do the stitching and mending—and fast—during all the fashion shows. She would whip those beautiful capes together in nothing flat.

We had the greatest crew. My makeup man, Harry Maret. He was the dearest and he was with me for years. I loved him very much and we were very close. I just adored him. And my hairdresser, Barbara Lampson, she lived in the Valley down there and was with me for years and years and years. She was one of my best friends. I just had the best people around me.

From *The Doris Mary Anne Kapplehoff Special.*

*John Dehner was a reporter, Jackie Joseph wrote for the Toluca Lake newspaper and you wrote for your own magazine—and you all started out at* today's world.

Yeah, isn't that funny? It really is.

*Doris Martin's bosses were quite different personalities, don't you agree?*

McLean Stevenson was so cute in the show. I really loved him as a person, and he was a wonderful actor. A funny man—and he did great takes—exasperated in the retakes. Of course, I was saddened when McLean passed away. He was so young. It was horrible—I just can't handle it. Almost all of my leading men have passed on.

I don't know why they didn't keep him. I think maybe the word around was that he was too goofy, that he couldn't run a magazine like *today's world* and be like he was. They wanted it to be more real, I guess. That wasn't my doing, the changing [of the actors], you know. I had nothing to do that.

Now, John Dehner could be very much in charge, and yet so funny at the same time. They just had a feeling that, they wanted someone rrreeallly out there—an egomaniac—which made it very funny. We were just rolling. He was one of the funniest men and a brilliant actor.

*The arguments you two would have—you'd jump on the desk...*

I'd put my feet up on desk and he'd throw them off.

*And you had one of the smallest offices in the world of television. You'd twirl on the chair to get to the file cabinet, climb around the desk to open the door. You would fall off your chair...*

Oh, John Dehner was my love. We would talk every few weeks and he was just precious to me.

Now every time I think of him, I could cry, is Peter Lawford. I just loved working with him as Dr. Lawrence. I thought we were really good together. We really bounced off each other. He never sounded like he was reading a script. And he told me the same thing, that it never felt like we were speaking from a script, that everything was from the top of our heads. And that's how our scenes worked. I thought we were really right together. I was really, really sad that he passed away. Also, Patrick O'Neal was just wonderful. I really liked him.

I had the cream of the crop. And I had such a wonderful time with all of them, so my shows make me sad in certain places and then gleeful in other places and I just laugh. I'm so grateful that God gave me the opportunity to do what I did.

*You and Rose Marie made a very good team.*

Oh, Rose Marie. She called me Do and I called her Ro. She used to crack me up all the time. It was really fun working with her. She's a terrific lady. She now has a lot of dogs because of me.

*I know you used to pester her about wearing all those fur coats.*

That was terrible! She would tell me, "Well you used to wear them!" And I used to tell her, "That was a long time ago. That was before I even thought about it." No one was talking about it then. Nobody knew the abuse these animals were enduring. Times have changed I used to tell her, "Get out of those skins!" She used to tell me, "You keep caring about them and I'll keep wearing them!" She was bad.

*We'd like to ask about some of your other co-stars. Another best friend on the series was Jackie Joseph.*

She is just incredible—so terrific. I used to call her Little Jackie Joseph. She was in *With Six You Get Eggroll*. She cracks me up and she was a very funny person. She had very special values to bring to the show. I came up with this idea: I told her, "You should wear an outrageous hairdo. And when Cy would walk by, he would just go bonkers looking at your hairdo. And of course, the hair was just absolutely normal for you to have these huge, high hairdos." And there are a lot of people like that. She loved it. She got the biggest kick out of it, and she played it to the hilt.

*Paul Smith?*

Wasn't he good? There's always one in every office. He was marvelous. Do you remember the show with the dancing school, with Larry Storch ["The Duke Returns"]? He was having a problem because somebody else had a dancing school. Rose Marie and I took dancing classes and I think Ron Harvey was in there, too. I loved that show. That was fun.

*Bernie Kopell and Kaye Ballard?*

He's a genius with dialects and everything. He just transforms himself. He and Kaye were brilliant together. And Kaye and I were really good together. "Wooooo! Have I got a fellow for you!" Always trying to fix me up with somebody—and she was like that in real life. I'd say, "Leave me alone. I've had enough!"

I loved Pallucci's Restaurant. We had such fun with those shows. It was so convenient that the apartment was located upstairs. With the terrace and the spiral staircase that I have right here in my house now. As a matter of fact, most of the furniture in the farmhouse and apartment I paid for all myself. We bought good things, antique things, and I ended up with everything. It was really my own. That apartment set had to be kept just so. I was always going around, "Eh! Finger marks on the doorway here!"

*A lot of the furniture used in the series was actually yours?*

Well, yes, because the producer in the beginning, Dick Dorso—Richard Dorso—was a wonderful person and I respected his taste implicitly. He said to me the studio can provide the furniture for the sets, as most of them do. But he also said, "You can also buy your own and have it when the show ends, and you can have just what you like." And he said, "You know me, I love antiques." And I knew all about him—he was just mad about shopping for antiques. He knew all about them—what was good and what wasn't. He said, "I can do all the shopping for all the things that you need. And then you can have them." I said, "I would like that, and I can probably supply a few of my own things from home." And I did that, too. So that's the way we worked it.

*The sets on the show were incredible in that they were eye-pleasing and looked comfortable. Your set designer was quite talented.*

Perry Ferguson was my designer and he designed everything. All the sets. And looking at all that furniture we had, he couldn't help but know and realize what I liked and how I would like everything to be done.

The farmhouse was wonderful. Just perfect, in every way. The outside, with the old porch swing, was so lovely. And then the office where we all worked was great. Perry was terrific. A wonderful person. Funny and funny to be with, and a great talent.

Everything he did for me was perfect. I could never walk on the set and say, "This doesn't look so good" or "You've done something different…" I never, ever thought that because he knew what to do. He always knew exactly what I would like. I don't know how that happened or if it was coincidence, but he knew.

It's nice to talk about Perry and his work because we had all those years together and I was so thrilled with the work that he did. And then I found out, of course, early on that his father Perry Ferguson—because the gentleman who worked for me is Perry Ferguson II—won many, many awards and he was great set designer apparently. I did not know him and I had never met him. I believe he had passed away when Perry came to work on my show. But everyone knew that name around the studio and in Hollywood.

*How was working with Billy De Wolfe like?*
He was one of my best friends. He was so, so good. He loved all my doggies. And Kaye Ballard just adored him, too. Now Kaye Ballard loved to have get-togethers. She loved to entertain. She would have so many people at her house, and the spaghetti would be flying! And Billy would be there and he'd say to me, "Clara," which was my funny name, "I'm picking you up at 6:30 prompt." He'd say it like that so I'd be ready. We'd go out and have a great time. We'd have such fun. We had a great time.

*Denver Pyle, who directed some episodes, too?*
Oh, Buck, my love! I loved him so. He was so good as my father. He really was. We had such lovely, tender moments. Bless his heart.

*James Hampton?*
He was so dear. Wasn't he just the cutest? Leroy—he was perfect to play the part. Such a kind heart, writing songs and making Buck upset.

*Van Johnson?*
He's another one who calls me Clara. He sends cards to me that are hilarious. He puts on the outside "Air Mail"—stamp, stamp, stamp. And draws a wild face on the back. So, so funny.

*I hear your mail volume is pretty awesome.*
Oh, don't even mention that! There is so much coming in and I just never catch up.

*How about Edward Andrews?*
Well, there you're talking about one of my favorite comedians. He was in so many of my films, that Eddie and I were like related. He was

just like part of my family. I adored this man. When I worked with him, he convulsed me. Very difficult to work with him. I would crack up all the time. We had to stop and the director would say, "Doris, pull yourself together. We've got to get this show on the road." But I couldn't help it. And John Dehner was that way too. They were just incredible to work with. All the people around me in my series and my films were incredible. I adored Eddie. There will never be another Edward Andrews or John Dehner, never.

*You had a lot of terrific guest stars on the series.*
The guest stars on the show were great. Lee Meriwether, who played Peter Lawford's nurse; Henry Fonda; Tony Bennett; Bob Crane; and Jodie Foster. Remember that? That cute little kid? Plus, we even had James L. Brooks as one of our writers. He wrote our guide episode, which is listed as our first, where I work for a women's magazine in New York.

*And the boys...*
Yes, as you know, when my series was on, I had two sons. Philip Brown—I love Philip so much—and Tod Starke, who played Toby. Tod was killed in a motorcycle accident at the age of 21. I was horrified when I heard that. I'm in touch with Philip, and he called years ago to wish me a Happy Mother's Day. He said, "For three years you were my mother, and you were the best mother I ever had." That was so sweet.

And there was Nelson—a dog among dogs—played by Lord Nelson. I loved him very much and I miss him terribly.

*The DVDs of the series earned great reviews in many areas, and several have remarked how contemporary the show looks.*
I'm so happy about that because I haven't seen any of it in it such a long time and life is so different now—but not really. It just seems in Hollywood, I think. And it is pathetic to me, it's very sad. I hate to see the women... I mean, it's not my business really, because I'm not involved any longer, but I like to see the ladies remain ladies. But they didn't. They do anything that they're asked to do. And it's... it's just crazy.

*But Doris Martin dated a lot in the last two seasons.*
Oh, well that's different.

*Everyone fell in love with her it seemed, from Patrick O'Neal to Peter Lawford...*
Yeah, and we had a great time. And I thought that was good. It was good for the show because it was natural. And it's the way life is because I had two young kids and I was, not divorced—they said I was a widow.

*They said your husband was Steve. So you were married to Steve Martin.*
That was in the show? That's funny. Was he a big star then?

*He was up-and-coming at that time and then did Saturday Night Live soon after your series went off the air.*
You know, when I discovered *Saturday Night Live*, it was after I moved up here. Terry used to always talk about it and say "Watch it," and I'd say, "That's much too late. I go to bed early." And then when I started seeing the *SNL* shows on the Comedy Channel, I flipped out over Phil Hartman. He was such a genius and it kills me that I can't write to him. I watch his DVDs constantly and can't get enough of his work. Oh, my God. And Dana [Carvey] too—so funny and talented. And the two of them together were just priceless.

*With your* Best Friends *series, was that shot over the course of several months or a year...?*
No, not that long. I don't know how long it took, but I know that we worked every day except Saturdays and Sundays. Terry did a lot of the work on that. That was fun. We worked at a beautiful place—I can't think of the name of it right now.

*A lot of people think that place was your house.*
Really? That's funny. They called that one my house? Oh my gosh. No, it wasn't.

*You also did two music specials as well as* The Doris Day Show *for CBS.*
That was very close to the time when Marty passed away, and when Terry told me that I was starring in a television series right away, I almost fainted. That's when I went to Palm Springs for a month with my mother, Marty's brother, and my hairdresser—my dear friend Barbara—and the five dogs, and Terry found a house for me to rent and we went there for a month.

When I started my series, I really wasn't ready for it—but I had to be, so I was. I worked hard—very, very hard—for a year I went through that, and then I realized that I had to do two specials. I had to rise to the occasion. I had to have fun. And I did it. And when I look at them, I'm so pleased with them. I was just so grateful—that's the word—I was so grateful for the companies, the crews, the producers, that did such great work on my behalf, and just plopped me right in the middle of it all and gave me the opportunity to sing the songs that I loved, and having that beautiful set with Perry Como. I adored Perry. He was one of my favorite singers of all time, and I didn't know him all that well when we worked together. But we got to know each other really well when we did that special. That was a highlight in my life.

Unfortunately, when we did that, it was agreed I would do his show when we could. It turned out that I was so involved with many things—knee-deep in everything! There was no time for me. I couldn't find time to rehearse because you have to rehearse when you do a special. You rehearse a lot when you do a special—it's every day and every day—and I couldn't get away to do it. I didn't get to do his special with him, and I regretted that. I missed seeing Perry after that, and would have loved to have worked with him again.

Drawing of Doris's home in Carmel.

*You did* The John Denver Special *in 1974...*

Yes, with *The John Denver Special*, the series was done and then I had plenty of time.

*The songs that you did with John Denver on your second special,* Doris Day Today, *were terrific.*

Oh, weren't they adorable? Every time I think of John, I could cry with the mention of his name. His accident happened not too far from where I live. He was living up here and we talked on the phone and had made plans to have lunch. When I heard that news [of his death] I nearly fell apart. But he was adorable to work with. We had a great time on that, and just laughed.

And sometimes I think about the time on the road with the bands. All the time we just laughed. In fact, I just got off the phone, talking with Frank Comstock [the talented musical arranger and friend from Doris's tenure with Les Brown and his Band of Renown. Comstock also arranged Doris's song "Secret Love" and her *Lullaby of Broadway* album].

*He lived near you, right?*

He lived in Huntington Beach—he and his wife, who I loved very much and has passed away—they and Ted Nash and Eve used to come up to my house to visit and stay with me all the time. And they got to know Carmel and all fell in love with Carmel. So Ted Nash asked me, in my free time, if I could find a house for them because he was still working in LA. He said, "I want to retire and come up and live there." So I found their house. It's right on the ocean.

*Any favorite episodes from your series?*

One that I loved was a man who came into the office and invited me to a premiere ["Doris Strikes Out"]. He was very handsome, but I had a baseball game to umpire. And I wanted to do both. I had to rush home and get dressed. And I was calling everybody out to make the game go faster. And they were really safe. Billy would say, "Mom! He was safe! How could you do that?!" "I said out! I'm in a hurry! Let's get this thing going." Oh God, I really enjoyed that. I had such a ball doing that one.

Another one I like that I was winging it all the way through was where I had a date with a man who hated women, and he was writing articles for the magazine ["The Woman Hater"]. Meeting me changes his entire view of women. So I had to change his mind again so he would still write for the magazine.

Well, there was a restaurant scene in the episode where the whole thing was ad-libbed. "I have a corn on my toe"—I mean, is there anything worse than for someone to say that? And I chewed gum and combed my hair at the table. I fixed my teeth. I asked him to hold my mirror so I could do that. I changed tables about four times. Then I hollered to the waiter, "Don't forget the ketchup!" And this was a fine French restaurant. And then ordering dessert: vanilla ice cream with chocolate on top and the chocolate ice cream with caramel on top and the strawberry ice cream with strawberry on top. Peanuts all over. "Don't forget the cherry!"

None of that was written. They said, "Come in and do what you want." And I thought of the most obnoxious things. First of all, I was late and I came in and I went "Yoo-hoo!" Then I said, "Are there any stars here? 'Cause I want to get some autographs." All these things came to me, things that I thought would be just awful. It was so much fun. And it was all ad-libbed.

*And you worked with many, many talented people in music, movies and television—Curtiz, Hitchcock, Previn, Harry James...*

Oh, God such great people! I just have been so grateful to have worked with such fantastic people. The actors that I worked with were the greatest. And the others in the films—not just the stars only—I loved them all. I was so blessed that God put me right in the middle of all of it. He took me out of Cincinnati and put me in Hollywood!

During the course of his latest interview with Doris Day, Pierre Patrick mentioned one of his favorite films (*Caprice*) and that with Jackie Joseph he attended the wedding of Eddie and Jill Miller who operate the Italian restaurant Rosa's in California. Pierre had sent Doris a photograph of the two of them at the reception. This led to a humorous exchange of lines between a devout trivia-filled fan and his subject (who obviously is not self-involved and very rarely watches her old movies). Their exchange sounded like it came from the pages of a TV sitcom script:

Pierre:     I went to a screening of *Caprice* at UCLA...

Doris:      You're kidding.

Pierre:     It's now become a cult film.

Doris:      I can't believe it. You know, Richard Harris and I would show up for work in the morning and I'd say, 'Do you understand this?' and he'd say, 'Not for a minute.' I hadn't a clue.

Pierre:     It's very much a contemporary movie and the kids love it because it has comedy, spies, suspense. It's fast-paced and you don't know what's going on until the end. It's kind of like a *Pulp Fiction* type of film.

Doris:      That is incredible. I can hardly believe it.

Pierre:     It goes to show you don't know what you're making at the time.

Doris:      That's true—especially that one.

Pierre:     *Caprice* is more of an intellectual film.

Doris:      That's why Richard and I didn't get it!

Pierre:     By the way, I went to a friend's wedding with Jackie her husband let me borrow her and you know who else was at our table? Your maid from *With Six You Get Eggroll*.

Doris:      Oh really! What's her name!

Pierre:     Alice Pearce. No, it was Alice Ghostley.

Doris:      Oh. That's right. Now just a minute, Alice Ghostley didn't play the maid.

Pierre:     Yes, she played the maid in *With Six You Get Eggroll*.

Doris:      Are you sure she played the maid?

Pierre:     Yeah.

Doris:      Or was she in a movie that I did with... oh, not *The Glass Bottom Boat*. Oh God, what was that other movie? I can't think of it because I can't think of the leading man. He was in *Do Not Disturb*.

Pierre:   You're thinking of Rod Taylor.

Doris:   Yes, Rod Taylor. I did another movie with him before I did *Do Not Disturb*. What was that one?

Pierre:   Well you did *Do Not Disturb* and then you did *Glass Bottom Boat*. Back to back.

Doris:   That's right. So *Glass Bottom Boat* Alice Ghostley was in.

Pierre:   No, that was Alice Pearce. You know the neighbor who was in *Bewitched*?

Doris:   Yeah, who was the neighbor?

Pierre:   Alice Pearce. Alice Ghostley was Esmeralda on *Bewitched* and she played your maid in *With Six You Get Eggroll*.

Doris:   Oh my God! And what was her name in the movie?

Pierre:   What was her name in the movie... She always had a day off in the movie, you know.

Doris:   Oh, she was so crazy in that. I loved her and I used to call her all the time and I remember calling her the name in the movie. And I can't think what it was...oh, it was Molly. That's what it was. She'd always say in the movie, 'Well, I'm off tomorrow, you know.'

Pierre:   Yes. 'Tomorrow's my day off!'

Doris:   So that was Alice Ghostley in *Glass Bottom Boat* and Alice...

Pierre:   Alice Ghostley was in *With Six*...

Doris:   *With Six You Get Eggroll*, and Alice Pearce was...

Pierre:   ...in *Glass Bottom Boat* and also *The Thrill of It All*.

Doris:     Alice Pearce was in *Glass Bottom Boat*?

Pierre:    Yeah.  She played your next door neighbor.

Doris:     Oh that's right.  And she was so funny, too.  So Alice Pearce…

Pierre:    Was in *Glass Bottom Boat*…

Doris:     That's what I said: Alice Pearce was in *Glass Bottom Boat* and Alice Ghostley in *Eggroll*.

Pierre:    And, if you're into trivia, the second Mrs. Kravitz  was in *Teacher's Pet*, *It's a Great Feeling* and *My Dream Is Yours*.

Doris:     Who was that?

Pierre:    Sandra Gould. The second one who played the neighbor on *Bewitched* after Alice Pearce…

Doris:     I don't remember that.

Pierre:    Now, did you know Sid Melton was in *The Tunnel of Love*? He played a delivery person.

Doris:     Was he really?  It's one I haven't watched.

Pierre:    Well, I'd better close for now.  Thank you again.  Love you Doris.

Doris:     Love you too Pierre.

Pierre:    Bye for now.

Doris:     Toodle-loo.

# Afterword
## by Donna DeLacy

It was an extremely busy day at Portrait of a Bookstore, the small independent store located in the Studio City area of Los Angeles, where I work as a bookseller and event planner. At Portrait we pride ourselves on two things. First, we're still in business after 23 years. Second, we're absolutely the most charming and cozy bookstore in the country, with lovely outdoor garden seating and a library-type room with a fireplace. The phone rings and I struggle to answer it while also dealing with a customer who is paying. The enthusiastic, almost bombastic voice of someone named Pierre Patrick on the line from New York City is telling me something about Doris Day and a book and television.

"Excuse me, Pierre, could you slow down and run that by me one more time, what about Doris Day (one of my personal all-time favorites)?"

"OK, Donna, here's the deal," he replied with the utmost patience, "I've written a book called *Que Sera, Sera, the Magic of Doris Day Through Television* with Garry McGee about her television show from 1968 to 1973. She has given permission for this book and is very supportive. I want to come to Los Angeles to do a book launch and we hoped your store might want to host our event. We expect a large turnout, and actually I can guarantee that it will draw a very big audience!" he said, his enthusiasm still at high pitch.

Well, let me just say that I've heard that claim countless times: eager authors who think the general public is just waiting to pounce on their book assure me that the reading/book signing will sell vast quantities of their book on...let's say, Midwifery in the Sixteenth Century. So I was more than a little skeptical of Pierre's claims of big attendance and yes, I understand that Doris Day has a large fan base and is still adored by many even though she rarely if ever makes public appearances.

357

Finally, through his persuasive and charming negotiations I agree to host the event. We arrive at a suitable date, order what I believe to be an excessive number of books to sell at the event, and we are all set...or so it seems.

Pierre calls a few weeks before his arrival from New York with the exciting news that Doris, who never attends events, preferring her quiet life with her animals in central California, has agreed to take a phone call and speak to the guests at the book launch event over a speakerphone. I can feel some of my skepticism slipping away. Next he announces that some of Doris' associates from the show will be attending and some of them will be doing informal talks. He asks if I can handle the additional good news and arrange for a speakerphone of some sort. I know perfectly well that we don't have a speakerphone that will deliver outdoors to our garden where the event will take place, but promise to do what I can to make it all work. Pierre mentions ordering more books but I remind him that we have ordered the maximum amount of books and that our small garden can only hold so many guests. After that number the fire department would surely be called for "unsafe crowding" or some such thing.

Sunday November 19th, the day of the event, arrives beautiful and sunny just like southern California is supposed to be. It's a hectic day at the bookstore with lots of preliminary Christmas shoppers out in force. I've hooked up a Public Address system with two big speakers and hope to work the phone chat with Doris Day through our regular phone. I've tested and re-tested the volume and feel confident that it will work. The books are safely in the office and as 3:00 nears we begin arranging chairs for the guests, who are scheduled at 4:00. At approximately 3:15 people begin to arrive and ask where they should go for Pierre Patrick's event. They are excited and some tell me they have flown in just to attend this book launch. I meet groups from Belgium, Germany, and a dorisdayicon.com group from Montreal. Good grief! No one has ever flown in from another country for one of our events. This is taking on new dimensions. By 3:30 all the seats are taken and we have an overflow crowd, now including actor William Suretté and his delegation from Canada! Pierre arrives and after hurried introductions he smiles at me and in that smile I see "I told you so" so plainly written that I have to smile too.

As events go it was a huge success for all. We sold every single copy of the book, and needed more (Pierre was right), since many guests were buying stacks of books to take home and share with others. Pierre was a wonderful author/host and orchestrated the event with the aplomb that spoke of his years as a producer. In the master of ceremonies role was

Jackie Joseph, Pierre Patrick, Rose Marie and Jim Pierson.

Jim Pierson, producer of *The Doris Day Show* DVD, who introduced the guests and explained that Garry McGee, co-author of the book, was unable to attend since he was on deadline for his next book on actress Jean Seberg. Doris' two best friends from her series were there: Rose Marie delivered some very funny lines in her talk and Jackie Joseph, who had written a wonderful review of the book in her newspaper column, was touching in recounting some of her memories of the show.

But of course the highlight was the phone call from Doris Day, who sounded just like she did on the TV show and in dozens of movies: a wonderful voice of a great vocalist that still has the famous lilt and softness we all love. She said that she loved the copy of the book that Pierre had sent to her and thanked him effusively. Doris answered questions and chatted with her longtime friends and fans, and seemed incredibly moved by the outpouring of love when the entire audience serenaded her with "Que Sera, Sera". I think everyone felt, as I did, that it was over too quickly and left us wanting more of Doris Day. We will have to wait, I thought, and hoped that we could get to know more of her through the engaging writing of Pierre Patrick and Garry McGee in this wonderful new revised edition.

# About the Authors

French Canadian-born Pierre Patrick (Patry) has worked in the recording industry for many years and produced the Grammy-nominated album *The Christmas That Almost Wasn't* starring John Lithgow and featuring celebrity guests including Jackie Joseph. Pierre won an Earphones Award for his production of *Peyton Place* with original star Tim O'Connor for Books on Tape. He has worked on several television shows, including A&E's *Biography*, along with many special events such as PBS's *Swing Alive—Les Brown's 60th Anniversary* (with Dolores and Bob Hope), *The Canada Day Celebration* and *The Grammy in the Schools* concert series. He has written several stories for the magazine *Television Chronicles* including the HBO series TINTIN. Pierre has also worked on many Doris Day On-stage tributes, CD and DVD releases. He manages *New York Times* discovery William Suretté. He is currently producing a new CD called *The Velveteen Rabbit Alive* with Beatrice Arthur, Marla Gibbs, and Brigitte Bardot, working on a new series called *Patty's Green* staring Jack Klugman, Ed Begley Jr., LeVar Burton and Patty Carver as Mother Nature.

As a writer, Jackie Joseph wrote for *The Tolucan Times* for three decades and, with Carolyn See, wrote several episodes for television, including the award-winning *Family* and *Barnaby Jones*. Most recently, Jackie played a 'sweet old woman' doing a testimonial for a 'Hood Bank' in Snoop Dogg's show *Dogg After Dark*.

Iowa-born Garry McGee is the author of popular culture books, including *Band on the Run: A History of Paul McCartney & Wings* [Taylor, 2003] and the reference book *Doris Day: Sentimental Journey* [McFarland, 2005]. In addition to various freelance production work on television movies and commercials, Garry is completing *The Last Wright*, a documentary film about the last standing hotel designed by Frank Lloyd Wright, which was awarded the IMPA Best Documentary Award (2008). He also produced the documentary films *Jean Seberg: In the American Style* and *Donna Reed: Reflections of a Wonderful Life*, which were honored with consecutive Iowa Film Awards.

Please visit The Doris Day Animal Foundation and the Cypress Inn in Carmel at www.dorisday.com.

# *The Legendary Movie Queen*

## STARRING ON THE SMALL SCREEN

### DIGITALLY REMASTERED!

### LOADED WITH BONUS MATERIALS!

### Available on DVD from

**MPI**
HOME VIDEO

www.mpihomevideo.com
Toll free: 1-800-323-0442
In Illinois: 708-460-0555

# They say there's nothing like a good book...

# We think that says quite a lot!

## BearManorMedia

P O Box 71426 • Albany, GA 31708

Phone: 760-709-9696 • Fax: 814-690-1559

Book orders over $99 always receive FREE US SHIPPING!

Visit our webpage at www.bearmanormedia.com

for more great deals!

CPSIA information can be obtained
at www.ICGtesting.com
Printed in the USA
LVOW01s0302030417
529390LV00006B/443/P

9 781593 933494